D0421893

HUMAN-CENTERED COMMUNICATION

A BUSINESS CASE AGAINST DIGITAL POLLUTION

HUMAN-CENTERED COMMUNICATION

A BUSINESS CASE AGAINST DIGITAL POLLUTION

ETHAN BEUTE • STEPHEN PACINELLI

FEATURING

JACCO VAN DER KOOIJ • DAN HILL, PHD • MATHEW SWEEZEY
JULIE HANSEN • ADAM CONTOS • LAUREN BAILEY • MARIO MARTINEZ JR.
VIVEKA VON ROSEN • SHEP HYKEN • MORGAN J INGRAM • DAN TYRE

**FAST
COMPANY**
Press

This publication is designed to provide accurate and authoritative information in regard to the subject matter covered. It is sold with the understanding that the publisher and author are not engaged in rendering legal, accounting, or other professional services. Nothing herein shall create an attorney-client relationship, and nothing herein shall constitute legal advice or a solicitation to offer legal advice. If legal advice or other expert assistance is required, the services of a competent professional should be sought.

Fast Company Press
New York, New York
www.fastcompanypress.com

Copyright © 2021 BombBomb™

All rights reserved.

Thank you for purchasing an authorized edition of this book and for complying with copyright law. No part of this book may be reproduced, stored in a retrieval system, or transmitted by any means, electronic, mechanical, photocopying, recording, or otherwise, without written permission from the copyright holder.

This work is being published under the Fast Company Press imprint by an exclusive arrangement with *Fast Company*. *Fast Company* and the Fast Company logo are registered trademarks of Mansueto Ventures, LLC. The Fast Company Press logo is a wholly owned trademark of Mansueto Ventures, LLC.

Distributed by Greenleaf Book Group

For ordering information or special discounts for bulk purchases, please contact Greenleaf Book Group at PO Box 91869, Austin, TX 78709, 512.891.6100.

Design and composition by BombBomb and Greenleaf Book Group
Cover design by Anna Hayes with Sarah Wagle
Graphics by Anna Hayes

Publisher's Cataloging-in-Publication data is available.

Print ISBN: 978-1-63908-000-7

eBook ISBN: 978-1-63908-001-4

Partof the Tree Neutral® program, which offsets the number of trees consumed in the production and printing of this book by taking proactive steps, such as planting trees in direct proportion to the number of trees used: www.treeneutral.com

Printed in the United States of America on acid-free paper

21 22 23 24 25 26 27   10 9 8 7 6 5 4 3 2 1

First Edition

TO OUR FAMILIES, TO OUR TEAM MEMBERS,
AND TO EVERYONE WHO TAKES A HUMAN-CENTERED
APPROACH TO THEIR LIFE AND WORK.

Contents

Introduction

We have a problem that hasn't had a name. As a consequence, we don't understand it well. But it's costing us more than we can measure—as individuals, as businesses, and as a society. Though it involves our technology, the problem is a human one. People cause it. People pay for its consequences. And, of course, people can solve it. The solution requires us to put people first and allows us to exceed our goals and be proud of how we do it. We propose an innovation in the way we communicate and connect with each other every single day.

At the risk of stating the obvious, everything and everyone has moved online. Virtually all of us and all of our activities are now available, well, virtually. We enjoy so many benefits from this shift. In digital environments, we increase speed and efficiency in our efforts. We extend the reach of our actions far beyond what we could deliver physically. This is true in our work and play. It's true when we're buying and selling, teaching and learning, connecting and communicating. Across multiple screens and interfaces, throughout the day every day, we've got so many reasons to get virtual.

But as we've complemented and migrated nearly every aspect of our real lives into digital environments, we've left something behind. Part of ourselves is lost as we mediate our experiences through screens. The benefits of this shift come with costs. While we enjoy the advantages of online opportunities, we also shed some of our humanity. People are minimized and even dehumanized in many digital experiences.

In virtual channels, we lack clarity. Tone, intent, and meaning are more difficult to express and to discern. We often misunderstand other people and are misunderstood ourselves. Miscommunication leads to confusion and frustration. We overwork in our attempts to achieve understanding. The toll of this friction is paid with emotional energy and precious time.

As a species, we have millennia of training in face-to-face communication. We've adapted and evolved to express emotions, read nonverbal cues, and build trust in person. So many of the innate skills with which we come equipped and that help us as highly social creatures don't serve us well in digital environments. When faces and voices are stripped from our messages, we lose context and meaning. Even when we can see each other in video messages and video calls, our emotions are dampened, our inflections are muted, and our motives are obscured.

We should spend as much time as possible face to face. We should start new relationships in person whenever we can. Once established, our personal and professional connections can be sustained and deepened through online interaction. That's one of the greatest benefits of our digital activity—quickly and easily keeping up with anyone at any time, no matter where they are. Today, however, we're not always afforded this sequence of events; we're not meeting as many people face to face as we were just a couple of years ago. Increasingly, our interactions start digitally and stay digital. This creates a gap that must be bridged.

This book will help you stay personal—and human—even when you go virtual.

POLLUTION AND MISTRUST

Starting digitally and staying digital has us fighting an uphill battle. Just as trust is down and bad actors abound in real life, mistrust and malfeasance proliferate online. Spam, bots, automation, robocalls, pop-up ads, spoofed accounts, phishing attempts, malware installs, data hacks, disinformation campaigns, and other forms of what we call digital pollution drive annoyance and anxiety. They hurt people, teams, organizations, and entire industries. As polluting activities become more nuanced, more sophisticated, and—dare we say—more human in their execution, each of us works harder to separate what's honest and safe from what's misrepresented and dangerous. And describing these threats is to say nothing of innocent and ignorant online behavior that adds complication and frustration to our experience.

Through countless generations of learning and evolution, our ancient brains have become adept at this discernment in physical spaces. Our powers of observation and intuition serve us everywhere we go, including into online spaces. But as we operate in digital channels, these innate, human skills are not as finely tuned. We struggle here—more than in real life—to know who and what to trust and to know when we're safe. As with pollution of our air, water, and soil, the costs of digital pollution are paid at every level, from the individual up through the entire society. Though they occur virtually, we pay for these ills physically, emotionally, mentally, and financially in very real ways.

> The **problem** is digital pollution—
> unwelcome digital distractions.

When we treat people like numbers, we break the bonds of trust. When we worship activities over outcomes, we frustrate and devalue the very people with whom our success is built. When we renew our membership in the cult of scale, we miss opportunities to make meaningful connections. Bringing an industrial mindset to a human endeavor leads to the misuse of tools and mistreatment of people. Betraying our stated values is a betrayal of ourselves and of others. We will never be perfect, but we must do our best to reorient our businesses toward a healthier future. And we must take the opportunity right now to realign our practices with current trends.

Many people suggest that attention is the currency of our economy, but it's not. Trust is. Attention is just one of its necessary precursors; when we pay attention, we actively and automatically judge sincerity, honesty, credibility, authority, trustworthiness, and many other characteristics of a person and situation. Trust is both grease and glue. Trust accelerates decisions, processes, and relationships. And trust makes good ideas, good people, and good outcomes stick.

We must find ways to build and maintain trust in a polluted digital environment.

RESTORATION OF THE HUMAN

One tool to help us restore some of the missing pieces of our humanity is video. Where typed-out text completely strips you out of your messages and faceless phone calls strip out your nonverbal communication, a video call or video message is infused with your face, voice, personality, expertise, enthusiasm, sincerity, concern, and all those rich, human qualities that connect us. Video restores so much of the data and input people need to actively and automatically read people and situations. It also helps people identify you as a real person and provides a verification layer that cuts through digital pollution and provokes engagement.

In short: Video is the next best thing to being there in person.

In *Rehumanize Your Business: How Personal Videos Accelerate Sales and Improve Customer Experience*, my coauthor Steve Pacinelli and I walk through a movement we call "relationships through video." This stands in contrast to the more familiar and traditional "marketing through video." We introduce the philosophy and practice of recording personal, conversational videos to improve our emails, text messages, and social messages.

Here in this book, we go wider than video messaging and deeper into human connection. In the pages ahead, you'll learn to be more confident and effective in:

Live, synchronous video meetings

Recorded, asynchronous video messages

Video calls and video presentations

Video in emails and text messages

Video in social feeds and social messages

Video for specific individuals and large groups

Video for known audiences and anonymous masses

Video for prospects, customers, employees, and other stakeholders

Sure, we're all basically equipped right now to execute these with an internet connection and a webcam or smartphone, but too few of us are attuned to what matters most . . . the person on the other side of our camera lens. We make video too much about our own needs and wants and not enough about other people. We focus too much on how we look and sound and not enough on how others feel and respond. Our videos even pollute when we go on too long, bury salient details, underuse emotion, or fail to show up in a spirit of service.

As we move forward together in life and in business, we'll be spending more time in virtual environments, not less. Technology only gets more powerful and less expensive. Video's use only grows. And the value of meaningful human connection will only rise, never fall. Our inboxes and feeds seem noisy now—and they'll only get noisier. To help, AI and machine learning will use behavioral insights to manage what we see, when, and where. The way others engage with our messages will affect our ability to reach them again in the future. So we must advance with a more human-centered approach, rather than retreating to unhealthy habits and digital shortcomings that have become so apparent they're now glaring.

The **solution** is human-centered communication—thoughtful digital experiences.

Fortunately, the benefits of a human-centered approach extend to all of our communication. When we think about others before we type a single word, before we click "Record," or before we join the video call, we improve the experience and the outcome. Our forethought results in empathy and provides a difference that people can feel. To offer it in digital spaces is to acknowledge a human and to extend a hand. We're reaching out in a way that creates connection, earns trust, and builds reputation—things that are increasingly valuable in an increasingly noisy and polluted world.

To help you employ human-centered communication more often and more consistently, my co-author Steve and I reached out to 11 of our expert friends and spent time with them in deep conversations. We've gathered their stories and insights here into one place to explore in a business context themes like:

Trust and relationships

Communication and connection

Service and value

Text and video

Noise and pollution

We also bring our own stories, insights, and experiences to this project. Steve and I have each been using video in a variety of ways and a variety of channels for nearly 20 years. We've each sent several thousand truly personal video messages and co-authored the first book on the topic, *Rehumanize Your Business*. Video training, podcasts, webinars, stage presentations—we've been openly sharing what we've learned for years. Like you, we've been on both sides of the digital pollution problem. And like you, we aspire to be more human-centered every day.

If you're already using video with some level of success in one or more channels, you can take the approach prescribed in these pages and achieve better results for years to come. If you're not using video consistently or well, we know why. You may lack confidence on camera. How do I look? How do I sound? Am I doing this right? Am I doing this well enough? If you're still showing up on meetings with your camera off or you've signed up for a video service but don't use it, you'll find help in this book. You'll liberate your spirit and unlock your potential as you come to understand that video is not about you.

Our approach to business, communication, and video must be about other people's needs, wants, and interests—*not* about our own.

THE GOALS AND STRUCTURE

Our two goals in this book are 1) to create awareness and provoke conversation about digital pollution and human-centered communication and 2) to help you connect with people in a more human way in digital, virtual, and online environments. While there's a heavy emphasis on live video meetings and recorded video messages throughout, most of what you'll learn can be applied to in-person and typed-out communication, too. Human-centered communication transcends any medium.

This book is philosophical and practical, but it's not particularly technical. You'll encounter some tool and tech talk, but you won't find specific tips to boost your social following or to properly light a studio. Instead, you'll learn to restore to primacy the recipient of your message, participant on your call, and viewer of your video. Putting others first is fundamental to productive, meaningful exchanges. You'll get stories, insights, and recommendations from more than a dozen business leaders, co-authors included, equipping you to increase emotion, connection, and trust online.

More than half of the allies and exemplars featured in this book have strong sales backgrounds, but it's not just for sales professionals. Because marketing, customer service, and customer experience have a significant impact on revenue and relationships, these functions are also well-represented in these pages. Insights into teaching, training, and presenting are here, too, as they're skills we all need. Several are founders, CEOs, and senior executives who provide leadership and management guidance here. Among them are a futurist, a professional actor, and an emotional intelligence expert.

No matter your role, your business, or your industry, you'll see your work in new ways and get ideas you can implement immediately.

You can read this book in a traditional, linear way—in sequence from front to back. Or you can read it in a nonlinear way, picking off single chapters as you prefer. Sequenced with intention, each chapter stands alone and they work together—especially in Part Two: Allies and Exemplars. That part of the book is the longest and it's bookended by an important setup in Part One and a helpful recap in Part Three.

In Part One: Pollution and Solution, we walk through the problem of digital pollution, the solution of human-centered communication, and the points of application in our businesses. In Chapter 1, you'll immediately identify with the causes, costs, and dangers of digital pollution before being formally introduced in Chapter 2 to the concept of human-centered communication, the pillars it's built upon, and a value-based framework to carry with you as you connect with people in virtual environments.

In Chapter 3, a view of the full customer lifecycle and the full employee lifecycle opens up to you, no matter the size or nature of your business. Jacco van der Kooij, Founder of Winning by Design, exposes fundamental flaws in the traditional sales and marketing approach and shows us a more customer-centric way forward. As he advises and as is reinforced through this book, "You have to stop the selling and start helping your customers to buy."

In Part Two: Allies and Exemplars, we feature 10 collaborators, each in her or his own chapter. Again, these chapters are sequenced intentionally, but can be read individually and in your preferred order. Each person shares insights into their own business journey, guiding philosophy, video strategies, and specific tips and tactics to be more human-centered.

We begin Part Two in Chapter 4 with Dan Hill, PhD, President of Sensory Logic; emotional intelligence expert; author of eight books, including *Emotionomics* and *Famous Faces Decoded*; and recipient of seven U.S. patents in the analysis of facial coding data. He shares the science behind our nonverbal communication to help us be more effective both face to face and in video. You'll learn how emotional resonance drives memory and motivation. The primary reason to communicate in human-centered and emotionally intelligent ways is because, as Dan tells us, "Everyone wants a sense of belonging and a sense of connection."

In Chapter 5, Director of Market Strategy at Salesforce, author of *The Context*

Marketing Revolution and *Marketing Automation for Dummies*, and marketing futurist Mathew Sweezey explains the importance of being personal and authentic in today's marketplaces . . . and tomorrow's. He breaks down the relationships among noise, attention, and trust and observes why "video becomes increasingly important for human-to-human connections" as we move forward in time.

In Chapter 6, Julie Hansen, professional actor, creator of the Selling on Video Master Class, and author of *Act Like a Sales Pro* and *Sales Presentation for Dummies*, shares the authenticity and alignment required for accomplished acting. She encourages us to step into our business roles with more presence and intention. You'll learn to "allow yourself to be passionate and commit to it," properly prepare before the camera turns on, and actively listen with your whole self. The key to all of it is focusing on the other person, not on yourself.

In Chapter 7, Adam Contos, CEO of RE/MAX Holdings, Inc. and former SWAT team leader (yes, as in kicking in doors, blowing things up, and saving people), invites us to ask the fundamental question, "How can I help you?" He shares the formula for emotional brilliance, walks us through his do-it-yourself approach to podcasting and video, and challenges us to look for return on relationship, not return on investment. Among his human-centered offerings is this axiom: "If you try to do good things for each other, then good things will happen in your business."

In Chapter 8, Lauren Bailey, Founder and President of Factor 8, a sales training company, and #GirlsClub, a leadership program for women, directly points out current sources of digital pollution. She also offers ways to rehumanize buyers, sellers, and sales processes because "just being 20% more human is a massive differentiator" right now. She explains how to demonstrate more personality and confidence in order to stand out, sell, and serve in more meaningful ways.

In Chapter 9, the CEO, Founder, and Modern Sales Evangelist at Vengreso, Mario Martinez Jr., explains why "sales is the art of helping" and balances the art with smart sales science. In addition to sharing 16 specific ways to use video messages and advocating for the use of virtual backgrounds, he helps us shift our focus from generalized personas to individual people. And more than in any other chapter, you'll learn ways to improve your remote work culture by being more fully human in your leadership role.

In Chapter 10, LinkedIn expert, personal branding coach, and Cofounder and Chief Visibility Officer at Vengreso, Viveka von Rosen, is a teacher. And in your own way, so are you—leading, managing, selling, and serving all involve education. Learn how she approaches video calls and video recordings for more effective training. Get some of the tips that earned one of her students 35 responses, 10 meetings, and three closed deals within the first 30 days of outreach to 50 C-suite executives. Find your confidence, turn up your energy, and "earn the right to the conversation" by putting others first.

In Chapter 11, Shep Hyken, a customer service and customer experience expert and *New York Times*, *Wall Street Journal*, and *USA Today* best-selling author of eight books, including *The Convenience Revolution* and *The Cult of the Customer*, balances technology and the human touch. In his experience, "you can't automate a relationship." Learn how he's evolved his virtual presentations to be more human-centered and when, why, and how he reaches out with video messages.

In Chapter 12, Morgan J Ingram, Director of Sales Execution and Evolution at JB Sales Training and a LinkedIn Top Sales Voice for three years running, puts people first in one of the more dehumanizing roles in business: sales development and business development. Having created more than 10,000 videos himself, he implores us that "we should add humanity into our prospecting outreach and stop being robots." How? By creating conversations, not presentations. By setting down scripts in favor of formulas. And by practicing and learning rather than perfecting.

To close Part Two, Dan Tyre, Sales Executive and original team member at HubSpot and co-author of *Inbound Organization*, declares that "always be closing" is dead in Chapter 13. Instead, "You help, not sell. You treat people like human beings." He explains why he can't live without video, how the use of video spread within HubSpot, how to deliver more human experiences, and why he stopped prognosticating about "the year of video."

See our **interviews** with
each of these experts at
BombBomb.com/BookBonus

In Part Three: Takeaways and Tomorrows, we tie it all together to recap key themes and top tips to help you take a more human-centered approach to your communication. Jump forward to these closing chapters and bounce back to the preceding chapters as you need and want to.

In Chapter 14, we bring together 10 high-level, human-centered philosophies and strategies shared by this group of experts throughout the book. Then, in Chapter 15, we help you cast the vision with your team and provide 10 specific tips and tactics shared by several of our allies. We close in Chapter 16 with a look to the future of human-centered communication.

"I don't think human-centered communication is necessarily a term," Mathew Sweezey told Steve and me in our conversation for this book, "but it totally should be."

We agree. And that's why you're here with us.

CONVERSATION, EXPLORATION, AND RESTORATION

We are neither judge nor jury on this movement away from digital pollution and into human-centered communication. As we'll confess, we've been polluters ourselves. But we know that immeasurable qualities make measurable differences in our lives and our businesses. We want to do work that matters with and for people we care about. As we explore these themes and set out on this mission, consider this your invitation to join us in the conversation. Join us in restoring people to primacy.

Prevailing social and cultural trends demand a more human-centered approach to all of the work we do. In the months and years ahead, consumers will seek more personal experiences, not fewer. Investing in and developing our employees only grows as an expectation. Human-to-human interaction only increases in value. The more virtual and mediated our experiences become, the more we crave clarity, sincerity, and authenticity from fellow humans. Your reputation and the way your stakeholders feel about you will increasingly affect your financial future in the forms of recruiting, renewals, and referrals. In the forms of conversions and commitments.

Innovation is often associated with technology; in this case the innovation is tech-enabled and human-centered. It's a commitment to develop new habits and implement new processes that put people first. Doing so creates sustainable, relationship-based advantages. Empathizing more effectively may require more initial effort than our current habits. Ultimately, however, it will deliver better outcomes for us and everyone around us. As technology advances, our unique human strengths become more valuable. We must focus our time and energy on those things that machines don't do as well as people and, at the same time, leverage machines to allow us to be more fully ourselves more often.

Human-centered communication breaks through the noise, reduces pollution, gains attention, delivers value, earns trust, generates engagement, and creates long-term business relationships. Doing it consistently teaches the people and machines involved in our communication processes that you're worthy of their attention, response, and trust the next time you reach out. And the time after that. Over and over again. In a positive, perpetual cycle. As digital pollution grows, human-centered communication becomes more urgent, more necessary, and more powerful.

Part One

POLLUTION & SOLUTION

CHAPTER 1

Digital Pollution

When you read the word "pollution," what comes to mind?

Wildlife slicked as millions of gallons of oil spill into the gulf? Skies shrouded in dense haze from billowing smokestacks? Illegal dumping of hazardous waste that leaches into the soil and groundwater? Perhaps nuclear meltdowns like Three Mile Island, Chernobyl, or Fukushima. Maybe toxic rivers like the Mississippi, the Ganges, or the Yellow.[1] Or the Great Pacific Garbage Patch, which is now more than twice the size of Texas and nearly three times the size of France.[2]

Our minds tend toward the egregious and dramatic examples—and rightfully so. Every year, pollution kills millions of people and other living things and harms tens of millions more. But its causes and consequences are often much more subtle.

When you read the words "digital pollution," does anything come to mind?

Think about the family member who spent several months, several thousand dollars, and several sleepless nights recovering from identity theft. Or your reaction to a bank alert about a potentially fraudulent charge. Think about the feeling you get when you return to your inbox after a week away. Envision the 2.4 billion emails being sent every single second.[3] Imagine how many of those emails are sent by machines rather than people. Realize that half of it is pure spam.[4] That's on top of the 4.5 billion spam text messages sent every year.[5]

Have you ever had a friend post on social media about her account being hacked? Definitely. And it comes with the caution not to accept the new connection request from a fake account using her name and photo. Have you ever received an alert that your personal information has been compromised in a data breach? Certainly. But you're desensitized to it at this point. Phishing attacks. Robocalls. Suspicious links and attachments. Questionable messages from unfamiliar people. These all seem endless and ever present. They're all around you.

Like environmental pollution, digital pollution's harms are real even when subtle. They're felt by each of us. They're experienced by the groups, communities, and companies of which we're members. This pollution costs us time and money. For example, the cybersecurity industry is projected to grow to a $173 billion industry by 2026, up more than 50% from 2020.[6]

But digital pollution also threatens the immeasurable and the priceless. Trust and relationships. Bonding and connection.

Because online content is faster and cheaper to produce and distribute than physical content, digital demands on your attention are massive and growing. The volume of noise alone threatens our productivity as we sift through it all. And it inhibits our ability to effectively reach people as they sort through their feeds and inboxes. Fold in selfish, greedy, and malicious activity, as well as exponentially more and increasingly valuable data, and it gets toxic quickly.

The assessments we have to make every time we enter a virtual environment aren't just "Does this matter?" or "Is this high priority?" but also "Is this safe or unsafe?" and "Is this real or fake?" Because we've moved online faster than we have evolved and adapted, humans aren't well-equipped for this. The automatic and subconscious assessments we make all day long in the physical world don't occur to us as often or serve us as well online. As we share our digital personas, others hide behind digital facades. Our vulnerability opens us to exploitation.

You and everyone you know is a stakeholder in our shared virtual environments of apps, platforms, networks, channels, and mediums. Every time you turn on or pick up a connected device (which is probably more often than you think), digital pollution affects you and your business. It affects employees and customers. It eats up time and expense. It threatens trust and relationships.

As with pollution of our air, water, and soil, you pay the costs of digital pollution whether you're a polluter or not—and whether you're a direct target or not. When we poison our physical environment, we poison ourselves—the air we breathe, the water we drink, the food we eat. Because we live, work, and play in polluted virtual spaces, we must observe and understand these digital forms of pollution, too. They poison us.

We'll begin by comparing and contrasting pollution, which we are familiar with, to digital pollution, which hasn't been explored nearly as much. The causes, characteristics, costs, and consequences of digital pollution must become clearer. Our human thriving and success depend on it.

CAUSES AND CONSEQUENCES OF POLLUTION

No one intends to create environmental pollution. It's a consequence. What pollutes our air, water, and soil is waste from a process with a separate goal. The goal of that process is value creation or value delivery—not waste, inefficiency, or pollution. So, while it's easy and rightful to demonize egregious polluters, we must also acknowledge pollution's correlation with rising living standards, increasing product and service availability, and wide-ranging benefits we enjoy every day.

Tradeoffs

We hate oil spills, but we love contact lenses, golf balls, cosmetics, N-95 masks, and thousands of other daily use, oil-based products.[7] We hate toxic mine waste, but we love our smartphones, which require ore minerals for their displays, electronics, circuitry, and batteries.[8] Our food, clothing, footwear, home furnishings, jewelry, electronics, household cleaners, travel, and other material wants and needs all create varying amounts of pollution.

Harmful but useful, energy production is one of the greatest sources of pollution. We're slowly mitigating some of its negative effects through energy-efficient production, energy-efficient products, cleaner-burning fuels, renewable energy sources, and energy conservation. But we're not solving the problem by removing furnaces from homes in Toronto or removing air conditioners from homes in Phoenix any more than we're solving the digital pollution problem by removing internet connectivity from our homes and offices. We make tradeoffs.

While we manage pollution through these compromises, we must guard ourselves against ignorance or complacency toward the status quo. False dichotomies, erroneous assumptions, outdated ideas, and broken models should not be accepted.

History

Because human-caused pollution is the dark side of so many lights, it's been with us for a long time. As early as the 1st century BC, Lucretius pointed out "the ill effects in the miners' complexions" and wrote, "How deadly are the exhalations of the gold mines!" In the same century, Vitruvius wrote that spring water coming from mining areas was harmful. Later, in the 1st century AD, Pliny the Elder noted how mine emissions affected animals.[9] Hundreds of years later, in 1306, Edward I of England issued a prohibition on coal burning in London. Court cases on groundwater contamination in Europe occurred as early as 1349.[10]

Sources

All along, pollution could be characterized by its source and its recipient—the mines and the mine workers in the observations of Lucretius. Sources are where the pollution comes from, where it's released. They include transportation, factories, agriculture, and household activities. Recipients are where the pollution ends up, what gets contaminated. They include people, animals, plants, air, water, and soil.[11]

When we can easily identify pollution's source, it's a point source. For example, an acute fish kill immediately downstream from a factory's effluent pipe. However, pollution also comes from nonpoint sources—diffuse, dispersed, generally prevalent, and harder to trace. For example, oil, grease, and chemicals constantly running off of parking lots and roads into our waterways. Or microplastics found at the greatest depths of the ocean, in Arctic and Antarctic sea ice, in our food supply, in our blood and our organs, and even in unborn babies.[12,13,14,15]

Costs

The costs of pollution range from the obvious to the obscured. Much pollution is a cost externalized by a business or organization onto the public. It's systemic waste that would be eliminated if not for the cost of doing so. That's to say, designing and implementing a highly efficient process could reduce harmful outputs. But rather than paying for these improvements, a company may simply release pollution into the environment.

Because it reduces production costs, pollution may seem to lower the retail price of products and services. But the full costs must always be paid. As stakeholders in this shared physical environment, you and I pay physically, emotionally, and financially.

We pay directly through taxes that support legislation, monitoring, litigation, and cleanup. We pay indirectly through our health, wellbeing, and healthcare spending. The most common causes of human deaths, like cardiovascular diseases, cancers, and respiratory diseases, are all exacerbated by environmental pollutants. A report by the Lancet Commission on Pollution and Health found that pollution caused 9 million premature deaths in 2015—16% of all global death. That year, pollution also cost us $4.6 trillion—6.2% of global economic output.[16]

One positive trend: Increasing transparency and accountability are putting some of the costs back onto polluters. Reputational damage and lost revenue are forcing some companies to clean up their acts. The same is true for digital polluters.

Regulation

Laws and regulations are in place to reduce pollution, but poor implementation and weak enforcement continue to be a problem around the globe.[17] Legislation tends to be reactive and one step behind. Enforcement tends to be understaffed and underfunded relative to the size of the problem. And even when found negligent, a polluter may face an insufficiently prohibitive punishment. For aggressive polluters, externalizing costs may be a conscious, rational decision; fines and legal fees may just be line items on the budget.

To the degree regulation is effective, the cost of compliance is a worthwhile investment. A study by the U.S. Environmental Protection Agency found the total costs of the Clean Air Act from 1970 to 1990 to be just over $500 billion. The middle-range estimate of the value of its benefits in that time was $22 trillion—nearly a 44x return on investment.[18]

Priceless Capital

Some of pollution's harms are irreparable; it can destroy the finite and priceless. Namely, natural capital, which includes the entirety of the world's natural resources like clean air, clean water, fertile soil, biodiversity, and healthy, balanced ecosystems. Natural capital doesn't show up on balance sheets or financial reports. To the degree it's immeasurable, it's neither visible nor valuable in a formal accounting.

This priceless capital is critical to human thriving and to human existence.

Some degradation can be restored, like replanting trees after a deforestation event. At a certain point, however, deforestation can become desertification, which is far more costly and difficult to restore—if it can be restored at all. Other consequences without remedy include the depletion of non-renewable resources, the extinction of species, and the introduction of tens of thousands of synthetic chemicals never tested for safety.[19]

Subjectivity

Though we all recognize the ills of pollution, we must also recognize that it's highly subjective. What's a tolerable or acceptable level? How near is the problem? How significant are the benefits? Who pays the cost—how and when? Depending on who's asking these questions and who's answering them, you get different answers. The source is likely more forgiving of pollution than the recipient. A visitor to a polluted area is likely more forgiving than the resident. Most pollution issues are NIMBY issues—"not in my backyard." Each of us tolerates pollution; we even support it through our consumer spending. But only when the costs and consequences are far enough away and sufficiently obscured. This is why people in poverty tend to suffer most from pollution.

A Human Problem

The pollution problem is a human problem. It's incredibly complex and invites to the conversation themes of ethics, justice, politics, economics, socioeconomics, sociology, healthcare, and beyond. We'll go no deeper here; our purpose is only to set up conceptual parallels to digital pollution. But there's a concrete connection between them, too.

The Connection

A Google search for "digital pollution" will serve up results about ecological footprints, energy consumption, and carbon emissions caused by our digital activity. When I ran that search, Google's homepage was tagged "Carbon neutral since 2007"; they're well aware of the energy demands of data processing and the pollution this creates.[20] Especially because of processing-intensive mining, Bitcoin alone is estimated to consume more energy in a year than entire nations, including Argentina and Norway.[21] A single Bitcoin transaction may be as energy intensive as nearly a half a million VISA transactions.[22]

The math gets complicated, but the point is simple: Our virtual activity drives both environmental *and* digital pollution.

CAUSES AND CONSEQUENCES OF DIGITAL POLLUTION

The term digital pollution is meant to capture the deterioration of virtual environments in ways that drive annoyance, frustration, confusion, anxiety, or fear. Potentially experienced anywhere we operate online, it reduces trust, transparency, and bonding. It tears at our social fabric. What's more, it dehumanizes us. We're suffering an epidemic of loneliness despite online connectivity,[23] an epidemic of facelessness that degrades online behavior,[24] and rates of depression and suicide that correlate with increased screen time.[25]

Unlike environmental pollution, digital pollution is often completely intentional—data hacks, phishing emails, malware installs, identity theft, and ransomware extortion. More often, however, it's quite similar to environmental pollution—negative consequences of a process with a separate goal. The goal is value creation or value delivery, but something in the execution creates adverse experiences for people. Think: robocalls, pop-up ads, spam messages, dumb chatbots, irrelevant pitches, fake followers, aggressive automation, unnecessary reply-all emails, and confusing comments.

The volume of noise and pollution we've created crowds, clouds, and complicates our online environments. As a result, messages that people want and experiences that people value may not reach them; this includes your customers. People and businesses that we know, like, and trust may not get the attention they deserve; this includes you.

Tradeoffs

Every technology has this in common: We can use it well or poorly. The printing press allowed knowledge and literacy to spread, but it also helped spread libel and slander. As publishing evolved into blogs and other digital formats, more people were empowered to spread valuable ideas, but misinformation spreads faster, easier, and further, too. Smartphones put access to all kinds of things into our hands, but many people struggle to manage screen time. Social media connects us, but it's also being weaponized against us resulting in social manipulation, isolation, and fragmentation.

Healthy, thoughtful, and responsible humans make the difference. We can use technology in ways that do no harm. We can benefit others, not just ourselves. The pro-social benefits of constructively using technology extend from each one of us out through our networks, organizations, communities, and all of society. The alternative is the degradation of digital spaces and the dehumanization of others. People and machines are lined up on both sides of this fight. The battle is a reflection of human nature itself.

History

Like environmental pollution's deep history, digital pollution dates back to our earliest days online. Self-replicating on infected computers until it crashed the system, one of the first malicious viruses, "Wabbit," appeared in 1974.[26] The first spam email was sent in 1978 to hundreds of unsuspecting people. Though it generated $13 million in sales of a new model of computer, "complaints started coming in almost immediately," according to its sender.[27] In the early- to mid-1990s, phishing schemes emerged on AOL with scammers appearing as AOL administrators to solicit login information from customers. That successful strategy spread to other internet service providers and expanded into using victims' email addresses to send spam emails.[28] What's believed to be the first online bank robbery? A $10 million hack in 1994.[29] The decades since are loaded with digital malfeasance of increasing variety, sophistication, and impact.

Sources

Digital pollution has point and nonpoint sources. Some problems are easy to track back to a specific source; others are so complex, distributed, scaled, and masked that their origins are unknown. Though entire industries and government branches have emerged to turn malicious polluters into known, point sources, many attacks go unsolved. Except for those clear cases in which otherwise legitimate sources send us emails we never asked for because we're on a list we never signed up for, pollution often *feels* nonpoint. It's a collective effect, generalized feeling, and persistent uncertainty. An acute incident like a stolen credit card number or spoofed social media profile occasionally spikes and validates our chronic unease.

Costs

As with pollution of our air, water, and soil, pollution online creates tolls paid by all digital citizens. Truly malicious polluters care nothing for the financial or emotional costs of their behavior; it's completely greedy or selfish. In grayer behavior, pollution is a consequence—a cost of production pushed out onto the public. Rather than investing time and money into cleaner lists, better segmentation, or human-to-human outreach, a company may do what's easiest—turn on automations and blast out messages hoping for some small percent of recipients to respond. In this way, the source pushes the costs onto the recipients.

We pay directly through taxes that support regulation, monitoring, and enforcement. Antivirus software, message filtering tools, and cybersecurity measures are direct costs, as is cleanup after incidents occur. The FBI recently called phishing "The 12 Billion Dollar Scam," and online identity theft losses were estimated at $16 billion.[30,31]

We pay indirectly for digital pollution through lost time, decreased productivity, heightened awareness, increased scrutiny, and reduced emotional well-being. Our fight-or-flight instincts in physical spaces don't translate as well to virtual spaces, so our brains and bodies work harder to make good decisions and safe choices.

Regulation

Laws and regulations like the CAN-SPAM Act of 2003 in the United States and Canada's Anti-Spam Law (CASL) that went into effect in 2014 support healthier online environments. Both address acceptable use of commercial digital messages. A couple of years later, the European Union enacted General Data Protection Regulation, or GDPR, which broadened protections to include consent, ownership, and privacy of personal data. A form of GDPR has been adopted in the U.S. with the California Consumer Privacy Act (CCPA) of 2018 and its addition, the California Privacy Rights Act (CPRA), which voters approved in November 2020. More than a dozen other states are working on similar data privacy protections, as is the U.S. federal government.[32,33,34]

But just because protections have been written and passed into law doesn't mean that enforcement is well-funded or effective. Many of the regulations are reactionary, a step behind. Issues related to humans' online existence are relatively new, extremely complex, and deeply philosophical. Issues of intent in commercial messages are more grounded, but still subjective. The best violations to pursue and prosecute, then, are the most egregious offenses—the visible tip of the proverbial iceberg, rather than the massive problem below the waterline.

Though there's a financial incentive for a source to permit environmental pollution, there's no financial incentive to create it. It's wasteful and inefficient. There is, however, a significant financial incentive to create digital pollution. Digitally scamming, swindling, and stealing can be done remotely, anonymously, and at scale. Automate the process, and it harvests ill-gotten gains while you sleep. As more valuable information gets digitized, the incentive to victimize people grows. With high potential for return on investment, malicious digital polluters may always be a step ahead of the law and its enforcement.

Priceless Capital

One of the most important aspects of digital pollution seems impossible to regulate: the drawdown on social capital. Like natural capital, social capital doesn't show up on balance sheets or reports. It's neither visible nor valued in a traditional accounting system. The term traces back to a book published in 1916 in which author Lyda Hanifan defined social capital as "those tangible assets [that] count for most in the daily lives of people: namely goodwill, fellowship, sympathy, and social intercourse among the individuals and families who make up a social unit."[35]

Trust, rapport, relationship, belonging, confidence, security, satisfaction, hope, encouragement, reciprocity, cooperation—these bind us together as families, teams, groups, companies, communities, cultures, and societies. We humans find meaning and purpose in our shared identities, norms, and values. They make things worth doing and empower us to get things done. They motivate our decisions and commitments. Social capital consists of immeasurable qualities that make measurable differences in our lives and businesses.

> **Social capital** consists of immeasurable qualities that make measurable differences in our lives and businesses.

When we treat people like numbers, when we do things online that we would never do in person, and when we say things digitally that we'd never say face to face, we burn social capital. When we poison digital environments, we poison ourselves. According to Pew Research, 79% of U.S. adults believe Americans have "far too little" or "too little" confidence in each other. Sixty-four percent believe Americans' level of trust in each other has been shrinking.[36] There's no calculating the cost of seeing each other and the world through this distrusting view.

Fortunately, we're a social species. Our emotions, thoughts, and behaviors are contagious. This damage can likely be undone. Social capital seems more renewable than natural capital. We need it. We want it. And we create it. In a *Harvard Business Review* article titled "Rethinking Trust," Roderick Kramer summarizes in this way: "In short, we're social beings from the get-go: We're born to be engaged and to engage others, which is what trust is largely about. That has been an advantage in our struggle for survival".[37] Our propensity to trust can be a weakness. We can be manipulated in person and online. But we're wired for and rewarded by building trusting relationships. Social capital can be restored.

Subjectivity

Stealing medical records or using a bot farm to bring down a legitimate website certainly seems bad. Even when intent seems malicious, however, digital pollution remains subjective. It's decided on a person-by-person, case-by-case, and moment-by-moment basis. You and I might receive the exact same message from the same source at the same time. I might find it tolerable or even useful. You might find it irrelevant and intrusive. Changing any of the variables—like the source, the timing, or the language—might change how you feel about that piece of digital communication, be it an ad, email, text, or anything else. And what appears to be innocuous to one of us may, in fact, be a danger to us both. Partly because of the difficulty in regulating what's subjective, polluting behavior proliferates.

A Human Problem

Just like environmental pollution, digital pollution is a human problem—caused by, paid by, and potentially solved by humans. Unlike environmental pollution, digital pollution isn't well understood and the conversation is just getting started. Hopefully you recognize its threat to all of us as stakeholders in our shared, virtual environments.

In perhaps the single best piece published on the topic to date, a *Washington Monthly* article titled "The World Is Choking on Digital Pollution," networking technology pioneer and Silicon Valley leader Judy Estrin writes, "We are right to be concerned. Increased anxiety and fear, polarization, fragmentation of a shared context, and loss of trust are some of the most apparent impacts of digital pollution. Potential degradation of intellectual and emotional capacities, such as critical thinking, personal authority, and emotional well-being, are harder to detect. We don't fully understand the cause and effect of digital toxins".[38]

Just as we don't have to accept the underlying assumptions, false dichotomies, or old models of environmental pollution, we don't have to accept the status quo here. We can work toward understanding and improvement—for everyone's benefit, including our own.

THREE CATEGORIES OF DIGITAL POLLUTION

To increase understanding of digital pollution, we offer this three-tiered taxonomy: Innocent, Consequential, and Intentional. The lines between these classifications are neither hard nor clear. The intent of the source is what differentiates them, but judgments of intent are made subjectively by each recipient. What each of us infers is based on what we're presented with in the current moment and on what we recall from the past. What's pollution to me may not be to you. What seems Innocent to me may seem Intentional to you.

1. Innocent Pollution

Innocent digital pollution is driven by carelessness, ignorance, or poor execution. It's a message or experience that is unwanted at the moment by the recipient, but with no ill intent from the source. It's one of those old chain emails from a family member with the expectation that you forward it on. It's a poorly punctuated or badly autocorrected message that conveys the wrong meaning and leads to confusion, frustration, or anger. It's an unintentional, clumsy click that communicates the wrong thing from the source and misleads the recipient.

Innocent pollution is experienced in that group text message or group LinkedIn message that you've found yourself in. It's somewhat relevant to you, but you'd prefer it as an individual message without all those replies from the entire group. Innocent pollution is the reasonable request in a digital channel from someone you know that uncomfortably feels colder and more curt than the request seems to deserve. It's the long and frustrating back-and-forth exchange in email, Slack, or a comments thread that could have reached clarity through a 30-second conversation.

Again, we humans have not yet adapted to our virtual environments. Entering them introduces unique challenges to clear communication and meaningful connection. We generally lack cultural norms, established patterns, and shared expectations to close the gaps. Most of us proceed into these spaces and behave just as we would in the real world without considering their nuances. Simple adjustments in our mindsets and actions, like those offered in Part Two of this book, can dramatically reduce Innocent pollution.

To illustrate how blurred these lines can be, think about whether you'd call this experience Innocent or Consequential. I received personal outreach via LinkedIn from a digital acquaintance whom I've never met or worked directly with. This person offered me the first chapter of his new book and asked to confirm my email address so he could send it over. I happily accepted.

Over the next four days, I received seven emails. I received 16 in the first month. Now at 59, they're still coming as I write this. On the upside, I did provide explicit permission for the first email, which delivered on its promise (the chapter of his book). On the downside, multiple emails greeted me as "%FIRSTNAME|UPPERFIRST%" and I never agreed to the dozens of emails I've received or any of the dozens still to come.

Is this Innocent? Or . . .

2. Consequential Pollution

Consequential digital pollution is the classification most like environmental pollution—it's a negative consequence of a process with a separate goal. Some sources may plead ignorance, but that excuse is quickly knocked out with a little common sense and a little attention to the feedback loop. A more honest assessment sees Consequential pollution driven by laziness, myopia, or greed. We don't want to put in the work, we don't recognize the ramifications, or we don't want to make the investment. We don't care as much about other people as we do about ourselves.

Consequential pollution is commonly experienced as irrelevant, unsolicited, poorly targeted, or overly aggressive messages. Some of it is straightforward spam. Some of it is dumb automation: the "Have you downloaded our app?" onboarding email, even though you downloaded the app two weeks ago and use it daily. It may also be experienced like this: You enter an email address for a webinar or a case study, then get a seemingly unending series of emails you never asked for or expected. Even after you unsubscribe, it keeps coming, along with a barrage of targeting ads that follow you from site to site. It feels more like an assault than an invitation.

> Consequential pollution is commonly experienced
> as **irrelevant, unsolicited, poorly targeted,**
> or **overly aggressive messages**.

If you've ever accepted a LinkedIn connection request and immediately received a four-paragraph, copy-and-paste sales pitch for something that's irrelevant to you, categorize it here. Spam texts, phone number spoofing, badly automated chatbots and menus, bait-and-switch on click-throughs, overly aggressive campaigns, artificial intelligence deployed on weak data sets and poor training—these tend to create negative feelings. And they crowd out things we actually need and want.

Many dynamics are in play with Consequential pollution, including subjectivity. As advertising innovator Howard Gossage wisely offered, "Nobody reads advertising. People read what interests them, and sometimes it's an ad." "Advertising" can be expanded to include any digital message or experience. What's irrelevant or toxic to me, might be helpful to you. You may feel elated to receive an unsolicited message—as long as it's helpful. Beyond the recipient's subjective assessment, though, are source considerations.

Tools and technology have become so powerful and inexpensive that they're easily misunderstood and mishandled. They may have been mischaracterized and oversold by the vendor. They may have been chosen and implemented poorly by the organization. The team may lack the time, skills, or resources to use a tool properly. They may not recognize or mitigate the negative consequences of their misuse. The team may lack the maturity, wisdom, or leadership to treat people as anything *except* numbers; they may not understand the difference.

Consequential digital pollution can be caused when disparate systems and data sources aren't talking to each other properly. The pressure on businesses to grow may be so strong that the negative effects of aggressive tactics are ignored; increased investment heightens expectations and often drives pollution. For example, my co-author Steve met a marketer in a well-funded, high-growth company with a $1 *billion* ad budget! Imagine the potential inefficiencies and externalities in a spend that large.

The demand for growth seems to require more emails, more ads, more everything. But this can be a trap. Because of diminishing returns and diminishing reputation, more isn't always better. Sometimes it's the fast track to Consequential pollution.

Consequential Confessional

As a marketer and a revenue professional, I've sent millions of emails over the years. I'm generally proud of the work I've done, but I confess to clicking "Send" on messages that weren't fully respectful of the recipients. For a time, providing your email address to my team meant you'd receive every newsletter and webinar invite until you unsubscribed or marked it as spam.

Several years ago, I helped launch a video training course. The marketing campaign provided significant educational value, even for people who didn't buy the course. But we delivered it through more than a dozen emails in less than two weeks, including six emails in the final three days. We supported this onslaught with targeted Facebook ads, too. The campaign wasn't thoughtless, but it was aggressive. As I segmented lists throughout the campaign, I began to see people as numbers—as opens, clicks, plays, purchases, unsubscribes, even abuse complaints.

Not surprisingly, some of those complaints arrived as angry email replies. I sent a truly personal apology video to each one, which almost always defused the situation. With sincerity I tried to make each person feel heard and valued. I had no desire to annoy or frustrate them, but I did want to sell out the course. With more focus on my short-term goal than our long-term reputation, I tried to "win" by increasing volume and activity. The negative consequences were a tradeoff.

Did it work? It's not easy to say. Is hitting the number "working"? What about the consequences to my personal reputation and to the company brand? What about the anger some felt? What about negative word of mouth? Could we have brought in the same revenue with a more patient and careful approach? Did the positive replies and purchases outweigh all of this? Because some of these things are not easily measured, we tend not to value or account for them.

Again, pollution is not the goal in the Consequential category. Value creation or value delivery is the goal. Pollution is a consequence we can manage well or poorly, even though we'll never do it perfectly. We can be good actors or bad actors in relation to it; our recipients get to make the judgment call.

3. Intentional Pollution

Though it seems the easiest to classify, even Intentional digital pollution is based on recipient judgments of the source's intent. Some seem selfish and malicious from the start: phishing schemes to install malware, gain personal data, or solicit cash. Various ways of stealing identities and creating accounts. System hacks to acquire seemingly secure data, create a ransom situation, or simply bring down the site or network.

But what about armies of bots on social networks spreading lies, conspiracy theories, and disinformation? What if the information is simply misleading rather than verifiably false? What if it advances an idea you support or an outcome you desire? What if, instead, the attack takes down a website for a cause you despise or an outcome you detest? Even Intentional pollution is subjective.

You might experience this type of pollution when you receive an email from a spoofed email address that looks legitimate. It appears to be from someone you know. But if you open the attachment, malware is loaded onto your laptop. In his TEDx talk "Human Hacking: The Psychology Behind Cybersecurity," Dr. Erik Huffman, the IT Director here at BombBomb with Steve and me, tells the story of receiving an email from his mom with the word "Help" in the subject line. A cyberpsychology expert, he recalls the personal concern for his mom, then red flags about the tone and language of the message, and finally calling her to confirm the message was faked.[39]

Attacks like these prey on human vulnerabilities in environments in which we're not as well-guarded. They may be against individuals, businesses, governments, organizations, infrastructures, or networks. The worst offenders have the biggest or broadest targets. There's enough money at stake to aggressively innovate. They remain a step ahead of current defenses and several steps ahead of the law. As long as they're successful, they'll maintain this edge.

Because you're reading this book, any pollution you're creating is likely Innocent or Consequential. But, again, you don't get to decide. Your recipients do. You know your intent, but you can't always make it clear. Often your recipients must infer it and they don't always come to rational conclusions. Reaching the wrong person at the wrong time with the wrong experience may create what feels like Intentional pollution for that person. Fair or not, you pay the price.

YES, VIDEO CAN POLLUTE

Human-centered communication is an antidote to digital pollution. In the next chapter, we'll define and characterize it and, in doing so, establish its relationship to video communication. But make no mistake that video, too, can pollute our digital environment.

Intentional video pollution includes deepfakes in which people's likenesses have words put into their mouths. They're synthetic but masquerade as authentic. They misinform or disinform while being offered as evidence. Consequential video pollution includes mass-blast or spray-and-pray distribution, as well as videos that mislead you with clickbait thumbnails or titles. Auto-play videos that have you rushing for the mute button or searching for the right browser window to close might be Consequential or Innocent. Each of these examples—and others you may already have thought of—degrade our online experience and make us question the source's motivations and intentions.

While most of us have increased our use of video to add a personal touch to our digital communication, we've increased the likelihood of creating Innocent digital pollution in the process. We typically show up on live, synchronous video calls without accounting for their shortcomings. The pages ahead include guidance from experts to help you show up with more thought, care, and intention. To increase engagement and to improve outcomes. In recorded, asynchronous video messages, we pollute by not thinking about the message or the recipient before hitting record, by not being clear and concise, by burying the most important ideas deep in the video, by failing to support those ideas with bulleted-list text, and by making other innocent, ignorant errors. You'll get guidance on this, too.

STOP DIGITAL POLLUTION

Because it's lacked a common name and definition, digital pollution has been easy to overlook. But you've seen it in micro form—an email or a connection request from an unfamiliar and perhaps suspicious sender. And you've felt it in macro form—the overwhelming sense of having too much to plow through to get to what matters. When you start to consciously notice it, you'll continue to see it more often. Talk about it. Screenshot it. Without shaming the relatively innocent, write about it and post about it. Start the digital pollution conversation within your company and within your professional network.

Each of us can be part of the solution rather than part of the problem. But it isn't easy. We've been there. To reach a number, we've executed strategies and tactics in ways we're not proud of. At the time, it seemed right . . . or at least justifiable. We rationalized that how we did it is just how it's done. It's how others do it, too. But what's normalized isn't necessarily right.

By definition, what's normalized isn't innovative. Whatever we're doing, we can do it better. We can change. Habits, norms, cultures, reputations, and fortunes can improve. It all happens one step, one decision, and one person at a time. Those who break out of standard practices in order to reduce negative experiences are moving in the direction markets are already headed.

Markets are people. They thrive on trust, transparency, reputation, and mutual benefit. Imagining that our interests matter more than our customers' interests doesn't make it true. What's bad for customers is bad for us. What's bad for any stakeholder is bad for us. Markets demand the respect of a human-centered approach. Regulations will eventually demand it, too. Every day, we should demand this of ourselves.

In "The World Is Choking on Digital Pollution," Judy Estrin wisely calls us to action: "We must now stake a collective claim in controlling digital pollution. What we face is not the good or bad decision of any one individual or even one company. It is not just about making economic decisions. It is about dispassionately analyzing the economic, cultural, and health impacts on society and then passionately debating the values that should guide our choices—as companies, as individual employees, as consumers, as citizens, and through our leaders and elected representatives."[38]

Pollution is a human problem with a human solution. And every one of us has a stake in it.

CHAPTER 2

Human-Centered Communication

We all know The Golden Rule: Treat others as you would like to be treated. It's present in nearly every major religious and philosophical system, including Buddhism, Judaism, Christianity, Islam, Hinduism, Zoroastrianism, Sikhism, Confucianism, Taoism, Baha'i, Rastafari, Shinto, Stoicism, Humanism, and others.[1,2,3] All express in one way or another that we should behave in ways for which we praise others. We should avoid behavior for which we criticize others. We should understand the consequences of our actions before we act. We should think as much about others as we do about ourselves.

The Golden Rule is simple and powerful. But we can take it a step further. Many people advocate for The Platinum Rule, which calls us to treat others as *they* would like to be treated. It shifts our mindset from inside-out to outside-in. It's about others' personal preferences rather than our own generalized rules; it calls us to know and understand individual people. Just as compassion goes a step beyond empathy by turning feeling into action, moving from Gold to Platinum asks more of us and gives more to everyone.

In addition to these rules, what else is a well-raised child taught? What other behaviors does an emotionally mature adult model? Honor your word. Say what you mean and mean what you say. Honesty is the best policy. Practice what you preach. Walk the talk. Walk a mile in another's shoes. Be yourself. Love one another. Tried and true, these ideas provide a good starting point for understanding human-centered communication.

What frustrates, confuses, annoys, or alarms you as you move through online experiences? Are you doing that to other people? Do you understand what they want? Have you asked? How much attention are you paying to the way people interact with your messages? Who's opening emails and who's unsubscribing? Who's clicking links? What's your response rate? What's in those responses?

Through tracking and analytics, feedback about people's behavior is easily available for most digital activities. To invoke The Platinum Rule: There's no reason to send a sixth follow-up message to a person who hasn't engaged with the first five or to the person who responded to the second message with, "No, thank you."

Every single email you send trains people to open or delete your next email. The same goes for every video, message, or experience you create. You're training us to engage or to ignore. You're giving or taking—making deposits or withdrawals. You're addressing relevant problems and opportunities or you're just making noise. You're helping others feel seen, heard, understood, and appreciated or you're helping yourself. With each click, you're improving or polluting our digital environment.

Impressions that train people to engage with or ignore you are only created if you can get their attention at all. Because of the volume of noise and level of pollution, you're likely finding it more difficult to get attention. We receive more messages than ever. They're harder to parse through and prioritize. Identifying the source and verifying its authenticity require more scrutiny. Intent is also harder to judge. We want to trust, but we can't afford to give every message the benefit of the doubt.

Our brains default to quick decision-making and work to protect our time, energy, and security. We dole out attention carefully. Though it's only 2% of our body weight, our brain uses 20% of our energy. "As an energy-consumer, the brain is the most expensive organ we carry around with us," according to Dr. Marcus Raichle, a professor at Washington University School of Medicine in St. Louis.[4] Mental calories are real, and we are optimized to conserve. In this environment, buying, begging, or stealing people's attention only gets more expensive.

Earning that attention is paramount.

No matter how you initially get a person's attention, reward them. Provide something timely and useful that entertains or benefits them. Demonstrate warmth and competence; show that you're capable of helping and that you'll do it with their best interests at heart. This earns you their precious time, plus the right to ask for their attention again in the future. Done consistently over time, you're building permission- and trust-based access to them. Failure to build positive familiarity results in your being ignored, deleted, or even blocked.

If all this sounds a bit transactional, that's because at some level it is. To support our survival and to conserve our energy, our brains identify patterns and create shortcuts. If a message or experience I provide you triggers a feeling of "this isn't for me or about me," "this isn't worth my time or attention," or "this takes too much energy and effort," then I get the "pollution" stamp in your mind. This establishes or reinforces a negative pattern. This is difficult to recover from; once a mental model is created, it's hard to break. If instead I leave you with the feeling of "he gets me," "this is for me," or "this is helpful," I'm part of a positive pattern in your mind.

Every touchpoint you create is emotionally experienced by a recipient. Each experience is evaluated against past perceptions in order to predict future outcomes. In this way, your reputation is formed from the earliest interactions. From there, it's constantly shaped by each message and experience you provide. As prediction machines, people are incessantly and subconsciously feeling their way around the physical and digital worlds, essentially asking, "Does this meet or exceed my expectations based on what I know about you from past interactions?" We respond accordingly, log new data, and prepare to make our next prediction.

No matter your role, business, or industry, your success is enabled by other people. You win when you work with and for others. When you treat people like people, not like numbers, you make them feel valued. You build social capital that's of long-term benefit not just to you, but to everyone. You support positive mental patterns that result in trust and engagement loops, which are reinforced through the digital interactions you rely on every day—every time you click "Send," "Share," or "Post."

> When you **treat people like people,** not like numbers, you make them feel valued.

Make your intent evident. Make your tone clear. Make the benefits apparent. Demonstrate warmth and competence in ways people can feel—even when you're not there in person. If you do these things consistently and well, you're part of the movement to make human-centered communication the norm. Your reputation and success depend on it.

ORIGINS OF "HUMAN-CENTERED COMMUNICATION"

Even though it captures a necessary innovation, "human-centered communication" isn't really a term. Yet. However, human-centered design has become a prevalent philosophy and practice over the past few decades, producing nearly 4 million results in a recent exact-match Google search. For comparison, an exact match search for "human-centered computing" produced about half a million results. "Human-centered communication?" About 20,000. Small, but promising.

The term "human-centered communication" elevates the conversation above any tool or technology. And it builds on the understanding and practice of human-centered design. Its characteristics are reinforced by our allies and exemplars throughout Part Two of this book and summarized in Part Three. The language is relatively new, but the underlying principles are as timeless and transcendent as The Golden Rule.

Roots in Human-Centered Design

In his 1980 book *Architect or Bee?: The Human/Technology Relationship*, engineer Mike Cooley coined the term "human-centred systems" as a call for work more satisfying to humans and production more useful to society.[5] His ideas are part of a larger, ongoing debate about the dehumanization of work due to specialization, mechanization, and automation. Another book to emerge from that movement is *Small Is Beautiful: Economics As If People Mattered* by E.F. Schumacher. Published in 1973, the book walks us through, among other concepts, the value of natural capital, the consequences of scale, the dehumanizing effects of automation, and the benefits of "technology with a human face."[6]

Today, finding the proper relationship between humans and machines remains a challenge. But it's not just about industrial factories and equipment anymore. Automation and mechanization are now digital, not just physical. Human-centered design applies to it all.

Founded in 1978, global design and consulting firm IDEO has practiced human-centered design since their inception.[7] Tim Brown, chair of IDEO, says that "human-centered design is about cultivating deep empathy with the people you're designing for; generating ideas; building a bunch of prototypes; sharing what you've made with the people you're designing for; and eventually, putting your innovative new solution out in the world."[8] It balances the needs of people (desirability) with the possibilities of technology (feasibility) and the requirements for business success (viability). "If you want to improve a piece of software, all you have to do is watch people grimace, and then you can fix that," says David Kelley, Founder of IDEO.[9]

IDEO's framework includes seven Mindsets (Creative Confidence, Make It, Learn from Failure, Empathy, Embrace Ambiguity, Optimism, and Iteration) and three Methods (Inspiration, Ideation, and Implementation).[10] These mindsets can be applied to most of the work you do. Same for the methods—you're sparked to create, change, or improve something; you generate ideas with people in mind; then you implement, learn, and iterate. IDEO's applied their framework to food waste, healthcare, technology, retail, publishing, education, and beyond. You can apply it to your business communication.

Other organizations offer their own approaches to human-centered design. For example, in *Innovating for People: Handbook of Human-Centered Design Methods*, the LUMA Institute describes the phases of Looking, Understanding, and Making, each with a suitable set of activities and characteristics.[11] The International Organization for Standardization has even created a standard for human-centered design, ISO 9241-210:2019—Human-centred design for interactive systems:

> *Human-centred design is an approach to interactive systems development that aims to make systems usable and useful by focusing on the users, their needs and requirements, and by applying human factors/ergonomics, and usability knowledge and techniques. This approach enhances effectiveness and efficiency, improves human well-being, user satisfaction, accessibility and sustainability; and counteracts possible adverse effects of use on human health, safety and performance.*[12]

What's human-centered starts with stakeholders in mind—the people it's for and the people it affects. It seeks human satisfaction and well-being while diminishing negative impacts. Impacts on humans aren't consequential, they're intentional; they're considered from the beginning and present by design. When undertaking this design process, it's not enough simply to know about these people. We must engage with, immerse ourselves with, and truly understand them. People are the priority.

That's not to say that we ignore business outcomes. For sustainable, long-term success, business needs are balanced with the needs of the humans involved in producing and experiencing those outcomes. And we don't just set up a process and let it run; we get feedback, analyze, learn, adjust, and iterate. In this way, we can design systems, processes, and procedures that treat people as people, that steadily improve, and that reduce pollution.

Human-centered design starts with empathy and understanding. But its success is in its compassion—acting to identify opportunities, improve processes, and solve problems.

FOUR PILLARS OF HUMAN-CENTERED COMMUNICATION

Too often, we "communicate" by just saying what we need or want to say. There's not much forethought. Not much care. We just type a message based on what we think others should hear, know, or do. Fortunately, this often works. Unfortunately, it also results in misunderstanding, missed opportunities, and diminished reputation.

Further, as Dr. Nick Morgan observes in *Can You Hear Me? How to Connect With People in a Virtual World*, the engineers who created the tools we use "didn't optimize the various kinds of digital communications for what humans need: data-rich, emotionally complex, fast exchanges of human intent and meaning, largely through the unconscious mind."[13] That's to say, our reliance on text-based communication alone is a reliance on data-poor, emotionally-limited, and highly rational processes. We're missing faces, voices, emotions, and nonverbal cues.

To help restore much of what's missing, more and more business professionals are blending video into their communication. Adding personality, improving clarity, and increasing response, video calls and video messages have one foot in the real world and one foot in the digital world. The emotional and visual nature of video matches the emotional and visual needs of every member of our social species. To truly connect, however, we can't just show up; we must be intentional.

A human-centered approach makes primary the needs and interests of our message recipient or call participant. Our messages are judged as digital pollution when they're not sufficiently attuned to our recipients—who they are, where they are, and what they need or want right now. We must understand the people we're trying to communicate with. And our goal isn't simply to be heard; it's to create conversations that further mutual understanding and mutually beneficial outcomes.

Guided by principles of human behavior and psychology, human-centered communication balances the needs of people (desirability) with the possibilities of technology (feasibility) and the requirements for business success (viability). It has an emphasis on digital channels but can be used anywhere. It has an emphasis on synchronous and asynchronous video but can be used with text and other mediums. It has an emphasis on professional communication but can also be used in personal contexts. It produces better engagement and results for your business, but it's also more satisfying and fulfilling for you as a person.

Below in Figure 2.1 is a simplified comparison of what the difference might look and sound like on an average workday. It echoes Lauren Bailey's SWIIFT[SM] ("So What's In It For Them?") approach to thinking about others; you'll learn more from her in Chapter 8. It's also aligned with Dan Hill's WIIFM ("What's In It For Me?") call to put yourself in others' shoes before reaching out; he's featured in Chapter 4.

DEFAULT APPROACH	HUMAN-CENTERED APPROACH
"Why didn't she open my email?"	"Why would she open my email?"
"Why didn't he reply?"	"Why would he reply?"
"Why didn't they play my video?"	"Why would they play my video?"
Reactive	Proactive
Backward-looking	Future-oriented
About the source	About the recipient

Figure 2.1 The Human-Centered Difference

By putting people at the center of your communication habits, you're making things easier and better for them. You're valuing their time and honoring their dignity. The difference is felt and increases the likelihood of response. Plus, you're creating a positive reputation. So this approach helps in the short term on a message-by-message basis and it also wins over the long term as you reinforce trust and confidence.

We believe there are four pillars of human-centered communication that help characterize this approach: Guidance, Identity, Verification, and Engagement. At the heart of the approach and supported by these pillars is Relationship.

Guidance

To adopt human-centered communication, you'll benefit from the support of a growing, like-minded community. To build business relationships, especially using video, you'll benefit from coaching on how to successfully integrate this new use of the medium into your workflows. Applying old habits from other channels doesn't allow us to properly use new ones; email isn't direct mail, websites aren't newspapers. As video norms and standards are still being set, you should look to pioneering peers and practiced professionals for guidance. You'll also learn and grow through the feedback you receive as a practitioner yourself.

Identity

Identity means that effective communication comes from leveraging your best asset—you—to create authentic, meaningful, and personal messages that help you connect with other people. You may have been told you're one in a million, but you're far more unique than that. You're one of a kind. What is unique to you distinguishes you. To be more human, you must come out from behind your keyboard and shed your cloak of digital anonymity. You must find confidence in yourself and comfort in your vulnerability. Doing so is a gift to others and to yourself. It's an invitation to true connection. Sharing your identity in this way makes the virtual more personal.

Verification

Your recipients have to trust and verify that you are who you say you are. Think back to our exploration of digital pollution. Innocent and Consequential pollution result when verification is made difficult. Often, we fail to provide any verification at all. Intentional pollution takes the extra step of misleading recipients into false verification. All of this produces friction for people who are assessing opportunities presented to them virtually. But you can't afford to get lost amid the noise. And you can't assume you'll get the benefit of the doubt. For everyone's benefit, you must make it easier for others to verify your identity and intent.

Engagement

Relationships are reciprocal; they require two-way communication. Your recipients need ways to respond to your messages and engage in conversation, regardless of the channel. This is the feedback loop that provides you guidance in your iterative processes; engagement helps you learn, adapt, and improve. It also moves opportunities forward. Engagement and exchange are the fundamental purpose of most of your business communication. As human-centered communication makes identity and verification faster and easier to discern, so too should it make engagement faster, easier, and more likely to occur.

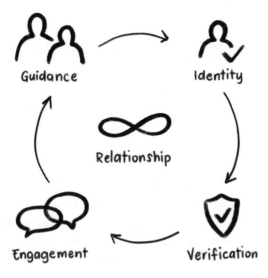

Figure 2.2 Four Pillars of Human-Centered Communication

Relationships

Relationships are at the heart of this approach, as you can see in Figure 2.2. At some level, every business is a relationship-based business—even those built on scaled, automated, and artificially intelligent systems. When people say "yes," they're not just saying yes to the specific opportunity you've presented. They're also saying yes to you—to the familiarity, trust, and relationship that you, your team, or your brand have built with them. Consistent use of human-centered communication will create more and deeper relationships, especially when you're confined to digital environments.

GIVE/GIVER

You may have noticed that the pillars of Guidance, Identity, Verification, and Engagement create the acronym GIVE, and including Relationship makes it GIVER. This is a reflection of the spirit and philosophy that underpin any human-centered movement.

"Life's most persistent and urgent question is, 'What are you doing for others?'" observed Martin Luther King Jr. in "Three Dimensions of a Complete Life."[14] Indeed, it is. We're to put others first. We're to lead with the give, rather than the take. We are a social species that has thrived through reciprocal relationships from the dawn of our existence. Some neurologists believe that The Golden Rule and its ethic of reciprocity is an evolutionary benefit that's hardwired into our brains.[15]

Through generations, we humans have learned that givers ultimately get far more in return than takers can acquire by taking. If you don't accept this as intuitively true, consider the research of organizational psychologist and Wharton professor Adam Grant. In a TED Talk based on his *New York Times* bestseller *Give and Take: Why Helping Others Drives Our Success*, he explains how being a taker catches up to you and how being a giver makes organizations better. His conclusion: "Success is really more about contribution . . . The most meaningful way to succeed is to help other people succeed."[16]

The benefits of giving are both measurable and immeasurable; givers are more wholly successful and more deeply satisfied. No matter our available resources, we can all afford to be more generous. As Rutger Bregman closes his sweeping book *Humankind: A Hopeful History*, "like all the best things in life, the more you give, the more you have."[15] Respect, trust, and love all work this way.

ALIGNING WITH PEOPLE AND MARKETS

You're likely already taking a human-centered approach at times, especially if you're more empathetic than most. Our goal is to increase conscious awareness of how we're communicating every day in order to be more intentional and to build new habits. We want to provoke conversation about human centricity and elevate its importance as a business practice. It's simply the right thing to do. But it's also the smart thing to do.

Aligned with People

To be human-centered means that we operate from humanistic values and a devotion to human well-being. In any human-centered system, process, decision, or function, we make the needs and wants of people primary, not secondary or tertiary. We recognize the intrinsic value of each and every one of our fellow human beings. We refuse to denigrate their dignity. This comes naturally when we're together in person. Sharing direct eye contact triggers our ethical and empathic impulses toward others. However, it requires conscious effort when we mediate our experiences and interactions through screens.

When we are children, we develop what psychologists call a "theory of mind." Slowly, and over many experiences, children come to realize that not everyone thinks, knows, or wants what they do. They realize that, in fact, every other person has his or her own unique beliefs, desires, hopes, intentions, and information that may differ from their own.[17] Humans develop this theory using a composite of memory, attention, face and gaze processing, language, the tracking of intentions and goals, moral reasoning, emotion processing-recognition, empathy, and imitation.

However, as we spend more time in digital environments, our access to facial cues, verbal cues, gaze, emotion—the very things that allow us to develop this theory of mind—is stunted, muted, or even eliminated. We threaten the development of theory of mind and its related functions when we trade real facetime for digital screen time, especially when we do so with a "just show up" mindset. To fully see others and feel seen ourselves in virtual exchanges, we must intentionally and consistently be human-centered.

Aligned with Markets

If we don't demand human centricity of ourselves and our team members on moral grounds, we should demand it on practical grounds; markets demand it of us. You're likely already aware that consumers, not businesses, are in control. And their expectations are higher than ever. As Mark Schaefer observes in the deeply researched *Marketing Rebellion: The Most Human Company Wins*, "Hyper-empowered consumers are less loyal, more informed, and less trusting of companies and brands than at any other time in history."[18]

Individuals can access and share nearly as much information as businesses can; this wasn't true just a generation or two ago. Customers' voices now matter more to a business's success than its advertising does. People's voices are more believable, more available, and more influential than corporate voices. The ubiquity of subscription models means more and more companies face potential one-and-done customer relationships with a single click to cancel. After a bad experience, customers don't have to return, and they can tell their family, friends, coworkers, and millions of strangers why.

At the same time, businesses face both hyper-competition and product parity, making differentiation more difficult. Starting a business is easier than ever and guidance to do so is widely available in YouTube channels, podcasts, blogs, books, courses, communities, and other educational materials. Sure, some of it is charlatans' work, but in this environment, most charlatans get exposed quickly (see previous paragraph!). Your product or service innovation? Your new feature? It can be copied by competitors in a matter of weeks, days, or even hours. In most industries, the barriers to entry are getting lower. Every day, the moat protecting your business gets narrower and shallower.

Continuing the decades-long trend of fragmentation, mass markets are steadily breaking down to markets of one. A segmented, persona-based approach is better than broad brushing, mass sending, and uniform treatment. But we can't just personalize; we must also get personal. Even in a scaled, volume-based model, personal experiences are necessary to create differentiation and to provide remarkable moments. And if they can be created on a human-to-human basis, all the better. All of this points to the need to make each and every customer feel seen, heard, understood, and appreciated. Customers once hoped to have their problems solved and opportunities capitalized upon in a personal way. This hope is now an expectation. And it requires a human-centered approach.

> We can't just personalize.
> We must also **get personal**.

But this approach doesn't start or end with your customers. How can we expect our team members to make our customers feel valued and supported if they don't feel valued or supported themselves? The growth, development, and success of our employees promotes pride and meaning in their work. This increases productivity and retention.

Our customers and employees are just two of several stakeholder groups we must consider. Investors, partners, suppliers, creditors, competitors, neighbors, schools, governments, and media are among the others. "A company absolutely cannot thrive and prosper at the highest level when you lose the trust of any of your stakeholders," writes Salesforce founder, chairman, and CEO Marc Benioff in *Trailblazer: The Power of Business as the Greatest Platform for Change*, a *New York Times* bestseller he co-authored with Monica Langley.[19]

Salesforce consistently earns awards and recognition as a best place to work, an innovative organization, and top CRM solution. For moral, social, legal, and financial reasons, Marc values all of the company's stakeholders, not just its shareholders. "Yes, our business is to increase profits, but our business is also to improve the state of the world and drive stakeholder—not just shareholder—value. And not just because serving the interest of all stakeholders is good for the soul; it's because it's good for business." Marc adds this caution: "There will be consequences for business whose leadership doesn't live by values like trust and equality."[19]

We're seeing humanity return to the conversation across industries, as with Lippincott's Human Era Index, which was produced through research involving more than 1,000 brands and 30,000 customers. They rated brands on three dimensions:

1. Do you truly care for and about your Customers?

2. Are you trustworthy, real, and authentic?

3. Is your personality vital and unique?

The average brand scored 6 on the index. Much beloved Southwest Airlines scored 6.9. Customer-obsessed and cult-followed Apple came in at 7.8. The most "human" brand across all industries? USAA, a nearly 100-year-old financial services organization, with a score of 9.4. The result of their human approach? A 98% customer retention rate.[20]

As for the human/machine relationship, many younger companies are building the bridge. Narrative Science focuses on data storytelling and aspires to make data and analytics useful, understandable, and accessible for everyone in your business. 6sense turns human behavior into intent data to help companies live out their anti-pollution promise of "No Forms. No Spam. No Cold Calls." Chorus.ai and Gong.io turn human conversations and interactions into data so we can better train, coach, and develop our team members, as well as make AI-informed decisions. These are just a few examples among many.

For every one of our stakeholders, we must honor prevailing trends and heed wise cautions about the dignity, value, and primacy of our fellow human beings. This is where the world is going. Language and ideas once perceived as "soft" have entered mainstream business culture and vocabulary—words like authenticity, vulnerability, transparency, empathy, and compassion. These aren't things humans want. They are things humans need. For centuries, markets have rewarded these qualities, even though they couldn't measure them. As mass continues to give way to niche, markets are demanding these qualities. Markets are people.

A PRACTICAL CONSIDERATION

Will this take more time? Can I afford for my team to take this approach?

This is a common concern and practical consideration. It's similar to concerns about the "green premium" when buying clean, non-polluting products. "Green" products are often associated with higher prices, but standard to substandard efficacy. This doesn't hold true with human-centered communication. It may take a little more time in the beginning, but this cost diminishes through practice. As for efficacy, expect it to be equal or higher in the short term and much higher over the long term.

Without being too flippant, here's a better question: Can you afford not to take this approach?

Your response rates, relationships, and reputation demand it. When immeasurables enter an equation, they look inefficient because their costs can be seen but their value cannot. To invest in them can feel like an act of faith. We can easily tally activity totals like volumes of voicemails, emails, or meetings. We can easily calculate ratios like reply rates and appointment set rates. It's easy to know what's working, but it's not so easy to understand why. What's missing from view but driving the why are immeasurables like trust and likeability, which are always in play. We all know that immeasurables affect every measurable outcome; it's irresponsible to ignore this fact.

Approaching the question more practically: Yes, you can afford human-centered communication.

It's not unlike any other transformation or innovation in your business. This will likely take more time as you figure it out and form the habit. As with any behavior change, it requires understanding, belief, and buy-in across the team. Without these, the effort fails. When communicating, you'll do more work up front to save your recipients time, emotional energy, and mental energy. And your team members may need additional coaching and feedback as they take on this new way of communicating. You'll find, though, that what's invested up front provides a generous return in the end.

Again, you're likely already communicating in a human-centered way. But you may not be doing it consistently, consciously, or as well as you could. Motivation, practice, and guidance will help you and your team cross over from "takes more time and effort" to "automatic, habitual, fruitful, and satisfying."

Where and when might you use human-centered communication day-to-day? In short: any time with anyone in any medium and any channel. The chapters ahead are packed with practical strategies and tactics to help you; Chapters 14 and 15 summarize them. And specific opportunities across the entire customer and employee lifecycles are described next in Chapter 3.

FOUNDER of
WINNING BY DESIGN

"What we're looking for now is authenticity."

A KEY IDEA IN THIS CHAPTER

Applying tools and technology in a customer-centric way.

CHAPTER 3

A More Human Funnel

Featuring Jacco van der Kooij

Damaging corals, fishes, sponges, and other animals isn't the goal. Tearing up plants' root systems and stirring up more than 20 gigatons of sediment every year isn't the objective. These are negative consequences of the widespread industrial fishing practice of dragging heavy nets and metal chains across the seafloor.[1] "We're using these large trawler fishing boats," observes Jacco van der Kooij. "And we kill entire ecosystems just to catch that one tuna."

Founder of Winning by Design, Jacco is a revenue architect, go-to-market designer, and business expert who, in this chapter, helps us bridge digital pollution and human-centered communication with what's going on in our businesses every day. He teaches a scientific and customer-centric approach to revenue growth on the Winning by Design YouTube channel, in hundreds of sales blueprints, and in several books. His fishing example perfectly captures the way some of our efforts look like success, but only if we ignore the consequences.

Jacco is from a small farming village in the Netherlands. Naturally, then, he provides us an agricultural example of these counter impacts. Heading down the California coast from his home in Silicon Valley, Jacco saw a gigantic machine that was "a stadium wide" harvesting a field. Getting more done in less time is a proper use of technology. "A tractor is a form of a force multiplier," he explains. "And a combine machine is even a force multiplier for a tractor." Now imagine taking that huge combine into the wrong field—there's so much potential for disaster. The wrong tool for the wrong job. Too much force. Significant negative consequences.

As we multiply force, we must be especially careful to do so in the right way and at the right time. Often, however, we're doing the careless equivalent of driving the combine into the wrong field. How? "We are creating processes around the technology," observes Jacco. "We've turned it around." The proper order is to design the process, then select the best technology to support that process. Tools are levers that magnify power, so when we get turned around and put the tools first, the likelihood and scope of negative consequences are magnified.

Here's a digital example: cranking out automated emails, calls, and texts from your entire sales team to the wrong audience. This can be like dragging nets across the ocean floor or shredding crops in the wrong field. This cranking has consequences. With new tools to manage their inboxes, your potential customers can block an entire domain as spam. With one click, they could become unreachable not just to you, but to everyone in your entire company. If your team is sending out undesired, irrelevant, or untargeted emails in a scaled system, your addressable market may be collapsing. And, as Jacco says, "your carefully nurtured brand name" is on the line.

In his YouTube video "How to Do Outbound Right | Sales as a Science #17," Jacco puts numbers behind this idea. In the scenario, a sales team generates $80,000 by sending out emails to 1,000 prospective buyers. You can see the assumptions in Figure 3.1.

POSITIVE METRICS

1,000 emails
x 4% conversion
40 opportunities
x 20% conversion
8 closed sales
x $10,000 sale
$ 80,000 revenue

NEGATIVE METRICS

1% unsubscribe/email
10 emails/sequence
99% remaining to power of 10
10% or 100 people lost
6 reps or 6 cycles
90% remaining to power of 6
470 people lost

Figure 3.1 Accounting for Negative Metrics

What if we want to double revenue to $160,000? Because we tend to focus on positive metrics and take a volume-based approach, the most common answer is to double the target list to 2,000 people. What we lose sight of, though, are the negative metrics. We look at the 4% conversion rate and ignore the 96% failure rate.

With this in mind, let's look at one of the costs of generating the $80,000. Assume a 1% unsubscribe rate and 10-email sequence, as Jacco does in his video. At that rate, we'd lose 100 of our 1,000 contacts over that sequence. Now assume we do this six times throughout the year or we have six team members running these sequences. The net result is that we'd acquire the new revenue, but we'd lose 47% of our target contacts. Nearly half! And that's just one measurable counter impact.[2]

Pick your cliché: biting the hand that feeds you, cutting off your nose to spite your face, killing the goose that laid the golden eggs. Somehow, it's become normal to behave in a way that shrinks our total addressable market while trying to generate revenue from it. And somehow, it's become normal to turn a blind eye to it. To be clear: We're not pointing fingers or moralizing here—we've been guilty of this ourselves.

This example is hypothetical, but the math works out, the assumptions are realistic, and several important ideas are illustrated. What looks like it's "working" may not actually be working. Volume-based approaches typically ignore negative consequences and focus only on positive metrics. These methodologies are outdated; a human-centered approach is the best way forward.

> "
> What looks like it's **"working"**
> may not actually be **working**.

Along with his team at Winning by Design, Jacco is an obvious ally in this movement against digital pollution and toward human-centered communication. As he writes in his LinkedIn headline, "Being kind and assuming positive intent will help you see the world from a different perspective."[3] His perspective helps us build a bridge from the first two chapters, to your business, and over to the stories of our allies and exemplars in Part Two.

THE BROKEN FUNNEL

You're likely familiar with the traditional sales and marketing funnel. We've included an example in Figure 3.2. The language changes depending on whose funnel it is, but it typically follows the AIDA structure (Awareness, Interest, Desire, Action). The final step, Action, is a purchase, commitment, sale, conversion, or another form of transaction.

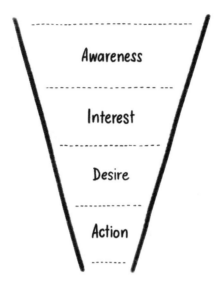

Figure 3.2 Traditional Funnel

Its flaws have been identified before, but we'll do so quickly again here. And we'll start with the fact that the physics are all wrong; people don't get into the top of your funnel and just slide down the side into a purchase. More importantly, the goal, perspective, and mindset are broken. Among the potential costs of adhering to its flawed simplicity are digital pollution, lost opportunities, transactional culture, and burned reputation.

The Goal Is Broken

The goal of the traditional funnel is to close the sale. However, this transaction is the goal line only in a transactional culture. A funnel that ends with a purchase says: We got what we wanted. But most businesses are relationship-based. The purchase isn't the end of a process; it's the start of a long-term relationship. Tacking on the word "Retention" or "Advocacy" underneath "Action" or "Purchase" is a move in the right direction but doesn't get us where we need to be.

In a subscription model, a purchase may not even be profitable for you. Instead, you must renew or upgrade a subscription over many months to reach profitability. Even if you're not in a subscription-based business, you rely on recurring revenue in the form of repeat purchasing, expanded purchasing, and customer referrals. No matter the model, a healthy business grows with and through current customers, not by creating a costly parade of one-time transactions. You want to grow the lifetime value of each customer, not just close deals.

The Perspective Is Broken

The traditional funnel is created from the seller's perspective. When it gets operationalized, we tally up the people and potential revenue at each stage, track conversion rates by stage, measure pace through each stage, and so on. Its purpose is accurate revenue forecasting. Its bias is toward getting the deal closed, not on developing the deal. For example, in five common stages of a sales funnel (contacted, qualified, demo, proposal, closed), four stages are dedicated to getting the deal done, but only one (qualified) is dedicated to discovery. And that's assuming qualification comes through a curiosity-based conversation. Regardless, the seller's needs and wants overshadow the buyer's.

The Mindset Is Broken

In Jacco's example earlier in the chapter, our default plan to double revenue from $80,000 to $160,000 is to double the top of the funnel. Double the calls. Double the emails. Double the connection requests. Double everything. This volume-based approach is driven by an alpha culture demanding that people and machines crank out activities, rely on size and force, and ignore counter impacts.

"That whole mindset is deeply ingrained into the typical sales culture," observes Jacco. But "there is scientific proof that shows that twice the volume does not bring in twice the results."

To illustrate, Jacco shares the story of the elusive four-minute mile. For years, it was thought to be an unbreakable barrier for runners. Most contenders had the mindset of running more and more, training more miles into their bodies. A doctor working in a hospital lab, Roger Bannister didn't have time for volume. Instead, he focused on interval training—shorter bursts to increase speed. One of his favorite track sessions consisted of three 1.5-mile runs at a swift pace. "What he learned is that running less made him go faster," explains Jacco. He was the first to break the four-minute mile barrier in 1954.[4,5]

Bannister's counterintuitive approach opened the door. Though three times as many humans have summited Mount Everest than have run a sub-four-minute mile (approximately 5,000 versus fewer than 1,500),[6,7] most major college track teams now have a sub-four-minute miler.

This story sets up the third of three of nonnegotiable principles of sales that Jacco shares with us. Each principle demands a better funnel with better processes and better communication:

1. Recurring revenue is a result of recurring impact.

2. People love to buy, but they don't like to be sold to.

3. The impact of marginal gain is better than volume.

Each of these principles helps fix the broken funnel.

THE BOW TIE FUNNEL

A better funnel is The Bow Tie Funnel, which Steve and I learned from Jacco's books and videos. As you can see in Figure 3.3, it's shaped like a bow tie. This funnel views the transaction, purchase, or commitment not as the end, but as the start of an ongoing impact journey. In this way, it involves your entire organization and starts from a more customer-centric perspective.

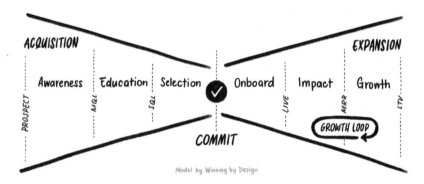

Figure 3.3 The Bow Tie Funnel

As we co-create with our customers their journey across the funnel into a positive growth loop, we work to deliver emotional impact (how it benefits the individual) and rational impact (how it benefits their organization). Impacts are problems solved, opportunities gained, and value delivered. The more we understand our customers and build trusting relationships with them, the more impact we can deliver. The delivery of impact earns us the right to revenue.

For a quick orientation to The Bow Tie Funnel, the three main stages are Acquisition, Commitment, and Expansion.

On the Acquisition side, which is typically the domain of marketing and sales, prospective customers become aware of their problem or opportunity, get educated on solutions, and select one of the providers competing for their business.

On that path, they're qualified by marketing (MQL) and then by sales (SQL), who work to earn a commitment.

When customers Commit, they're onboarded into the product or service and guided to initial impact. Helping them achieve that desired outcome generates monthly recurring revenue (MRR). As we continue to provide impact for customers, they grow and expand with us, increasing lifetime value (LTV) over a long-term relationship.

Even if you don't use this language to describe your business, you can use The Bow Tie Funnel. No matter the size of your team or your customer base, this model applies. Whatever your product or service may be, you can view relationship building, value delivery, and revenue generation through this lens.

The Goal Is Better

With this funnel, the sale isn't the goal—customer impact is. It doesn't end with a purchase; it looks to an ongoing growth loop. It is inherently customer centric.

This bears out Jacco's first principle: Recurring revenue is a result of recurring impact.

The Perspective Is Better

The Bow Tie Funnel takes the customer's perspective. Their benefit (impact) is a necessary precursor to our benefit (revenue). It demands we stop selling and start helping. It demands we think first about their needs, not our own.

This reinforces his second principle: People love to buy, but they don't like to be sold to.

The Mindset Is Better

The path to doubling revenue isn't to double the top of the funnel, it's to create more impact for your customers.

Math fact: 10% to the power of seven is 1.8. Therefore, creating a 10% improvement in each of the seven main stages across The Bow Tie Funnel will nearly double revenue. Improving a conversion rate from 4.7% to 5.17% is a 10% improvement. An incremental, human-first approach builds trust, minimizes counter impacts, and grows revenue.

This exemplifies the third principle he shares with us: The impact of marginal gain is better than volume.

Stakeholders of Highest Priority

This funnel doesn't just apply to the customer journey. You can also use it to think about your employee journey. Potential hires need to be aware of the opportunity, get educated on your company, select between options, and make a commitment. New team members must be successfully onboarded, achieve the impact they expected, and learn, grow, and develop with you for years to come.

Because a remarkable employee experience is a necessary precursor to a remarkable customer experience, our employees are stakeholders of highest priority. As we think about marginal gains for customers, we should also think about improvements at each stage of an employee's journey with us. Just as your customers can become your best source of new customers, retained revenue, and expanded revenue, your employees can become your best source of new employees, innovation, and productivity.

Human-centered communication treats employees like people, not like variables in a math equation or cogs in a machine.

BENEFITS OF VIDEO IN THE FUNNEL

Whether your organization is large or small, you should be able to map your people and processes to The Bow Tie Funnel. In smaller businesses, one person may cover multiple stages. In larger businesses, entire teams may be dedicated to one aspect of one stage. From there, consider the communication you're providing along the journey. Look for spots to be more personal, human, and effective by adding some video. Your customer experience and your employee experience both benefit from this effort.

We already mentioned the Winning by Design YouTube channel—that's just one of several ways Jacco uses video. Having built a successful career in sales and sales leadership, he recalls the days of meeting customers in person, especially for bigger deals. Today, however, he's seeing million-dollar deals done between people who've never met face to face. And video is a primary driver of this shift. Here are four of his insights about video communication to improve the impact journey for your customers and employees.

Trust

"Trust is no longer just based on meeting in person, getting to shake hands, and looking at body mannerisms," Jacco explains. "The reason we seek personal contact is because we believe, as human beings, when we see another person in their natural habitat, that we get a good idea of who that person is." It's about creating trust.

And it's based in the science that Dan Hill has dedicated his career to and shares with us next in Chapter 4. In short: It's about the human skill of reading people's faces and emotions.

But being there in person isn't the only way to do it. "We can do that through video, too. But with video, we combine that with a track record," Jacco says, referring to our online history, social profiles, websites, online reviews, and overall digital presence. "We are now looking at different signals to build trust."

"Video has created that transparent feel," he explains. "It represents an authentic being." Authenticity and trust are highly complementary. Both are fundamental to healthy relationships.

Independence

We've all learned that video has made us independent of place. We can simulate an in-person experience with anyone, anywhere in the world, as long as each person has a camera, internet access, and software to connect. More than half of the global population and almost the entirety of professional workers in high- and middle-income countries meet these criteria.[8] We work remotely. We communicate remotely. We meet remotely—independent of place—on video calls. But we have to be there at the same time. It's synchronous.

The next big realization is that video makes us independent of time. "We're going to see a far bigger impact," Jacco anticipates. "It's no longer just place that we become independent of. It's time." We can send a video to someone on a Friday afternoon and she can watch it over the weekend. We can send a video to 15 people and each can experience us in person at their own convenience.

This asynchronicity in delivering a personal and human experience provides a significant benefit that still seems underused today. Further, videos on websites, YouTube channels, LinkedIn feeds, LinkedIn profiles, email signatures, and other places help people know us before they ever meet us. This empowers potential customers and potential employees alike to prequalify us by experiencing us through video.

Efficiency

"To record and deliver a video with an accurate message takes me far less time than to write an email. We think that video takes longer, but it doesn't," Jacco says. "The density of words, the need to reread it, and to correct the words in an email—to do this takes far longer than just saying it in a video." In a two- or three-minute process, Jacco makes a few quick notes, does one or sometimes two takes, and sends the video. He estimates a similar email takes him five to seven minutes to write, reread, edit, and send.

As a caution, Jacco notes that we have a tendency to try to correct our videos like we correct our typed-out text. But that's a mistake. "We need to let go when we shoot videos," according to Jacco. "You just need to be okay with whatever you shoot. Be okay with it. It's you. Don't worry about it." When we include our imperfections in our video messages, it's an invitation for others to connect with us. When we include those flaws, we don't just save time: "The person on the other side actually starts to pay attention."

Professionalism

One of your responsibilities as a pioneer in the movement of human-centered communication is to focus on professionalism. One of the best ways to do this: Be clear and concise. "The ones who are killing our business right now are the ones who are just walking around and giving us a stream of their consciousness," Jacco observes. He also cautions that distracting filters and silly effects detract from video's potential as a professional tool.

Before hitting "Record," professionals focus on who the video is for, what its purpose is, and how best to communicate it.

EMPLOYEE EXPERIENCE AND CUSTOMER EXPERIENCE

The mechanical aspect of employee experience (EX) and customer experience (CX) is the full range of touchpoints and interactions across The Bow Tie Funnel. You can apply human-centered communication almost anywhere at any time in this funnel, including but not limited to:

The tools and tech you buy—and how you set them up.

The systems, processes, and cadences you design.

Any time you click send, post, or share.

Any time you get on a phone call or video call.

In person or online.

On laptop or on mobile.

In meetings and presentations.

In video posts and video messages.

In documents and slide decks.

With employees, customers, and every stakeholder.

More powerful than the mechanical aspect, however, is the emotional aspect of EX and CX. Their essence is *how we make people feel*. When we make people feel better about themselves, about us, about our team, about their problem or opportunity, and about our relationship, we motivate behaviors and enhance memories. We'll go much deeper into this in the next chapter. Here, "better" is a catch-all for the most appropriate feeling for that person at that time—confident, secure, accomplished, smart, attractive, inspired, valued, trusted.

Because video provides the closest approximation of an in-person experience, it offers the greatest potential for communication clarity. More importantly, it provides the greatest potential for emotional resonance. As you evaluate the journeys your employees and customers are on, you're looking for places to be more authentic, intentional, and clear. You're looking for moments to enhance feelings, not just knowledge. You're looking for touchpoints to add video.

Three characteristics of those moments serve as signals to use your camera rather than your keyboard:

1. Making a personal connection.

2. Managing emotion and tone.

3. Breaking down detail and complexity.

When you want people to feel like they know you before they meet you or you want to remind people what it's like to work with you, video is better than text. When you have an emotionally charged message to communicate, whether positive or negative, start with empathy and reach out with video. When you have a detailed or complex message, share your screen to walk and talk through it, put it in layperson's terms, and help people understand.

As you look again at The Bow Tie Funnel, you should begin to notice opportunities to use more video. An entire book could be written on this. In fact, we already wrote it. In *The Video Adoption Guide*, we provide dozens of use cases for video across every stage of The Bow Tie Funnel. Not just for your customers, but also for your employees and for people within your professional network.

Get **The Video Adoption Guide** free
at **BombBomb.com/BookBonus**

For our purposes here, we'll provide a sketch across the customer lifecycle. And you'll get many more ideas and examples throughout the rest of this book. In Figure 3.4 is a simpler version of the funnel, followed by the main problems you're trying to overcome and a few examples of how to do so through a human-centered approach.

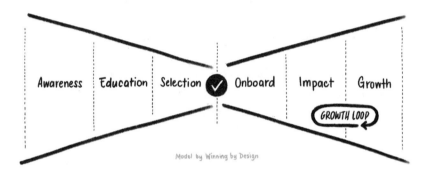

Figure 3.4 Video Across the Funnel

In the Awareness stage, it's hard to stand out and get attention. You're competing with a significant volume of noise and digital pollution. Human-centered communication breaks through, puts a face with your name, and generates replies and conversations.

+ Outbounding to potential customers or replying to inbound opportunities with personal video messages.

+ Pairing a video message with a voicemail; refer to the other in each message.

+ Providing live or recorded video training about the problem or opportunity.

In the Education stage, it's difficult to encourage the right people to give you their undivided time and attention by scheduling and showing up for appointments, calls, and demos. This is both a symptom and cause of insufficient trust.

+ Providing service-oriented, context-rich nurturing with invitations to connect directly.

+ Setting and hosting meetings, demos, or appointments.

+ Following up after appointments with video to restate salient points, readdress any concerns or objections, tap into the initial excitement, and draw the vision of a better future.

In the Selection stage, it can be hard to have people answer "yes" to these critical questions: Do I like you? Do you listen to me? Do you make me feel valued? Do you understand me? Can I trust you? Affirmative responses are prerequisites to getting a commitment, and they can be hard to come by digitally unless you take a human-centered approach.

+ Presenting every proposal, contract, or offer in a video call or with a screen recording through video.

+ Engaging and empowering your internal champion(s) and introducing yourself personally to other decision-makers through video.

+ Making peer-to-peer video introductions between, say, your CTO and their CTO.

At the Commitment stage, you're up against two common phenomena: cold feet and buyer's remorse. Both require the momentum of trusting relationships.

+ Sending "thank you" videos to every decision-maker.

+ Sending peer-to-peer "thank you" videos from, say, your CRO to their CRO.

+ Introducing the next team members involved in the relationship, like an Onboarding Manager, Customer Success Manager, or Account Manager.

The Onboarding stage is critical for the long-term health of the customer relationship. As points of contact change, new relationships must be built. The door is open here for miscommunication, which neither party can afford.

+ Providing a setup and training sequence that includes some video instruction.

+ Following up to reinforce key aspects of training sessions, to provide feedback, and to acknowledge early wins.

+ Warming up relationships with your team members through personal introductions.

In the Impact stage, customers are notoriously difficult to get a hold of. They may revert back to old habits if new behaviors and solutions are not reinforced. Without strong relationships and consistent communication, they could be at risk for a future churn event.

+ Setting, confirming, holding, and following up after account reviews.

+ Providing consistent account updates in video messages when you can't schedule a call.

+ Enhancing positive feelings at milestone celebrations or managing negative situations that inhibit impact or progress.

In the Growth and Growth Loop stages, you're challenged with departures within your organization and your customer's. And any cross-sell or upsell may feel like a completely new deal to the original decision committee or to a new one. Human-centered communication reinforces relationships and makes sharing and engaging easier.

+ Introducing additional problems or opportunities with which you can help.

+ Setting up, confirming, hosting, and following up on customer interviews.

+ Providing more peer-to-peer communication from, say, your CEO to their CEO.

Again, this is just a quick sketch. These videos may be live calls or recorded messages. The messages may be truly personal to each person (human-to-human) or recorded once and used over and over again as appropriate (evergreen, sent one-to-one or one-to-many). Truly personal messages can be more specific, helpful, and valued than generalized videos.

As a reminder, the feeling you create and emotional resonance you provide are what you're trying to enhance. With personal connection, emotion, tone, detail, and complexity in mind, look at your customer lifecycle, employee lifecycle, and even your personal network to find moments to be more human with video.

WHAT PEOPLE WANT

"What we're looking for now is authenticity," Jacco declares. "I believe that ultimately, this is what we want. People want transparency."

For too long, we've been trained to create the appearance of perfection. The shine and gloss. The impression and illusion. The effort and expense. The call for authenticity is a call for substance over style. When we drop the facade, we can devote our effort and expense to what matters most: creating recurring impact for people.

Our sales calls and our recruiting interviews start long before we ever meet in person. Our reputations precede us now more than ever. Our first impression is often made virtually. Word of mouth has been with us for millennia, but its effects are wider and deeper digitally. Now is the time to get intentional about authenticity, transparency, and human centricity.

Part Two

ALLIES & EXEMPLARS

DAN HILL PhD

PRESIDENT
of Sensory Logic

"If you can take in the face, then you get a
sense of the emotions and of the person
you're dealing with."

A KEY IDEA IN THIS CHAPTER

Driving memory and motivation through emotional intelligence.

CHAPTER 4

Emotion, Memory, and Motivation

Featuring Dan Hill, PhD

In Chapter 2, we mentioned books published in 1973 and 1980 calling for the rehumanization of people's dehumanized work experiences. More than a decade earlier, in *The Magic of Thinking Big*, David J. Schwartz advocated for a leadership and management approach he called "Being Human." Published in 1959, the book cautions against a mechanical leadership style. David writes, "Of all things people don't like, perhaps the most disliked is being treated like a machine. The cold, impersonal efficiency expert is not an ideal." But through his recommended leadership style, our actions can say, "You are a human being. I respect you. I'm here to help you in every way I can."[1]

When Steve and I connected with Dan Hill, PhD, to talk about human emotions, facial expressions, and emotional intelligence (EQ), he referred to Schwartz's "Being Human" approach while recalling his career transition from academia and state government into the business world. The period was the 1990s, but what Dan experienced over the next decade of his career had likely been true for generations before and at least a generation since.

"Emotional elements were never getting acknowledged," Dan found. The "professional" environment refused to embrace our full, human reality or a whole, real person. Emotional literacy was low. Emotions were not welcomed. Should they ever emerge, they'd be ignored or dismissed.

It's likely an echo of our heavily industrial past—treating "official" business in a mechanistic way and conducting it exclusively to produce the desired output. Any dehumanizing effects are accepted as necessary consequences; emotions must not threaten precision or production. Micromanage as needed. Limit transparency. Play politics. Ignore the fact that people are checked out. Stay focused on the task at hand. Measure everything you can; ignore what you can't.

The result: It's "horribly inefficient," says Dan.

This model is built on the illusion that "you're going to walk through the door, you're going to supposedly put your emotions aside, you're going to focus on a joint objective, and you're going to move forward with great dispatch and efficiency." As with pollution, there are tradeoffs to be made and a healthy balance to seek, but it's a fool's errand to try to suppress human emotion.

Business culture has progressed since then, as has Dan. Since he left the corporate world, he founded and runs his own company, Sensory Logic; authored eight books, including *Emotionomics* and *Famous Faces Decoded*; earned seven U.S. patents in the analysis of facial coding data; and hosts a podcast, "Dan Hill's EQ Spotlight." He's analyzed political leaders for *The New York Times*, CNN, and dozens of other leading news outlets. He's assessed team chemistry, trades, and draft picks for professional and collegiate sports teams. Dan has provided human insights for businesses of all kinds.

While Dan is enthusiastic about where this field is heading, he tempers his exuberance by observing that the growth in EQ books, articles, and stories likely outpaces the growth in EQ readers. He also recognizes that males still occupy the vast majority of leadership roles, and for them emotions are "an away game" rather than a home game. Broadly speaking, many professionals still don't recognize, understand, or appreciate the power of emotions. "They just think that it's nonsense. It's irrational. It's soft." Perpetuating the problem is the fact that people in power have lower levels of empathy.[2]

This helps explain why 85% of employees are disengaged at work, collectively costing organizations approximately a half a *trillion* dollars per year.[3] When we build real relationships between employees and managers, we generate real results; companies with a highly engaged workforce are 21% more profitable.[3] As you'll see, we must connect emotionally in order to engage humans.

The challenge today is not only overcoming the aspects of business culture that dismiss emotions, but also doing so in digital channels that dampen our emotional expression. For its visual and emotional qualities, human-centered communication in person and in video will help.

"When you can take in the face, you get a sense of the emotions. You get a sense of the person who you're dealing with," Dan shares with us. "You're dealing with people. Business is people to people. It's not B2C. It's not B2B. It's people to people."

THREE DISTINCTLY HUMAN QUALITIES

We tend to think of ourselves as logical beings, but we're actually emotional creatures who rationalize our decisions. As Dan writes in *Emotionomics*, "People's decision-making process is primarily quick, emotional, and subconscious; in a word, it's intuitive. The bottom line is that people feel before they think."[4]

Neither thinking nor feeling is unique to humans, but in our conversation about rehumanizing business, Dan shared three things that are.

1. Speech/Vocabulary

"One of the first things that distinguishes us is our ability to have greater flexibility with vocabulary," Dan says. But too often "we just pull back into little chunky phrases and jargon that a machine could automate and utilize just as easily as we could." When we communicate using clichés and jargon, fail to discover and use our own unique voice, and find ourselves inflexible in the moment, "that's a real squandering of a potential advantage."

A human-centered approach, then, demands that we separate ourselves from the bots and machines by adding authenticity and adaptability to our verbal and written expression. "What has to happen with your speech is to actually have it be in your own voice, to have it be saturated with your own experiences, and to be adaptable in the moment based on what other people are saying," Dan recommends. "If you're going to make a connection, we don't want to feel like we're just talking to bullet points from a PowerPoint presentation. We want a real, genuine human being who's responding to us."

Finding your voice in any medium or channel is a challenge. We worry about how we'll be perceived, whether we have real value to offer, what we look and sound like, and so much more. The best way through the challenge is action. Our voice isn't actually waiting to be found or discovered. Instead, it must be actively developed through practice.

2. Emotional Flexibility

Whether in a meeting or in a message exchange, we've all experienced it: In an instant, the tone, mood, and emotions change. You didn't see it coming, but there's no mistaking it now. Immediately, you must figure out how to deal with the moment, the people you're sharing it with, and the emotions you're all experiencing. Should you retaliate, drop out, solicit an ally to fight back, or wait it out? Your ability to read the situation and adapt is critical to successful communication.

Humans experience seven primary emotions: happiness, anger, contempt, surprise, disgust, sadness, and fear. Seventy percent of how we emote is in happiness and anger. Humans universally and intuitively express the seven primary emotions through our faces in 23 specific ways, per the Facial Action Coding System (FACS). Reading these expressions is also universal across cultures and innate to every human. As Dan says, it's not "rocket science," but it does take practice to do it exceptionally well. He teaches us to develop our skills of reading facial expressions in *Famous Faces Decoded*.

Here's a quick list to decoding facial expressions as a primer. Try to put these on your own face as you read and train yourself to start recognizing these emotional cues in the faces of others.

- Happiness is like a hug or a welcome mat, as the corners of our mouths go up in a smile.

- Anger is like a fist with compression in our faces, narrowed eyebrows, and tight lips.

- Contempt is a feeling of superiority with the tension of anger, but the lift of a smile.

- Surprise is wonderment with eyes wide and eyebrows high as we pay attention, take things in, and stay quiet.

- Fear overlaps with surprise and primarily differs with the mouth pulled wide in an "egads" expression.

- Disgust is visceral rejection with a wrinkled nose, flared upper lip, and protected mouth.

- Sadness slows us; wrinkles form a mid-forehead "puddle" and the corners of lips sag to form an "upside-down" smile.

Because we have more facial muscles than any other species on Earth and because our faces are the only place on our body where our muscles attach directly to the skin, these facial expressions of emotion are clearly fundamental to the human experience. We're also equipped with the flexibility required to read others and react in emotionally effective ways on the fly.

"The machines are going to get better at these things," Dan tells us. "But if there's a lack of flexibility in adapting to and reading the nuances and making the adjustments, that's where we're going to retain the advantage over the machines." The leading companies working on machine-reading of faces and emotional expression are 60% to 70% accurate right now for six of the seven primary emotions; fear wasn't measured.

Dan expects that machines will improve; they improved from 30% a decade ago, to 45% a few years back, to 65% or so today. In 10 to 15 years, Dan predicts they'll be 90% accurate, but only in ideal environments. We humans, on the other hand, can fight through weird framing, bad lighting, faces turned to the side, variations in skin tone, and other variables that machines can't. And our reactions are more subtle, nuanced, and evolved, where machines still react more crudely by specific rule sets.

Our ability to read, respond, and react intuitively, universally, and innately serves us well in person and in video, though tone and mood are suppressed in virtual spaces. In human-centered communication, we must consciously pay more attention to others' emotions and consciously express our own more overtly.

3. Sense of Mortality/Need for Vitality

"We are the only animal that knows that there's an end to this game," Dan adds. "We have a sense of mortality." This is a practical observation rather than a morbid one. Our heightened consciousness of our mortality and that of our families forces an interest in acquiring status and resources. Today, this drives an interest in our careers and livelihoods. Well beyond a basic "fight or flight" instinct, this deep awareness of the finite nature of our time together in this human experience drives so much of our behavior.

"We are terribly concerned about how we keep ourselves vibrant, vital, and in the picture," explains Dan. "We need allies. We need our own energy. We want connections. We want resources, whether it's a salary, power, a new title, or a corner office." To resolve these concerns and fears, we work to connect and communicate in ways that build relationships. This is best done reciprocally—through giving and not just through seeking, taking, and hoarding.

A human-centered philosophy and practice expands our social network, demonstrates our vitality, provides access to more resources, and helps provide the deep sense of security we need.

MOVERE: THE COMMON ROOT

Unlike rational thoughts, emotions are action oriented. This fact is captured in *movere*, a Latin root shared by the words emotion and motivation. Motive, motor, motion—they all come from this root word. In contrast to overthinking and "paralysis by analysis," movere conveys movement and making things happen. If there's no emotion, then there's no action. "Emotion is a fuel," says Dan. "One of the big fallacies of corporate life is to imagine that you can drain the gas out of the gas tank and somehow the car is still going to run. It's simply not going to happen."

> If there's **no emotion,**
> then there's **no action.**

Emotions drive both behavior and memory. "We will remember the last Zoom call," Dan explains. "We will remember the dynamic and how it went or how frustrating it went. We will remember the last meeting with the manager or the last year-end review." We remember the warm, sincere "thank you" message or the annoying unsolicited text message. These emotional charges don't just affect our immediate experience, they drive memory and, therefore, our future behavior.

In addition to being emotional creatures, Dan says that "we are really visual creatures by evolutionary standards." For efficiency, processing of input starts in the back of our original brain with the visual cortex. That is to say, we think in images. From there, we may kick it up into the limbic system, the emotional brain. And "the emotional part sends 10 times as much data to the rational part as the other way around. That's just how the brain is wired because everybody feels before they think."

Visual activity in our original brain and emotional activity in our limbic system are subconscious. "About 95% of our mental activity is not fully conscious. It might be as much as 98%," Dan shares with us. "So most of the ball game is actually below the water level." Even when decisions get kicked up to our rational brain, the decision is influenced if not already made by our subconscious. Several studies have shown that our brains seem to make decisions several seconds before our conscious awareness of the decision.[5]

The vast **majority** of our mental activity is **visual, emotional, and subconscious.**

The takeaway here: We must infuse the messages and experiences we're creating for others with an emotional component if we expect something to happen as a result. If we're to move someone in thought or action, we must be emotionally expressive, engaging, and resonant. And we should be as visual as possible. Again, most decisions and conclusions are being made subconsciously. This favors video as a key component of our communication.

An important reminder is that we create patterns, models, and shortcuts to save time and energy. These help drive our subconscious decision-making. Digital pollution creates negative patterns and increases the likelihood that we're ignored, deleted, or blocked in the future. For the way it engages and serves others, human-centered communication reinforces the opposite pattern and behavior.

COMMUNICATION THAT MOVES PEOPLE

Reading text is a cognitive exercise—conscious, rational, and calorie-consuming. For survival, we do as little rational processing as possible. And as we just learned, the more we think, the less we feel. The less we feel, the less likely something is going to happen. Emotion is tied to motivation.

Further, eye-tracking studies that Dan's conducted reveal that we don't read very carefully. Effective reading requires about one-fifth to one-third of a second of attention per word—an average rate of 250 words per minute. But we extensively skim and the vast majority of text isn't absorbed. In short and in Dan's words: "It's amazing how little people read."

And yet, here we are, decades after the introduction of text-based email and decades into its fragmentation across text messaging, social media messaging, Slack messaging, and other text-based channels. Even for our most important messages, we restrict ourselves to plain black text on a plain white screen. And we hope other people will labor through it. Unless we're exceptional writers, this doesn't leverage our preference for visual and emotional engagement. There's a loss of tonality that produces misunderstanding. Along with that are typos and autocorrections. These all diminish our ability to effectively communicate with typed-out text alone.

If you have to communicate with text:

+ Send a short email with the sole purpose of trying to get on a phone call or video call.

+ Don't give feedback in a long email if you want to move people to change.

+ Use visual metaphors, contrast, and emotionally loaded words.

For clarity and connection, move more of your communication to video. As Dan reminds us, we have two eyes and two ears to help us see faces, hear tone, and make meaning. The likelihood of reaching people effectively and generating action goes up when we get visual and emotional. "That's where the opportunity is and that's what gets sidelined" when we rely on text, according to Dan.

"If you think you're going to drive great results through a text-based message—blasting it out to people—you are utterly fooling yourself."

Have you had positive results from text-based messages before? Of course you have. So has Dan. Same with Steve and me. But in our daily communication, we have room to improve. We can be clearer. We can achieve more by connecting emotionally, not just cognitively.

EMOTIONALLY INTELLIGENT VIDEO

Based on his expertise and years of research, here are some of Dan's recommendations for creating video that moves people and builds connection.

Be "On Emotion" (Not Just "On Message")

As marketing leader and best-selling author Seth Godin wrote, "Communication is the transfer of emotion."[6] And emotions are contagious. If we want our prospects or customers to be excited about an opportunity, we must be excited ourselves. And yet we've all experienced a flat, bored, distracted, or robotic representative of an otherwise exciting opportunity. To only train our teams on the "right" things to say and the "right" order to say them is incomplete. How we say something is as important as what we say.

Being "on message" is about what you need and want to say. Being "on emotion" is about what others need and want to experience. Tailor your message for the person you're communicating with—their motivations, their concerns, and their preferences. Being on emotion means that you're present in the moment with others. You're still working toward a specific objective or outcome, but you'll get better results by shifting your focus, being attuned to the mood, and staying flexible.

With human-centered communication, "you're not just bombarding them. You're not lobbing missiles over the castle wall." Instead, in Dan's metaphor, "you actually know who lives in the village and you are connecting with them in ways that matter to them. You speak with them and back to them based on how they're responding. It's a lot more give and take."

Keep It Short (Video Calls and Video Messages)

Over the years with Sensory Logic, Dan has tested all kinds of television ads and sales pitches for a variety of companies in a variety of industries. The consistent finding: The longer a pitch went, "the less effective it was—almost always." Keep it short. If you have to go longer, break it into modules, and consistently provide people a sense of progress and direction. Higher quality content helps sustain attention and interest, but you can't hold people as long as you might think.

Focus on Authenticity (Video Calls and Video Messages)

"You might think that production values are going to save you, but authenticity is going to save you more than production values because it comes back to trust," Dan informs us. "I still want to know: Are you my ally once I've given up the money? Are you going to be there for me if there are shortcomings?" Before people commit, they need to feel not just that you're competent and capable, but also that you care. In Dan's experience, it comes down to this: "Do I like you? Do I trust you? Do I feel like you get me? Do you care about me?"

That's not to say that production values don't matter or that they're at odds with authenticity. The better our camera, lighting, and microphone are, the easier our viewers can detect subtle cues in our faces and voices that help them understand and connect with us. If we can't see you well, we can't read you well. In *Can You Hear Me?*, Dr. Nick Morgan explains that the undertones in our voices carry the emotional content, but that undertones are often stripped or compressed for digital transmission, including over the phone.[7]

Focus on authenticity first. Consider improving production values to make that authenticity clear, obvious, and accessible.

Open Strong (Video Calls and Video Messages)

Open with a good question. Open with a statement that acknowledges your understanding of their pain or where they're coming from. Open with something unique and personable. Open with a compelling image—showing or describing it. "You want momentum right away," Dan advises. "Sales is about small yeses that lead to the big yes. But a lot of videos are a series of not-quite-interesting, a-little-bit-better, and it's-getting-kind-of-long." Starting strong gets you the early yes that builds necessary momentum.

Don't Use Scripts (Video Calls and Video Messages)

Dan takes this lesson from legendary San Francisco 49ers coach Bill Walsh, a two-time NFL Coach of the Year, three-time Super Bowl champion, and Pro Football Hall of Fame member. Bill would plan the opening of the game—approximately the first 10 plays—then coach to the situation from there. Likewise, you shouldn't script the entire game, the entire call, the entire video, or the entire experience.

Dan only plans the first few minutes of a presentation precisely and recommends the same for your videos. "I think a script works well only for about two to three sentences" because they may not be your words, you may not feel them, and you may not even believe them. The result is a loss of authenticity, sincerity, and emotion. "That's all going to come through," Dan cautions. "It's not going to be hidden on a video. And so I think you could get them some sprinklings and some orientation, but I don't think most people can pull off a script."

Forcing yourself or others to adhere to a script doesn't create a good experience for anyone.

Don't Fake It (Video Messages)

If you're in a bad mood, should you be recording and sending a series of video messages? Dan says no. "A different activity is the answer . . . we are mood and emotion creatures so I think that can be difficult." We can't just shut off our emotions and imagine ourselves into another place. "That's not very human. I don't think most people can do that nor should they probably do that to themselves, actually. There's an emotional injury involved in faking it."

Obviously, with scheduled meetings and calls we often have to work our way through even if we're not in a positive emotional state. But with video messages, pause, take a walk, or do something refreshing and then come back to the task. We humans can detect discrepancies between what you're saying and how you're saying it. It's hard to fake it.

Read the Room (Video Calls)

Making the shift to human-centered communication requires just a little more intention—at least until you've made it a habit. Instead of simply showing up on a video call or presentation and reacting, take care to actively read the room and decode faces using the facial decoding list we included previously.

"You've got real powers of observation. I think it's absolutely doable," says Dan of reading others' faces on your video calls. "You've just got to find it intellectually intriguing so that you have some fun with it and then realize it's actually really productive and beneficial—conducive to your career—so you should pay attention and get better at this because it's good for you."

Many salespeople, account managers, and others wonder: If I have, say, seven or eight people on a Zoom call, should I try to read them all? Dan says no. When your time or attention is constrained, focus first on the person who's likeliest to make the buying decision. Then, try to identify and emotionally engage the decision-maker's natural allies or key influencers. Pay attention to their faces and expressions and stay in touch with them emotionally throughout your time together.

As much as possible, you do want a sense of the entire group, not just those key participants. Ask for feedback along the way, especially when you notice changes in someone's facial expression or changes in the overall mood of the group. The best approach is to engage everyone, even if you don't have the capacity to decode every face. And if you have the privilege of being there in person, all the better (and easier!).

Teach in the Round (Video Calls)

During his time in academia, Dan's best class was the one in which he circled the chairs and facilitated an open discussion. He didn't speak first, dictate the topics, or control the conversation too tightly. When it was his time to speak, he intentionally incorporated what he heard from others. "I was trying to weave threads and basically bring it all back together. And half the class at the end of the semester said, 'This is the best class I've ever taken at the university, bar none.' And I think it's because of that trying to weave and incorporate, allow them space, and not impose."

As mentioned in the previous tip, you may not be able to actively read the details of every person's face. But you can read the overall tone and engage everyone. Ask and listen. Bring each person in—by speaking or through the chat window. Seek true discovery around the problem, issue, or opportunity at hand, then find and weave the threads. As Morgan J Ingram recommends later in Chapter 12, don't give a presentation. Instead, create a conversation.

Show and Adapt to Emotions (Video Calls)

"Emotional engagement is how you get into the game. If there is no emotion going on, then there's no motivation going on and nothing that's being said is memorable to anybody because it doesn't have any meaning for them," Dan reminds us. On calls and presentations, we must create emotional engagement; we must show our own emotions and adapt to the emotions of others. We shouldn't just plow through the planned material and hope to save time for Q&A.

We've all worked with the proverbial brick wall who doesn't show or adapt to emotions. Failing to appropriately respond can come across not just as tone deaf or insensitive, but even offensive or inappropriate. Pay attention to people's reactions and ask about them during the call. Adapting on the fly to, say, a team member's sadness, concern, or excitement continues the momentum.

"You've got to show engagement to get engagement," says Dan. "You've got to be adaptable to the river that you're swimming in."

A SENSE OF BELONGING

Authenticity. Sincerity. Vulnerability. What's long been thought of as soft or irrational in a business context has always been our source of strength. Even though we've not always used these words, we've always understood their power. Salespeople have long known that the in-person visit was most effective to connect with and move people. That's because human emotions and facial expression are foundational to trusting relationships.

"Everyone wants a sense of belonging and a sense of connection," Dan says. "We want to feel connected closer—on safer, better ground with somebody. We all want that." Introvert, extrovert, or ambivert, you want this. You need this. And our businesses and organizations need it, too.

Human-centered communication incorporates these strengths. It's an invitation we make to others to connect in a more holistic and satisfying way. And in the next chapter, Mathew Sweezey builds from that truth and shows that markets need and want it from us, too. Markets, after all, are just people.

MATHEW SWEEZEY

DIRECTOR of MARKET STRATEGY at SALESFORCE

"Human-to-human interactivity is the basis of life."

A KEY IDEA IN THIS CHAPTER

Breaking through the noise and earning trust.

CHAPTER 5

Noise, Attention, and Trust

Featuring Mathew Sweezey

When we ask better questions, we get better answers. When we ask how to make our marketing better, we make only incremental improvements. But when we ask why our marketing isn't working, we get a better answer . . . and a new perspective.

Over the past few years, researcher, marketer, and futurist Mathew Sweezey allowed that question—"Why isn't our marketing working?"—to guide his work. His learnings from that journey are shared in his award-winning, nine-part podcast series *Electronic Propaganda Society* and his book *The Context Marketing Revolution: How to Motivate Buyers in the Age of Infinite Media*. This revolution doesn't call for new marketing ideas. Rather, Mathew calls for a new idea of marketing. This slight shift in words drives a dramatic shift in ideas, activities, and outcomes.

Director of Market Strategy at Salesforce and author of *Marketing Automation for Dummies*, Mathew's an ideal person to invite into this conversation, especially at the intersection of noise, attention, and trust. Attuned to the importance of human centricity, he offered a challenge when he joined me on The Customer Experience Podcast, which I host on behalf of BombBomb:

> *If we put humans at the center of everything, if we put humans at the center of our business, if we put humans at the center of what marketing should be, if we put humans at the center of economics, we see a very different approach.*[1]

Similar to human-centered communication, Mathew's proposed context marketing revolution puts the needs of our customers first. To break through the noise and motivate people to act, the messages and experiences we create must help people achieve their immediate goal in the moment. Our job is to consistently get them to their desired outcome faster and easier. How we make people feel in those moments provides sparks of emotional connection and establishes roots of trust.

THE HUMAN MOTIVE

Our motive, mindset, and goal at the outset of an activity significantly affect the outcome. If we're in a relationship-based business built on trust, why not put humans first? Why not make primary the needs and wants of the people for whom we're creating messages, experiences, products, and services? The motivation to humbly serve in a customer-centric way differentiates the experience and improves the result.

In recalling E.F. Schumacher's groundbreaking economics treatise, *Small Is Beautiful*, Mathew explains that "if economic theory is completely based on a profit motive, and it doesn't include a human motive, then you end up removing the human from the outcome. You end up with a completely mechanical process that's inhuman and that isn't good for humans. Hence you end up with a society that is optimized for the wrong thing."

A small shift in the initial approach dramatically changes the trajectory and end result. If we start with our own interests in mind, negative consequences are externalized to our stakeholders. If we start from a human-centered perspective, everything changes.

One of the reasons this is resonant with Mathew is how he was raised—to be bold with ideas, empathetic with others, and kind to himself. Just as Dan Hill cautioned us in the previous chapter not to divorce emotions from business, Mathew suggests that we stop trying to separate our personal and professional lives. We should be generous in our personal lives and in our professional lives. We should honor the dignity of every person in our personal lives and in our professional lives. The commercial basis of a relationship shouldn't change how we view or treat people.

An eight-year team member at Salesforce, Mathew points to founder and CEO Marc Benioff, who's been outspoken about the responsibility of business to serve all stakeholders, not just shareholders. The company's 1-1-1 pledge to donate 1% of equity, time, and resources has generated hundreds of millions of dollars in grants, several million hours of volunteer time, and tens of thousands of free or heavily discounted products for nonprofits and nongovernmental organizations.[2] This isn't just a moral consideration; it's a practical and financial consideration.

Customers don't just prefer a human motive and orientation—they're increasingly demanding it. As a complement to his context marketing revolution, Mathew recommended to us Mark Schaefer's *Marketing Rebellion: The Most Human Companies Win.* In the book, Mark makes it compellingly clear that customers have won all three of their rebellions so far (against company lies, secrets, and control). Like Mathew, he warns that incremental improvements won't take our businesses where we need to go. And he explicitly calls for a human-centered approach to marketing as the only way forward.[3]

Get links to the **books**, **videos**, and other **resources** mentioned throughout this book by visiting **BombBomb.com/BookBonus**

Why is it the only way? Because hyper-competition and product parity are becoming the status quo. In most markets, customers can obtain approximately identical value from a variety of sources for approximately the same price. In this commoditized environment, the most human business wins. Yes, we must reduce the time and effort it takes for customers to get the value they seek from our product or service. But the more we can use tools, techniques, and mindsets to treat people like people and provide human-to-human interaction, the more we differentiate ourselves.

Here are some questions to ponder in your business:

Do we use human-centered design to design products, services, and experiences?

Do we deeply understand our customers and actually listen to individuals?

Do we deliver outcomes that customers need/want in the moment they need/want it?

Do we invest in reducing the time and effort it takes to achieve those outcomes?

Do we have a reason to exist beyond a pure profit motive?

Are we empathetic with all of our stakeholders in these activities?

Drive past the affirmative or negative answer to the why or why not behind your answer. As you do, you'll find yourself thinking through themes Mathew talks about with us here: noise, attention, trust, and context.

THE AGE OF INFINITE MEDIA

In today's and tomorrow's marketplaces, our messages and experiences must become more human-focused, beneficial, desired, valued, sought out, and algorithmically-supported. When successful, we rise above the sea of noise, get attention, create conversation, and earn trust. When unsuccessful, we sink beneath the waves. How did we get here? When did the noisy raindrops turn into today's deluge?

Mathew tracked "noise" back to the year 1900, when it consisted primarily of print advertising. As he traced the evolution of noise over the next 120 years, he made a key observation: As new media enter the picture, noise levels spike and settle on a new, higher plateau. With the arrival of radio, there was a spike and then a new norm in noise levels. With television, a higher spike and higher plateau. Next the internet, higher still. Then social media . . . and a dramatic change.

At this point, growth in noise became exponential.

Back on June 24th, 2009, we left the age of limited media and entered the age of infinite, according to Mathew's research. On that day, individuals overtook businesses as the largest creator of noise. Today, each of us is incredibly well-equipped to contribute to the din, with our cameras, keyboards, devices, and digital profiles. Also contributing are an ever-increasing number of machines that are now internet-connected. Think about all the alerts, updates, and notifications from your smartwatch, doorbell, exercise equipment, kitchen appliances, and other devices. The demands on our attention are higher than ever.

Not all noise is bad. Everyone says they hate ads, but when Mathew's gone a level deeper with consumers, most have a few ads they remember, love, and want to tell you about. You probably have one, too! One of Steve's favorites: the beautiful and powerful "Like a Girl" ad from Always that debuted in Super Bowl XLIX. Not only was it groundbreaking, but it was also released within a year of the birth of his daughter and reinforced for him the message of empowerment with which he wants to raise his daughter. The point: We like some of this noise. We want, need, and even pay for some of it. Noise is good when it's desired, permission-based, and helpful.

An essential element of this subjectivity is contextual relevance. Noise I may perceive as pollution right now may have been useful and appreciated a week ago or a year from today, but . . . I don't need this now, I don't want this now, and I didn't ask for this now. I may already have made the purchase decision. The problem may have dissipated or been solved. A more important concern or opportunity may have moved up in priority. I may simply have been in the wrong mood or mindset in the moment.

We pay our limited attention to ads, email, alerts, and other digital noise for the promise of a payoff. We're driven by our current interests and hate to be disappointed. As individuals, businesses, and brands, then, our noise must make strong promises, deliver on those promises, and thereby meet or exceed each person's expectations. The promise of the subject line, headline, opening statement, or visual imagery that captures attention must reward that attention. We must provide a positive return on our recipient's or participant's investment of attention. This closes the trust gap and earns future attention and engagement.

"Trust is the currency of human relationships," argues Mathew. "The more trust I have with you, the more time I want to spend with you, the more value I give the words that you say, and the more value I give to our relationship. Trust is such a powerful thing." Whether person-to-person or customer-to-company, trust is based in the judicious use of people's time and attention. And consistency in this is key. You're reinforcing mental models and perceptual patterns about you and your business in the minds of others.

> **Trust is the currency**
> of human relationships.

The more consistently I honor and respect you in whole—your needs, wants, time, and attention—the more you'll engage with me now and in the future. To the degree this can be tracked and digitized, algorithms will help fast track or sideline demands on our attention, just as they do with our Google searches, social feeds, and inbox organization. The ideal situation is one in which contextually relevant opportunities from trusted sources are separated from the noise for us; machines will intuit our mental models based on the who, what, when, where, and how of the ways we've chosen to interact and engage.

THE CONTEXT FRAMEWORK

Mathew's context framework, which he details in *The Context Marketing Revolution*, helps us deliver opportunities and solutions to people that are needed or wanted in the moment. Its purpose is to provide a holistic approach to serving others as they need and want to be served. No silver bullets and no black-and-white answers. Rather, he offers five characteristics along continuums to think about what, why, and how we're delivering messages and experiences. Considering these characteristics will help us become more contextually relevant for people in the moment.

The Five Characteristics (and Their Continuums)

Available (Forced, Direct, Organic)

How is our message or experience made available to people? How is it encountered or found? Forced availability is an ad that interrupts the video you're trying to watch or a box that pops up over the story you're trying to read. The ideal is that people look for or ask for it organically—and that it's immediately available in that moment.

Permissioned (Implicit, Explicit)

This continuum only has two characteristics—implied or explicitly stated permission. Some prior engagement gives you implicit permission and creates the expectation of hearing from you. When someone overtly gives you permission to reach out—"Yes, sign me up!" or "Yes, please reach out"—that's explicit.

Personal (Mass, Segmented, One-to-One, Human-to-Human)

Mass is delivered in the same way for everyone; it's uniform except, perhaps, for some personalization through variable data. Segmented gets to smaller, more targeted groups based on shared characteristics, such as industry, title, age, purchase history, subscription level, or other criteria. One-to-one gets one message to one person at one time and may be delivered by a person or by a machine. This used to be the apex of this large continuum. The new apex is human-to-human experiences, which "break through not because they are personalized, but *because they are delivered personally*."[4]

Video's traditionally been used in a mass or segmented way. They're now easily sent one-to-one, but that's not necessarily personal, especially when automated and triggered. Human-to-human video is the peak. Mathew says,

"Brands must learn a new possibility for video across the entire customer journey and how to elevate the medium from a one-to-one to a human-to-human approach."

Authentic (Tone, Empathy, Consistency)

This is the most subjective element in the framework and its characteristics aren't offered here as a continuum. "We say that someone is authentic when he or she acts in a way that we intuit as congruent with their inner selves," Mathew writes.[4] Tone and voice must be true. Empathy and care must be demonstrated. And they must be infused into a message that's consistent and aligned with the channel it's delivered in.

Purposeful (CSR, Branded Action, Co-action)

Purpose is your reason for being beyond your product or service. It starts with corporate social responsibility (CSR)—adopting a stakeholder orientation and giving time or money. Branded action involves more overt and visible activity on the company's behalf. The pinnacle is co-action and co-creation with customers, communities, and other stakeholders. Through co-action, people aren't just interacting with messages and buying your products; they participate in campaigns, events, and experiences aligned with your shared values.

To consistently take actions reflecting the right end of the continuums is to be more contextually relevant and more human centric. We should aspire to have more of our messages and experiences be . . .

organically sought and available,

with clear and explicit permission,

delivered from one human to another,

with authenticity and empathy,

driving co-action toward shared purpose.

If your market isn't especially competitive or commoditized, you just need to be more contextual than others. In advanced markets, you must be the most contextual. It all starts by thinking about the human beings for whom you're designing products, services, and experiences from the very first step. It starts with human centricity.

THREE WAYS TO HELP MORE HUMANS

To orient yourself and your team toward human needs, to be of service and value, and to be more contextually relevant, here are three of Mathew's recommendations.

1. Start from the Inside

A remarkable customer experience has a necessary precursor: a remarkable employee experience. If you want to drive revenue growth, invest in the experience of your employees. In the words of Tiffani Bova, Mathew's colleague and Global Growth and Innovation Evangelist at Salesforce, "The fastest way to get customers to love your brand is to get employees to love their jobs."[5]

Tiffani's quote comes from a recent Forbes Insights study of customer experience (CX), employee experience (EX), and revenue growth. The causal links work this way:

High EX drives high CX.

High CX fuels revenue growth.

High CX reinforces high EX in a feedback loop, but it doesn't drive it directly.

This matches the findings of Harvard Business School's James L. Heskett, W. Earl Sasser, and Leonard A. Schlesinger, which were published in *The Service Profit Chain* nearly 25 years ago. They found that direct investments in employees drive their satisfaction, retention, and productivity (EX). They proved that EX drives customer value, satisfaction, and loyalty (CX). And they showed that CX drives revenue growth and profitability.[6]

In the Forbes Insights study, 89% of executives at revenue-growth leaders agreed that better EX leads directly to better CX. Companies with high EX and high CX have nearly double the revenue growth as those that do not. In the same study, executives ranked "Go beyond charitable giving to strengthen communities" as the second most likely way to improve CX, second only to "Increased tech investment" (34% vs 35%).[5] Why is this important? It supports the idea that a stakeholder orientation motivates both employees and customers, as well as Mathew's call for purpose-driven co-action.

Employee experience is far deeper than the list of perks and benefits that come with the job. They matter. But they don't matter nearly as much as what it feels like to work for you and your company. Do I feel seen, heard, understood, and appreciated? Do I feel challenged and supported? Are you investing in me and empowering me? Am I being treated as a person, rather than an expense, a revenue source, or another number? People want safety, flexibility, and compassion. Investing time and attention in your employees is more important than investing in physical or material improvements in working conditions.

Not only is this approach more effective and satisfying for leaders and managers, it's also better for your employees, your customers, and your revenue growth. It sets the cultural tone and demonstrates "how we do it around here," which is consequently felt by your customers. How you treat your employees is the foundation for your reputation and your long-term success.

2. Rethink the Way You Communicate

Our default approach to communication asks questions like these:

How do I get someone to do what I want them to do?

What are the right words? What do I need to say?

A human-centered approach to communication asks different questions:

If I was that person, what would get me to engage in a positive way?

Why would she respond or engage? What's in it for her?

How can I help?

As Mathew writes in *The Context Marketing Revolution*, people want to be worked *with*, not worked *on*. As Jacco put it in Chapter 3, people love to buy, but they don't like to be sold to. Persuasion is fine, but manipulation and coercion are not. The challenge in making this shift is getting your team members out of their own way, giving them permission to ask better questions, and getting buy-in throughout the organization.

Both manipulation and persuasion seek to influence people and affect outcomes. So, what's the difference?

"What matters in identifying manipulation is not what kind of influence is being used, but whether the influence is being used to put the other person into a better or worse position to make a decision," according to Robert Noggle, professor of philosophy at Central Michigan University.[7] For example, is your use of fear helping or hurting someone's decision-making process? It comes down to intent, which is also a key factor in our judgments of noise and pollution.

Look back at those two sets of questions and think about how you and your team are communicating through personal messages and automated messages. If it's not human-centered, it may not be "working." Remember, a 2.2% success rate is also a 97.8% failure rate.

3. Add Video to Your Communication

We've already said it and we'll say it again (and again): to be human-centered with your online communication demands that you be more visual, more emotional, and more human. With video, Mathew says, "I can see your expressions. I can see the nonverbal cues that you're giving me. I can build trust in a way that I cannot build by any other method or medium. It's a very empowering thing. It can be very human."

But video itself is just a medium; people and their motives make the difference.

"It's not the medium that is human, it is the fact that it allows two humans to connect in a naturally human way. Face to face is the easiest way that humans can communicate back and forth because we are multi-sensory beings," Mathew explains. "We have all these senses available to us to then make these determinations. So video allows us to be the most human that we can possibly be at any moment with someone else. The only thing greater than this is actually being in the room."

IMPROVING YOUR VIDEOS

So often, you can't be in the room. So often, a video call or video message would be better than its alternative—typed-out text. So how can we make the most of our video communication? In Mathew's experience, watching videos back, soliciting feedback, and leveraging new tools will help.

Practice and Playback

Mathew's career started in sales and an early influence was *Zig Ziglar's Secrets of Closing the Sale*. One of Zig's recommendations in that book: If you want to be good at selling, go buy a tape recorder, record your calls, listen back, put yourself in the other person's role, and learn to improve the way you use your voice. That's happening every day now with tools we mentioned in Chapter 2, Chorus.ai and Gong.io, but with two notable differences.

First, we're typically hosting, recording, and playing back video calls rather than phone calls. Second, we're not necessarily doing what Mathew and Zig recommend: putting ourselves in the other person's role. This is the heart of human-centered communication—empathy, understanding, learning, and growth.

Your first phone call, your first video call, your first video message, and your other firsts tend to be awkward, uncomfortable, and worse than all the others that follow. If you want video to be powerful, you have to work at it. To improve at anything, you must put the effort in. It's a learned behavior and new skill. Mathew confessed to Steve and me that he was not a natural presenter; it took him a long time to get comfortable on stage and he continues to work on it.

The key, though, is not to look at yourself through your own eyes. It's to think first about the other person. To put yourself in their place. Review your videos through their eyes. Imagine their experience. It sounds simple. And it is. But making this shift is powerful in its effect on your perspective; it will make you better.

Honest Feedback

We learn and improve through feedback on our work and our performance. Video shouldn't be any different. Create a group of trusted people who'll give you honest feedback about the way you communicate on your video calls and video messages.

As Mathew sought feedback from customers about their experiences, he noticed that they often struggled to articulate their feelings and thoughts. Your people may struggle to provide feedback about your videos, too. Here's Mathew's advice:

Ask for specific and structured feedback.

Ask three or fewer questions.

Make them easy to answer.

Don't ask, "How was my video?" Instead ask, "On a scale of 1-5, how [X, Y, or Z] was this?" Warm, honest, confident, persuasive, clear—whatever you're working on, ask about it simply and specifically.

Production Quality

We've got screens everywhere. There's more video than ever. The speed of uploading, downloading, and streaming will only get faster—and higher in quality. It's easier to produce and distribute than ever. "Now that everyone does it, we have to then up our game," Mathew says.

As new tools make it easier and less expensive to increase production quality with graphics, animations, image quality, shot selection, source switching, and more, Mathew feels that we must take advantage of the opportunity. But it must be done in service of the viewer. "If we use these new things without human-centered communication, I think that we end up in a regression," Mathew predicts.

Just as we shouldn't take the same old emails that convert at 1.7% and turn them into video scripts, we shouldn't take the same webinar that's a thinly veiled sales pitch and dress it up with flashier graphics and animations. That's not progress. That's an incremental improvement or even a regression. The opportunity before us is a new concept of video communication.

WE ONLY INCREASE IN VALUE

Technology will continue its advance and it's up to us to make sure it serves us. As we turn over some share of our responsibility for effective communication to new tools, we must keep foremost in our minds the currency of trust. We've already become somewhat like cyborgs, leveraging technology to extend ourselves. But we must not outsource our strengths and soft skills. Their value doesn't fall away in the future. Instead, it only grows.

An entire book, *Humans Are Underrated: What High Achievers Know That Brilliant Machines Never Will*, was written on this topic by Geoff Colvin, Senior Editor at Large for *Fortune* Magazine. Its theme is captured in this passage from the opening chapter: "The new high-value skills are instead part of our deepest nature, the abilities that literally define us as humans: sensing the thoughts and feelings of others, working productively in groups, building relationships, solving problems together, expressing ourselves with greater power than logic can ever achieve."[8]

The new high-value skills aren't *new* at all. They're already in us. What's new about the skills of connecting, communicating, and collaborating with other people is their increased value. The value of other skills may diminish. The way some people put food on the table may change. Some career tracks may dead end. Some livelihoods are threatened by new apps, tools, and automations. In the face of these threats and changes, we need to reinvest time and energy into what's uniquely human, because the value of truly personal experiences won't fall. It'll only increase.

"As we move forward in time, I think that video becomes increasingly important for human-to-human connections," Mathew predicts. That's because it's intrinsically linked to these high-value skills that reveal our deepest nature and our greatest strength.

CREATOR of the SELLING ON VIDEO MASTER CLASS

"Allow yourself to be passionate and commit to it."

A KEY IDEA IN THIS CHAPTER

Being the best version of the real you that's appropriate for the situation.

CHAPTER 6

Preparing to Be Present

Featuring Julie Hansen

"What can I do to really get out of myself,
get in front of people, and find my voice?"

This brilliant question occurred to Julie Hansen years ago. At the time, she was confronting the fact that she didn't feel as confident on the job as other people seemed to be. The answer to her question? Acting classes. "For me, the opportunity was to express myself and gain confidence, which worked," Julie explains. "But it also helped me to see that sales is a role."

This intersection of acting and sales is where Julie has since spent her career. Her acting classes led to years of professional acting with roles in more than 75 plays, commercials, and television shows, including HBO's *Sex and the City*. During that time, she also worked in sales. "The same skills I was using to win parts were helping me win more business," Julie says. She spent two decades as a salesperson and then sales leader in the technology, media, and real estate industries. "As I got into management, I started coaching others on how to step into roles that were sometimes uncomfortable."

Often, the people she was working with simply needed to bring more of themselves into those roles. "I see so many salespeople who have left their personality at the door. There's a piece of you that is engaging and personable; let's find that piece and bring it on camera," observes Julie. "And that's what coaching people to be authentic and to project on camera is all about—finding those unique parts of them and allowing them to express that."

Ten years ago, she turned this unique solution into a company: Performance Sales and Training. Julie also authored *Sales Presentations for Dummies* and

Act Like a Sales Pro: How to Command the Business Stage and Dramatically Increase Your Sales with Proven Acting Techniques and created the Selling on Video Master Class. She works to make connecting and communicating through video more natural for people. Her goal for students: "being as real as you can but being the best version of the real you that's appropriate for the situation and the confines of the medium."

Preparing in advance so you can be present with the other person. Turning up emotions and expressions a little so other people can clearly read them through their screens. Building trust by aligning yourself, your message, the subtext, and the other person. Julie's expertise and coaching in these areas make her a strong ally in the movement toward human-centered communication.

Reading, listening to, and interviewing Julie was eye-opening for both Steve and me; her teaching challenged some of our long-held beliefs. We thought that acting didn't have a place in human-centered communication—that acting was associated more with being fake than with being human. As you'll see, we couldn't have been more wrong.

ACTING AND AUTHENTICITY

Every day, we play multiple roles within our personal and professional lives. Just within the realm of parenting, we might play good cop, bad cop, chef, teacher, nurse, coach, and therapist. All in the same day! Friend. Leader. Sibling. Manager. The various roles we play are each a little different, but we put as much of ourselves into every one of them as we can.

The same is true of acting roles. A common misperception is that acting involves being someone or something that you're not. Without a level of authenticity and connection between you and your character, what results is the worst type of acting. To be a great actor, you must find and express parts of yourself in the role you're playing.

To illustrate, think about some popular movie characters. Try Jennifer Lawrence as Katniss Everdeen in *The Hunger Games* and the late Chadwick Boseman as Black Panther. Could you see Emma Watson, most familiar as Hermione Granger in the *Harry Potter* films, as Katniss? Could you see Jamie Foxx, one of the most famous performers in the world, as Black Panther? Same script. Same lines. Same scenes. Completely different experience. Try this with a few of your favorite characters; plug in a variety of actors. You'll start to see how much of themselves excellent actors bring to their roles.

> In **every role** you play,
> find and express parts of
> **your authentic self**.

The same is true in our business roles. They come with some parameters, guidelines, and recommendations, but we make them authentically our own. Think about one of your best team members. Think about their job description. Then think about the difference between what the job looks like on paper and what it feels like performed in real life. Or think about the person who had the job before them. Same title. Same responsibilities. Same tasks. The difference in the experience is based on how much each of us brings to our roles.

Unfortunately, not everyone steps into their role authentically. "When people think about business, it's business-like. We're talking business. We get into business mode and presenter mode. It's all very nice and polite—and boring," Julie laments. "It doesn't show any personality. It's what we imagine a businessperson should be like." This is bad acting. You belong in your business role. We need and want you.

"By being authentic in our roles we can be honest, be open, and give people an opportunity to identify, empathize, and trust," she says. These are the dynamics of human connection; we're giving what we hope to receive. And when we do it in videos, the camera doesn't lie. We can be ourselves and thereby extend an invitation to others. Or we can be robotic and curb a connection. Human-centered communication calls for authenticity.

Turning Everything Up (A Little)

Before you meet "Super Viv" in Chapter 10, we'll share something she has in common with Julie: awareness that being on camera dampens your emotional expression. Because the camera takes off 10% to 30% of your energy, "you have to amp it up." Knowing that some of it won't read on the other person's screen, Julie coaches people to really bring their personalities in full.

Practice runs with her clients often go something like this:

Client: (Delivers something that's very "flat, uninteresting, and salesy")

Julie: "Let's try it again. And I want you to just talk to me like I'm your best friend. And you just found out something exciting. Just let loose, go over the top, and be bigger than you think is necessary."

Client: (Does it again with more energy)

Another person on the call: "Wow, that was so good!"

Julie: "How did that feel?"

Client: "That felt good, but it was way too big."

Another person on the call: "No, that's right where you need to be."

Turning it up is *not* inauthentic. It's still you, but in an elevated state. "These are the aha moments some of the people experience when they realize they can bring their personalities," says Julie. To simply pass information along, you may want to just type it out. To connect, communicate, influence, and inspire, you need to turn on the camera and turn yourself up a little. Smile. Bring natural excitement. Use more variety in your voice. Express yourself.

> Turning up your emotions and expressions is **not inauthentic**.

Good acting and good communication both start inside you. But they're not *about* you. We must put ourselves into the role in order to reach other people. "It just starts with getting in touch with the intention that you're trying to communicate to the other person," Julie explains. "But if you don't have [a clear intention], it's going to be really hard to manufacture excitement and energy and have that read as real." The result is overexpressing, overemphasizing, and orchestration. In other words, bad acting.

Leveraging Your Real Estate

Emotional intelligence and facial coding expert Dan Hill, featured in Chapter 4, says that "the 25 square inches that feature our eyes, nose, and mouth is the richest visual territory on the planet."[1] Julie advises us to use this valuable real estate with purpose. When we don't, we default to "resting business face" (RBF), a flat face with neutral to negative emotion.

Wearing this blank expression feels like disinterest to the people we're trying to engage. And it brings us down. Research suggests that our expressions don't just convey our emotions to other people; they may also allow us to experience our own emotions more fully.[2] For example, putting on our "game face" has been proven to enhance performance.[3] We must be ready, willing, and able to access our emotions.

"One thing that I love about acting is that it's very connected to learning to open up, warming up, vocalizing, and stretching out your facial muscles, so that you have ready access to them," Julie advises. Our head, shoulders, and face carry much of our meaning; they help communicate our intent. Julie asks, "If I turn the sound off, could I tell whether you're giving me good news or bad news?" Our body language should be doing that for us.

This requires us to connect with what we're saying and the "why" behind it, just as actors invest themselves in their scripts. Also like actors, we must be in touch with our own faces and bodies to physically express our intention and motivation. For decades the cultural norm and status quo in business has been to rein in emotion and to wear a "professional" facade. The pendulum is swinging back toward fuller expression and whole people.

Fighting Fear and Taming Tension

Steve and I have taught "comfort on camera" for years. As it turns out, there's a better goal: confidence on camera. You want being on camera to feel familiar, but not tension-free. Comfort leads to leaning back, rather than leaning in. It may also lead to the dreaded RBF. "The camera reads energy, and it reads that from your voice, your face, your body language, and even how you're sitting," Julie says. "So, if I'm sitting back where I'm comfortable, I could be super interested, but it still looks like I'm not as interested as I could be."

Seeking confidence on camera, then, makes more sense than seeking comfort. But both are better than what most of us start with: fear, tension, or anxiety. "To deal with that fear, first acknowledge that it's real," Julie advises. "This is an unnatural thing that you're doing, and it brings up a lot of personal doubt and questions and seeking some kind of perfection that isn't there."

The best way to make the unnatural feel more natural? Practice. Turn your camera on during meetings, even if you'd prefer not to. Record and send video messages, even if you'd rather delete them. This is good practice. But Julie advises that you take it a step further by reviewing your videos after you've sent several of them:

> We know we don't like how we look on camera, but we don't really know what that means. As opposed to just a generalized 'I look terrible and I don't know what to do about it,' look at it in different buckets. Record yourself, objectively go through it, then ask, 'Okay, how was my eye contact? How was my lighting? How were my facial expressions? How did I come across?'

Play it back. Break it down. List out the areas of improvement—eye contact, facial expression, emotive quality, movement of your hands and body. What's distracting? What might help bring your ideas to life? For example, you might try to physicalize things on purpose, like counting or listing things on your hand. Work on these things in a focused, consistent way. In Julie's experience, "you start to feel more confident just taking it one area at a time."

> Build confidence by working on **one area of improvement** at a time.

As you work to face your fear, build your confidence, and improve your delivery, also remember that you're the only one expecting perfection from yourself. We need space to make errors when we're live on video or when we're recording video. Without that space, even minor errors that don't really matter will grab our attention, trip us up, and take us out of the moment. At that point, we're instantly lost in the middle of the video. Just as we must in real life, we should just keep going.

PREPARATION, CONFIDENCE, AND ALIGNMENT

In acting, a character's life doesn't begin the minute the curtain goes up or the camera turns on. As an audience, we're joining them in progress. They've been somewhere, done something, or had a conversation. This is what helps a scene take off. "It's very difficult to start from nothing, ramp up the energy, and ramp up the scene," Julie says.

And when you think about it, the same is true for our video calls and video messages. "Most people don't hit their sweet spot until about 20 or 30 seconds into the video. Now they're cooking, but they may have lost people by then," Julie cautions. "So you've got to bring that friendliness, interaction, availability, and connection right from the start."

We need to create what Julie calls the "Moment Before," an alignment of your internal state, your message, your purpose, and your audience. What's happening the moment before you click Start, Join, or Record? What is the other person's moment before? Creating answers will create valuable momentum. As opposed to just showing up, you're propelled into the scene. And this is just one way to prepare.

Preparation

"When we are uptight or nervous, our body sends those signals that make us get more inhibited. It's much harder to express yourself if your body is fighting against you and trying to protect you from the fear," says Julie. "You've got to warm up, physicalize, and keep your energy flowing. And then be confident in what you're going to say and be clear on your intention for saying it. Ask yourself why you're talking to this person right now."

This is how you prepare for human-centered communication. Thinking about the other person, gaining clarity and confidence about why you're connecting, and aligning your mind and body to deliver. From there, it's like any other performance. Trust that you know what you're doing. Let go when the camera turns on. And just focus on that person, staying in the moment and adapting on the fly. "You can't be thinking 'What's my next line?' or 'I want to move over there' or 'I wonder if that light is too bright.' You have to really focus on the other person."

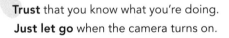

> **Trust** that you know what you're doing.
> **Just let go** when the camera turns on.

To be prepared:

+ Practice the content. Know it and internalize it, but don't memorize it word for word.

+ Practice being on camera. Look at the camera. Move on camera. Get familiar.

+ Know what's in your frame before you start the call or the recording.

✦ Be intuitive once you're on. Don't think about these things consciously. Rely on muscle memory.

✦ Let yourself go. Create space for errors and imperfections so you don't get tripped up in the moment.

Confidence

Self-confidence starts when we stop being hyper-critical of ourselves. We tend to look around at everyone else and subconsciously wonder how much we can be our true selves. Instead, Julie says, "you have to trust that what you have is unique and allow that to come out in whatever you're doing."

In Julie's experience, when we operate with a lack of confidence and an "I'm not enough" mindset, we often embellish. We put on an exterior that isn't connected with what we're saying, why we're saying it, or what we're trying to accomplish. "That's where it starts to get phony," Julie explains. And the problem is that confidence and guidance are the reasons you're in these calls, conversations, and videos.

"If people could just read something online and say 'Yeah, I'll take it' then salespeople would be looking for more work, but that's not the case. Buyers still need to get that confidence instilled in them that this is the best option and the reasons why," Julie explains. "That hasn't changed. The tools and technology have changed, but we still have to make that connection. When people are more cautious and uncertain, we have to help them have more certainty and knowledge. They need to feel like they're going to be safe and that they're making a good decision. And that's because of you, the person."

Julie observes that at a very basic level, we're delivering information and answering questions. "If that were enough, it wouldn't matter how you did it. But it does matter," says Julie. "It matters because people aren't just listening to the words. They're listening to your authority, your credibility, your reassurance."

We want to show up as a fellow human who authentically believes what we're saying and who inspires confidence and trust. "When all that aligns, that's pretty magical. That does a lot more than words on paper." We'll keep learning about how critical confidence can be with Lauren Bailey in Chapter 8.

Alignment

Trust is built by aligning yourself, your message, the subtext, and the other person. You have to believe that the opportunity is worth the other person exploring and that the opportunity can help that person. You have to believe that you can help that person.

"When you're passionate about it and you can express that appropriately in front of the camera, that can be so powerful. Those are the videos that get watched," Julie explains. "It doesn't matter if you flub a line here and there, people respond to that, so those really break through. Unfortunately, those are the minority of the videos out there."

"On the negative side, if you're *not* aligned with what you're saying, your body will betray you in some way. If you're not totally in sync, it's going to show in your eyes. It's going to show in some nervous tic. Something is going to read as off," cautions Julie. "Your customer won't know what it is, but it's going to cast a seed of doubt." From that seed of doubt grow uncertainty and risk, not confidence and trust.

Be clear about what you're saying, why you're saying it, and why it's valuable to the other person. Allow yourself to be passionate about it and to commit to it. "Commit 100% to letting someone fully appreciate why you're excited about this and convey that to them," Julie advises. "Then they get to be the judge."

LISTENING AND BEING PRESENT

Once you're prepared, confident, and aligned, let go. The purpose of letting go is to be fully present for the other person, including active listening. When we let go, we invite the E, engagement, from the GIVER framework shown in Chapter 2. We let go of scripts, we stay adaptable, and we create space for conversation.

Listen with Your Entire Being

This mantra, "Listen with your entire being," came to Julie from an acting coach and is absolutely critical to every one of our live, synchronous video calls. It reminds us to do more than hear the words being said. How does this person sound? How does what they're saying feel? What is their face saying?

"This is something you can't do unless you're really present in the moment," Julie explains. "When you can really open yourself up to listen, to respond, and to not be afraid to go off track, that's when you connect." For example, when someone says something with a tone that indicates that there might be something more to the story, you can ask a follow-up question. "You can't pick up on those things if you're nervous about what you're going to say next."

"Listening on video is very challenging, because the impulse is, 'I want to look at their image while they're talking,'" Julie explains. But when we spend too much time looking at our screen instead of into the camera lens, "it feels like you're not interested." Even if you're not distracted, it can still make people feel unheard.

Add Punctuation

Julie offers this recommendation, "Add punctuation," as an encouragement to incorporate the equivalent of a comma, period, dash, or ellipsis to your recorded, asynchronous videos. When we're together in person or on a video call, the conversation is more natural. We pause and create breaks. We let people set down and pick back up their ideas. We often let moments sit. In our video recordings, however, we tend to get going . . . and go, go, go!

Being present with someone who isn't there with you "is in the high end of challenges" for people who are recording videos and for actors who are recording part of a scene without their scene partner. We have to add punctuation, even if it feels unnatural. We must pause, wait, and let the idea hit. It creates a much more dynamic flow and feels more like a real conversation. Adding punctuation brings the video to life. "This is definitely trickier to do than it is in synchronous videos, but it's possible."

The alternative is a punctuation-free zone. "We are so afraid that if we pause, they're going to lose attention," Julie says. "So it's just this verbal onslaught. This happens sometimes in real life, but it happens a lot more in video, even with experienced people. I see them just rushing through." The irony is that instead of *preventing* people from tuning out, this firehose of information actually *causes* people to tune out. When we pause, we demonstrate our own presence and invite people back into the message.

We thought about writing these paragraphs without any punctuation but decided that even though it was a fun idea it wasn't a great idea That decision comes in part from our deep internal need to give in to perfectionism come across as polished and professional and demonstrate our competence Giving in to these feelings is something that experts in this book have encouraged you not to do So we restricted it to this paragraph alone We hope it wasn't too confusing or annoying Thanks for your patience And remember to be present enough to add punctuation to your recorded videos your conversations and your writing It's a gift to your recipients.

AN AUDIENCE OF ONE

Shifting our focus from a generalized persona to an individual person is what others want and need from us. It's also at the core of human-centered communication. For the sake of efficiency, we can't make every single message or experience truly human-to-human. At the same time, we must take care not to sacrifice rapport, intimacy, or connection—no matter the audience. Whether it's for one person or for a group of people, each video is for an audience of one.

Efficiency vs Connection

Very often, we find ourselves making a video or a call over and over again. One message created 5 or 10 times in a row and delivered to 5 or 10 different people. In these cases, when we're cranking out a series of similar activities for different people, a common tendency is to slip into robot mode. Almost as if it's all one task. But that's a mistake.

"I understand that there's a need for efficiency," Julie says from experience. "But when you have that practiced recording that you're going to do for several different people and it's 90% the same every time, that doesn't make it a good recording. If you're not thinking of who you're talking to every time and having a unique performance every time, it's going to read as rote to your audience."

"Being efficient means blocking out anything new," explains Julie. When we slip into efficiency mode, we look to uniformly knock out a series of activities. With video, it's "Hey, Bob." "Hey, Joe." "Hey, Jill." Instead, we should think more about "Who is Joe?" "Can I see Joe?" "Am I looking at Joe?" "Am I imagining Joe?" Just having that basic connection with each person doesn't take much time. And it gives that same practiced video a new life each time.

Think about the other person. Be present with them. Tailor the message a little. Provide a unique performance. Make a connection. "If you went to see the same show two nights in a row, it would be different. The actors would still be saying the same words, but it will be different because there are different things going on," Julie reminds us. Think about each person as an individual, not just a segment, a persona, or a task.

Rapport and Intimacy

When we create an audience of one in our virtual communication, we create rapport and intimacy. Mediating our experiences through screens presents some challenges, but it also comes with opportunities. For example: On our video calls, "we're much closer now than we would be if we were sitting in a room together, so we have this pretty amazing level of intimacy." To capitalize on it, we must think more about them, see their face, read their expressions, and make it a conversation. "That's when things slow down and when our real emotions come out."

Making eye contact is Julie's top tip for building rapport and relationships. Of course, we struggle with this on video calls as we shift our focus from the screen to the camera. To help, turn off your view of yourself and move the other person as close to your camera as possible. The less your eyes are moving around and the more eye contact you make, the more confidence you inspire.

Pausing also helps, so don't rush or make it a monologue. And pause longer than you think you need to. "When we're in front of a screen, we tend to be more passive in general. And we're used to people just talking at us and we'll just let you talk. So you have to make it very clear if you expect an answer by pausing and by using the right intonation. Make the question sound like a question, not like a statement."

As part of your preparation and in order to build rapport, expect the best from the other person. Before you start the call or recording, imagine the other person being interested in what you have to say. There's no upside in imagining anything less. "Imagine this person is really interested, that they need this, and that they're excited," Julie suggests. "There's no downside to that and it brings out the best in you."

Those are a few rapport builders. But what about rapport ruiners? To stay human-centered, Julie advises you to avoid:

Failing to involve other people.

Talking over people.

Not providing space and pauses.

Not actively listening.

Not being willing to go off-script.

Failing to acknowledge important things you're seeing or hearing.

Upstaging your customer, your team member, or yourself.

Julie says we upstage others when our attitude is that of "putting on a show." When we act in this way, it's almost as if we're treating the other people as props while we "get our lines out." "No matter what you have planned, the other person is going to affect that. You may have planned out a presentation, but that person may have a different plan in mind. Ultimately, you have to be flexible. It's more important that you let them feel like they have a part in the conversation and have some control over where things go than sticking to your plan."

Reality and Proximity

"If somebody told you 10 years ago that you'd be able to be in a CEO's home, you'd say, 'Wow, that would be awesome.' So, here we are. You're at home. They're at home. There's just a different level of connection already. You can leverage that by using your own environment," Julie observes. She knows many people who use green screens and recognizes that there are good reasons to use them, but they can also create distance. Showing our real background "creates more opportunity for rapport-building and connection. It makes you real." We reveal more of ourselves and learn more about others in our natural settings.

Whether live or recorded, video brings us psychologically closer to others. If you're both sitting within two feet of your camera, you're within what anthropologist Edward T. Hall calls "personal distance" of the other person—less than four feet apart. Best-selling author David Meerman Scott writes about this in *Fanocracy: Turning Fans into Customers and Customers into Fans* and explained it to me on The Customer Experience Podcast:

> People intellectually know they're just on camera, but your subconscious and mirror neurons tell you that you're actually in close, physical proximity. You're in the personal space of the person on the screen. This is an incredibly powerful way to build fans by establishing a close, virtual proximity.[4]

Creating this closeness through video in your real, personal setting gives you "an opportunity to really be your best, authentic self in this authentic environment with someone else in their own environment," Julie says. "That's where some magic can really happen."

IF YOU HAVE A MESSAGE

No one is wired for video. It's unnatural. Some people happen to be good at it without much effort, but that's rare.

"Even actors who are good on stage pretty universally have to learn how to project and communicate on camera," Julie says. "But if you look at the spectrum of different types of actors who are on television and movie screens, it's clear that anyone can become effective on camera."

In order to humanize our communication and improve our results, we must become effective on camera, too. "It's so much easier to turn someone down or not pay attention if they're on the phone or in the inbox. I've done it. We've all done it," Julie says. "It's much more difficult to be in front of another human face and deny that they're a real person and categorize them as just another salesperson. So it automatically puts you on a more equal footing with another person, and I think that's something we've always strived for in sales. Why not use that?"

In short: "If you have a message and if you have something you're passionate about, there's no reason you can't be on camera."

ADAM CONTOS

CEO of RE/MAX

"Nobody can hear you right now."

A KEY IDEA IN THIS CHAPTER

Forsaking yourself and completely understanding the other person.

CHAPTER 7

"How Can I Help You?"

Featuring Adam Contos

Adam Contos, CEO of RE/MAX, had an epiphany several years ago. It was an epiphany of why things like social media and podcasts matter. He had just been named Senior Vice President of Marketing and was attending Social Media Marketing World where he met the event's founder, Michael Stelzner. Part of their conversation went something like this:

Michael: "What's the name of your podcast, Adam?"

Adam: "I don't have one, Michael. Why do I need one?"

Michael: "Because nobody can hear you right now."

This conversation was a turning point for Adam. Michael's response sparked an insight into the importance of visibility and the power of "parasocial relationships." These relationships allow people to invest their time, attention, and emotional energy in a one-way manner that builds a relationship with someone they've never met.[1] They're created through visibility, which comes through publishing your ideas online and reaching the people who want to see and hear your ideas.

Adam immediately linked this need to be seen and heard to a philosophy he'd long held: "What we're all in business for is to help people." The ultimate questions for your business then become "What problem are you solving?" and "Who are you solving it for?" Once you've got clear answers, you almost have a duty to make yourself and your message available to everyone who needs it. Getting in front of the camera and microphone allows you to help people in a more personal way—even people you've not yet met.

So Adam began producing videos for social media, as well as a podcast. His efforts were based on a simple, powerful premise. "I knew if I could help people, then people would listen to what I have to say. But I needed to deliver good solutions," he explains. "So I thought let's ask the question 'How can I help you?'" This customer-centric question set him up for a journey into human-centered communication.

You might be reading this and thinking, "This isn't for me." Maybe YouTube channels, live streaming, or podcasts seem daunting. But sit with Adam for a while and learn from his experiences and expertise. Audiences are built one person at a time. If you promise to help people, they will come. When you deliver a good solution, they will stay.

In this chapter, you'll see how mindset and intention can guide human-centered decisions and actions in parasocial relationships. You'll learn the formula for emotional brilliance. And you'll hear three mantras to encourage you to enhance your visibility and presence in virtual environments.

A DIY JOURNEY

Nearly 20 years ago, Adam appeared in his first RE/MAX video, a highly produced piece about real estate agent safety. A professional production with professional actors. They even hired a national television news anchor to do the voiceover work. Since then, he's been in other videos with large budgets and long timelines, spoken on stages large and small, and worked with production crews throughout.

Though he's now the CEO of a publicly traded company that ranked as the top real estate brokerage franchise for eight straight years on *Entrepreneur*'s Franchise 500 list,[2] Adam prefers a do-it-yourself (DIY) ethic.

Adam describes the majority of his videos in this way: "I'm sitting in my basement in my own little personal studio. In a closet, practically." He's set himself up in an extra room, adding a wood wall, a few lamps, and basic equipment. He owns a green screen and several backdrops, but never uses them; they feel fake to him. "[People] don't want to see you in a full production. But they do want to see you in a high-quality environment with high-quality audio and visuals, knowing what you're talking about, and staying in front of them regularly to deliver value."

If you're a business owner or leader, you can follow Adam's lead. You don't need to wait for big budgets. You don't need to hire in specialized skills. And you definitely don't need a television news anchor to narrate your videos. Instead, you just start, then iterate.

Adam began his video journey by challenging himself with "30 in 30": recording and sharing 30 videos in 30 days. It's a great way to gain experience and develop the habit. At first, he recorded everything on his iPhone. Over time, he's slowly built up his equipment and sophistication. Whenever he wanted to upgrade, he Googled things like "best vlogging camera" and "best podcast mic."

Today, Adam uses a nice Canon DSLR with a high-quality lens that beautifully blurs the background, a $29 lavalier microphone from Amazon, and an ATEM Mini from Blackmagic Design to switch between camera shots. He mostly does live video and avoids the time and effort of editing. Now, he's appeared in hundreds of live videos on Facebook, hundreds of videos in his own channel and the RE/MAX channel on YouTube, and hundreds of live and recorded videos in LinkedIn and Instagram.

Then he moved on to podcasting. His friend and podcast producer Mark Labriola II of Brand Viva got Adam going with his show, Start With A Win. From there, he learned the process and equipment and has started other podcasts on his own. He's now been podcasting for more than three years and has created thousands of virtual relationships with his guests and his listeners. I've enjoyed the privilege of being both a listener and a guest myself; Adam and I talk about rehumanizing business on Episode 42 of Start With A Win.

Get links to the **podcasts** and **people** mentioned throughout the book by visiting **BombBomb.com/BookBonus**

THREE MANTRAS FOR LESS HIDING

As the old saying goes, "They don't care how much you know until they know how much you care." Adam can't stress that enough. If we're going to help people as the foundation of our business, we must share knowledge. Competence and knowledge are necessary, but not sufficient in communications. We must also demonstrate warmth and build trust when transferring that knowledge.

People naturally seek human connection and shared values, even in buying decisions. "They want to know that you're a human being. People want to have something in common with you before they want to do business with you. Functionally, it goes down to the root of kindness, which is caring about each other." This is the warmth to support your competence.

Here's a less familiar saying: "Leaders lead, and hiders hide." Our fear of criticism and lack of confidence keep us quiet. But—counter to what we might think—when you put others first, you make yourself seen and heard. You bring solutions to problems. You open up for engagement and conversation with others. You lead.

This, then, is a call to create and share helpful ideas in more human ways. Video helps us be seen and heard. It empowers us to help and serve. It enhances connection and relationships.

Here are three mantras that drive Adam's communication philosophy:

1. "Presence creates trust."

"People don't do business with a company whose leadership they don't trust because they don't want a transaction," says Adam. "They want a relationship." Even when a decision looks rational and transactional, people still want to know that you'll be there for them if or when something goes wrong.

When you can't be physically present, you can be psychologically present. Even in the absence of physical proximity, video creates psychological proximity. A nearness. A sense of knowing. When people spend time watching you on a screen or listening to you in their earbuds, you have presence with them. Adam builds trusting relationships in this way—often before he ever meets someone in person.

Presence also opens us up for the commonality we seek in others. As prediction machines, humans value what's common, known, and familiar, because this allows for more accurate predictions. With no basis or foundation to confidently predict the future, we're uncertain, uncomfortable, or even scared. That's why building parasocial relationships is so effective; people discover things they have in common with you.

2. "Top of mind is first in line."

"I may have never met them before, but when I go to events people come up to me and say, 'I've been watching your videos, thank you,'" Adam shares. "I give them a hug most of the time because we have this relationship as human beings. We share challenges. We share thoughts and philosophies. And you can tell that first time you talked to them that they know who you are."

Visibility and presence keep you top of mind. When you're teaching, sharing, and helping based on your expertise, you're top of mind in a trusted way that's tied to a specific problem or opportunity. At that point, you're first in line when that problem or opportunity arises. So human-centered communication helps with the "when" behind people's buying decisions, not just the who, how, and why. Because everyone's needs change over time, we must maintain presence with people.

"I've had people call me from other companies and say, 'I want to become a franchisee of your company.' And I ask, 'Have we met?' Then they say, 'No, but I watch your videos and I know who you are. I know what you're about and I want to do business with you.' You're closing deals without having to close deals," explains Adam. "And it's not about closing deals. It's about building relationships that lead to deals and to longevity of relationships."

3. "Focus on ROR, not ROI."

"It's amazing for leaders to be putting themselves out there in a very vulnerable manner," Adam says. You will be rewarded for your time, effort, and authenticity. But the rewards aren't always easy to see. Trust and relationships are not easily measured or quantified. So, instead of focusing on a transactional view of return on investment (ROI), Adam recommends focusing on what his friend Ted Rubin calls return on relationship (ROR). In fact, *Return on Relationship* is the title of a book Ted co-authored.

Even if you can't track specific dollars, you can track other metrics, right? Definitely. But Adam doesn't pay much attention to total view counts. Instead, he focuses on which people are commenting, sharing, engaging, and repeatedly watching. Being attuned to the behavior of individual people helps him deepen digital relationships and sometimes bring them into real life.

The returns here aren't just about relationships or revenue, by the way. Among the transferable skills Adam's developed through his video work: Confidence in public speaking. Managing tone and tempo. Ideating and creating messages. Telling better stories and telling stories better. The leadership and communication skills he's developed are as valuable as the relationships he's developed. In the short term and in the long term.

Leaders lead. Hiders hide. When we get out from behind our keyboards, make ourselves available in authentic ways, and seek to serve others, we enjoy the benefits of communicating in human-centered ways.

THE HANDSHAKE DEAL

Trust and relationships. That's what Adam's mantras are based on. "We're all in the human business," Adam says. "And if you keep that as your North Star—that you're a good person dealing with good people—this philosophical foundation allows you to accomplish anything."

This healthy perspective implies trust—and even faith—in other people.

A long-standing, trust-based practice that's fallen out of favor is the handshake deal. After centuries of doing a significant share of business this way, most people feel it's not safe to look someone in the eye, get a verbal commitment, and shake on it. Taking people at their word seems unsafe. "No," counters Adam. "If you *can't* do a handshake deal, then it's not safe. A handshake deal meant more to society and more to human nature than you can possibly imagine."

Adam doesn't think you should fire your legal team, operate on blind faith, or actually revert to handshake deals. Negotiated, revised, and eventually signed contracts provide protections and benefits for both parties. But how do we get to the contract faster? How do we minimize the expensive, back-and-forth revisions? How can our digital signature mean as much as our eye contact and handshake?

These questions are answered with one word: integrity.

Adam believes that we must create business relationships in such a way that others would take you at your word alone if they had to. To do so in his own life, Adam focuses on how others want to be treated—then serves those wants and meets emotional needs. Emotions, in his view, are the currency of relationships and the driver of trust. Naturally, then, he appreciates the value of video. "When you look at how communication occurs, I think you're doing yourself a disservice as a communicator if you're not using the most emotionally charged delivery that you possibly can," asserts Adam. "And if you can't be there in person, video is the next best thing."

> You're doing yourself a disservice as a communicator if you're not using **the most emotionally charged delivery** that you possibly can.

EMOTIONAL BRILLIANCE

The head of an organization with more than 130,000 agents in more than 110 countries around the world, Adam calls emotional intelligence the most important leadership trait. "As a leader talking to other leaders, the number one thing that I instruct people to understand is controlling your emotions and using them appropriately." But he goes beyond the common concept of emotional intelligence, seeking to develop "emotional brilliance" in himself and in others.

This term came to him by way of Dr. Cathy Greenberg, co-author of *Emotional Brilliance*. Brilliance happens when emotional intelligence meets emotional maturity. The former is about accurate understanding and appropriate expression of our emotions. The latter is about emotional control and choice management. Why are these so important in business? Adam explains:

> *If you can't manage your choices, you're never going to be able to manage how you respond to other people. So you're going to allow other people, the flow of their decisions, and their communication with you to just come and go with what's easy and convenient, as opposed to what's effective and what moves that relationship forward. Ultimately, you can't do a business deal unless you combine emotional maturity and emotional intelligence, because you're not going to do what's best holistically for either side of the transaction.*

Notice that his explanation includes a consideration of the needs and wants of the other person. This is key. "In order to truly have emotional intelligence and reach this emotional brilliance level, to be that sensei of communication, you have to forsake yourself and completely understand the other person."

> To be that sensei of communication, you have to forsake yourself and **completely understand the other person**.

Emotional brilliance lays the groundwork for human-centered communication. The emotional intelligence to read and adapt to others' needs and wants, plus the emotional maturity to manage your own emotions and engage appropriately. Too often, we lose control of our emotions—and it can happen fast. Society perpetuates it and businesses often exploit it. Online, a lack of emotional discipline often results in digital pollution. Our call here is to reject polarity, condemnation, judgment, and fault-seeking and instead appreciate the other person in all of our digital communication.

For better or worse, video captures and conveys your emotion. This is a strength, especially if you're on the path to emotional brilliance. It can also be a weakness if you lack maturity and discipline. Being human-centered isn't about turning your camera on. It's about connecting emotionally through the camera.

TIPS FOR YOUR JOURNEY

When it comes to getting started with video or audio, Adam says the biggest mistake you can make is overplanning. Because "done is better than perfect," Adam encourages you just to start. He did invest in training courses about how to create video, how to launch products, how to script out your topics, how to improve your vocal techniques, and other related subjects. But it's all useless without implementation. The learning never starts or sticks until you apply it.

In the spirit of sharing, Adam offers these ideas picked up from those courses and from his implementation:

+ Don't read scripts, especially if they're written by other people. To be effective, you need to speak more from your heart.

+ Don't use a teleprompter. If you need to, create bullet points and keep them near the camera.

+ Use basic copywriting formulas like Problem/Agitation/Solution. The problem creates a hook right off the top, makes a promise of value, and tells viewers whether or not the video is for them.

+ Spark curiosity by asking a question that viewers don't know the answer to. This open loop in people's minds is engaging and attractive. The question could be the premise for your entire video.

+ Ideally, you'd share the most valuable ideas with the highest production quality. Realistically, if your production value is lower, the value of your ideas must be higher. "Yes, a crappy video is better than no video, but the reality is that a great video is amazing."

+ Don't worry about how you look or sound. It doesn't matter. "We're all self-conscious and that's just because we're humans," says Adam, who confessed that he, too, dealt with these common fears.

As anyone who's undertaken this journey will tell you, your earliest efforts are going to seem bad. So get the bad done. That's how you get good. If you approach every video in a human-centered way, it's basically impossible to fail. "People just want to know that you're doing something for them," observes Adam. "And they're not going to judge you." When you do get feedback, it's reciprocal—they want to help you because you've tried to help them.

ANYBODY CAN DO IT

"Business is not about *what*, it's about *who*. And video is not about *what*. Video is about *who*," observes Adam. "If you correlate that, then you've got a winning concept that can help you help other people. And they like to help your business as a result."

> Video is not about **what**.
> Video is about *who*.

The opportunity to build trust through presence and visibility is available right now. And it's equally available to every one of us. "I don't care whether you've got nothing but an iPhone or an Android in your hand or you're a billionaire. The cool thing about this is that anybody can do it. Anybody."

Adam's concern is that people will read this, internalize a thought like "I want to do this," but fail to act. Though many video pundits will, Adam won't threaten these people with a do-or-die message. "They're still going to exist. They're still going to be there. They'll still find a way to do business. But are they truly making the impact on an audience base—known and unknown—that they could be?"

Don't let fear keep you from making an impact. Listen to yourself. Understand the reasons or excuses you're giving yourself. Sharing a lesson he picked up from entrepreneur, author, and motivational speaker Jim Rohn, Adam encourages video-timid people to consider the two pains we suffer in life: "The pain of discipline from doing a little bit every day. And the pain of regret from doing nothing and missing the results down the road, because you can't go back and redo it."

Before we share leadership insights from two more CEOs in the next two chapters, we'll close with encouragement that perfectly summarizes Adam's offerings here: "If you've got the right thing in your heart and you go out there with video and you deliver that, you're not going to do wrong. You're going to help yourself. You're going to help others." Human-centered communication isn't about any one particular medium; it's about this mindset guiding your decisions and actions.

FOUNDER & PRESIDENT
of Factor 8 & #GirlsClub

"Just being 20% more human is a massive differentiator."

A KEY IDEA IN THIS CHAPTER

Building self-confidence and restoring pride to the sales profession.

CHAPTER 8

The Decade for Sellers to Shine

Featuring Lauren Bailey

Lauren Bailey has three main goals: working with happy employees, maintaining a full sales pipeline, and helping people transform their lives. She's Founder and President of Factor 8, a sales and sales management training company that specializes in working with virtual sales teams. She's also Founder and President of #GirlsClub, a sales leadership program for women. Transforming lives sounds lofty, but Lauren brings it down to earth in practical ways over the next several pages.

An at-home worker for more than a decade, Lauren's career was transformed by a Fortune 1000 client she worked with. She jokingly says they "bullied" her into turning her camera on during video calls. Though she was resistant at first, the benefits—and therefore her transformation—were immediate. "It was amazing how much faster we got things done. How they would understand the point I was making more quickly. How I could see these nonverbal signals throughout the meeting," Lauren recalls. "I loved it."

"There's nothing that moves you into a trusting relationship faster than connecting with someone at a human level," Lauren explains. When she can't be there in person, video's become her virtual go-to. She started adding videos to blog posts in 2016. She started using video calls in 2017 for client meetings and internal meetings. A year later, in 2018, she launched an on-demand training platform, which included a significant amount of video. In 2019, she began using video emails and video messages.

"I think the reason video works better for me is the level of authenticity that I try to bring. And I try to make that part of my brand," Lauren says. "I'm perfectly fine messing up in front of everybody and being really, really human." For her, more authenticity creates more connection. And more connection creates better results. Today, those results are outsized. "The truth is we're in this wonderful opportunity right now in the sales industry in America," she observes. "Just being 20% more human is a massive differentiator. So we've got to use that."

By turning her camera on, Lauren reaches more people in more meaningful ways; it's been revolutionary in her business. But it's not the medium that makes the difference. It's her mindset. Lauren operates from a spirit of service and seeks to give, rather than take. Many people start the day thinking, "I'm going to close some deals today." Lauren starts the day thinking, "I'm going to get out there and change some lives today." The difference is felt.

> "
> It's **not the medium** that
> makes the difference.
> It's **your mindset**.

As the founder of two companies, Lauren initially struggled with openly sharing the purpose and mission behind her work. Would anyone care? Would people wonder, "Who do you think you are?" Over the years, though, she's overcome the imposter syndrome so many of us feel. She's grown to embrace this vulnerability and openness. Being transparent about her beliefs and values has accelerated her successes. Further reducing her fears is the validation of positive feedback. She'll hear from people who attended her training 10 years ago who share how it has transformed not just their work, but also their lives.

She's come to see "sales training" as human development. Behavior change is the goal. Real change requires us to be open and to get personal. In virtual environments, she's found this nearly impossible to do without video coupled with a human-centered approach. The most popular #GirlsClub programs Lauren's ever offered were the ones with live, interactive video sessions in which women directly connected with one another. It creates "such an impactful experience."

In the pages ahead, look for an honest view of where the sales profession has gone wrong and a hopeful view of how to get it back on track. See the thread that runs through and ties together confidence, video, and sales. Hear a few success stories and learn how to help your team transform to achieve similar outcomes, no matter what industry you're in. Throughout, notice the human-centered approach that guides it all.

A POINT OF PRIDE

"As the customer journey changed, as our employment rates changed, and as venture capital got deep into software companies and sales teams, it was a convergence of events," observes Lauren. We noted in Chapter 2 that engineer Mike Cooley and economist E.F. Schumacher cautioned decades ago that increased specialization of roles delivers mixed results and tends to dehumanize employees. Lauren sees the same thing in sales today. Further, the unrealistic growth expectations, high failure rates, and intense revenue pressures that come with venture capital investments tend to drive behavior that dehumanizes our customers.

"In these last five years, the average lifespan of a sales rep has gone down almost 50%. A business development representative's [BDR's] lifespan is now under 15 months. In a lot of companies, it takes them three to six months to get ramped up. The last few months they're looking for their next gig. So, you've got six to eight months of actual productive time with a sales rep," Lauren explains. "The right thing to do is to work with these humans—to teach them how to do the job, to help them love sales, and to stay with the company."

Instead, what she sees is that companies often "throw them on the fire like logs." Employers rush out to find 50 more BDRs. Managers equip them with 15 tools. New reps receive no more training than they used to. Lauren's kicker here: "And we're going to try to solve this whole problem by providing a script!?"

Exacerbating the problem is a fundamental change in buyers' needs. With advances in marketing, technology, and communication, buyers are better educated and deeper into their journey when they engage our salespeople.

"They need a higher-level person, but our salespeople now have less training, less tenure, less background, and less experience. We used to hire them with two or three years of experience, a college degree, and experience in a competitive sport," Lauren explains. Today, however, hiring standards are down and so is buyers' trust. A HubSpot survey found that just 3% of us trust salespeople, barely edging out stockbrokers, lobbyists, and politicians.[1]

"We have over-tooled. We've put on higher expectations for rapid growth. We've overspecialized. And now we've got reps whose leaders are focused on the science over the art," Lauren summarizes. The result? Our people are serving as "cogs in the wheel of the sales engine, not connecting with customers, building relationships, or adding value." They're following prescribed activities in a prescribed manner using words that have been prescribed to them.

"So many of our sales tools dehumanize people," Lauren observes. But something more human, like video, doesn't fit the status quo in most companies. "Hell, you're afraid to let them write their own emails," she says. "If you don't have a culture that invests in the development of your people or in the forging of buyer-seller relationships, then you'd be afraid to arm them with a tool as powerful as video."

Where do we go from here? We focus on human-centered communication. We must put our employees first by investing in and developing them. Their improved knowledge, confidence, and emotions are then passed on to our customers.

"This is our decade as sellers," posits Lauren. Being in sales should be a point of pride, not something we "hide" from people at dinner parties with creative job titles and roundabout job descriptions. Lauren anticipates the return of curious questioning, active listening, virtual sales skills, and greater adaptability. Now is the time to come together and raise the bar in the profession.

This requires a shift to a culture of learning and growth. It requires a shift to deeper customer understanding, industry knowledge, and business acumen among our team members. With this shift, we can rehumanize our salespeople and the sales process. With this rehumanization, we can restore customer confidence and trust.

THE ROLE OF CONFIDENCE

The restoration of customer confidence begins within each of us. It begins with self-confidence. Like our emotions, our confidence is contagious[2]—when we believe in our own vision, others begin to believe in it too. Developing self-confidence, then, is a gift to others. But many people struggle. We think that in order to be confident, we must be perfect, or pretty darn close. We think that if we can become perfect, we can avert judgment, avoid shame, and preserve our good standing.

Of course, perfection is impossible. And our brain tends to miscalculate risks, resulting in fear. Though it's irrational, it feels real to us. One of the best antidotes to nervousness, doubt, and fear is brave action. When we act, we build momentum and confidence. And we find our success in that confidence. "When you have that self-confidence, you'll dial the phone again," says Lauren. "When you have self-confidence, you go for it and send a video. When you have self-confidence, you're okay if there's some hair out of place in that video."

Confidence isn't just about our actions; it's also about our thoughts. We each have an inner critic that wants to be heard and needs to be managed. It tells us stories, but they may not be true. This topic itself deserves an entire book; many of them have been written, including *The Gifts of Imperfection* by Brené Brown, *You Are a Badass* by Jen Sincero, and *The Confidence Code* by Katty Kay and Claire Shipman. Each will teach you that confidence is built through beliefs, as well as behavior.

Lauren has observed a gender-based confidence gap and it's one supported by research. Women tend to be more perfectionistic than men,[3] which drives self-criticism and limits self-confidence. Women report not feeling good enough or ready enough. In Lauren's experience, this makes it tougher in sales and in video, where women should have a natural advantage. Women are proven to have higher interpersonal sensitivity,[4] more compassion,[5] and better communication.[6] These all suggest that video is an ideal medium for women.

It comes down to being okay with your flaws and even making fun of them a little bit.

Something salespeople share regardless of gender is that many didn't set out to be in sales. They often find themselves in sales because someone saw potential in them. Something that attracts people and connects with people. In the face of self-doubt, return to that vision. "There is something about you that influences, that convinces, that builds credibility and trust," affirms Lauren. "And if you believe that, then you're doing yourself a disservice by not turning on your video because people buy from people."

Especially in competitive and commoditized markets, the differentiator is you. When we buy, we're not just buying based on price, features, and benefits. We're buying based on trust in and relationships with people. The dynamic is the same for employees, who join companies but leave bosses. People make the difference. Confidence makes the difference.

Confidence and credibility aren't qualities you assign to yourself. They can't be self-proclaimed. Instead, you must demonstrate them. They must be experienced by others and assigned to you. Trust that others place in you is based on the credibility you demonstrate and the confidence you inspire.

Lauren offers a few tips on how to exude more confidence. She recommends eliminating "upspeak," in which you end phrases or sentences with your voice going up. Upspeak can sound as if you aren't confident in what you are saying—which in turn reduces a customer's confidence as well. She also recommends reducing qualifying language (phrases like, "I could be wrong, but . . ."), which can make your statements feel less certain. Lastly, she encourages "taking up your space" with a confident, upright posture, rather than shrinking down or folding in. Certainly, there's nuance here; you want to mirror the culture and context you're entering.

Confidence in yourself is one of the most powerful qualities you can develop. Putting your confidence on camera is one of the most powerful ways to communicate it. No matter which feelings, thoughts, or actions you anchor yourself with, Lauren reminds us that "we have to make sure our voice and our image is projecting that belief and confidence."

True confidence isn't arrogance in our abilities. It's turning from our own deficiencies toward putting others first and serving them through our expertise. Confidence is all about being human-centered.

THREE AHA MOMENTS WITH VIDEO MESSAGES

For years, Lauren's been using video in meetings, in blog posts, on social media, and in training programs. The most recent addition to her communication mix: video messages. Here are three experiences on her journey that made it clear that video messaging dramatically improves our ability to engage others.

1. Reaching Busy Leaders

To make #GirlsClub a success in transforming lives and careers, Lauren relies on volunteers. Who are they? Busy executives in demanding positions. How does she express her deep appreciation to these generous people? By sending simple, personal "thank you" videos. Lauren reflects on the first time she sent them.

I got so many replies. It energized me to keep going. People thanked me for sending them a "thank you." To be clear, they're putting in 800 times the effort, but it felt personal to them. The responses that came back to me let me know that they felt seen and that they were grateful. It was awesome. You just don't see that very often. And I got a ton of them.

2. Breaking Through Noise

Lauren's team launched a Top 25 Companies Where Women Want to Work campaign. They reached out to their community seeking sponsors and nominations. They'd sent text-based emails and posted on social media. But when Lauren reached out to their subscribers with a video email, the response was different.

I had four new sponsors in the pipeline. I had five calls set up for the next week. This was not the first time people heard about this. But I sent a video, and now they're getting the message right from me. They could feel the emotion. They could connect to me as a person. They were able to reply to a person they felt like they knew.

3. Increasing Conversion Rate

"For every 1,000 women who come to check out the #GirlsClub website, we get one applicant to the program," Lauren shares. "That is a 0.1% conversion." But when they are referred by their manager, the conversion rate is 65%. That's 650 times higher. The difference comes from human connection and personal encouragement. And video messages provide that support.

> *In essence, we appeal to the woman herself. What it takes to increase that conversion rate is personal encouragement. When a sales leader says, "I think you'd be great. Have you ever considered management? I've got a program for you," she takes off like a rocket. But when she's got to gather the confidence to go to her manager and say, "What does it take to . . . could I maybe sort of, kind of, should I . . ." When she's got to get the permission, the funding, and the time, she can get shut down.*

> *Because of that, I have to over-connect with those women. My job is to create a personal touch and say, "Hey, I know that you've been interested. This is important. Investing in yourself is important." That's belief in yourself. It's a personal, emotional decision. And that requires the connection through video.*

> *It's shocking, the difference. People can receive 200 emails from us. But when I sent a video out saying, "Hey, I saw you came to the site and I just wanted to say that I'm so happy. I really hope to see your name in there. Here's my cell phone if you have any questions." Now they've connected with me. And they can feel that I believe in them. And it helps more of them say 'yes' to themselves and sign up.*

In each of these cases, video was simply the medium. The real difference was Lauren—the clarity, sincerity, and intent she conveys.

LEADING AND MANAGING VIDEO ADOPTION

If you've got the mindset and culture to support it, growing the use of video within your organization is likely something you're working on. Lauren started her career in corporate training and has firsthand experience with the challenges of behavior change, technology adoption, and personal transformation. Here are a few of her insights specific to getting your team on board with video calls and video messages.

The Manager Makes or Breaks It

"Nobody likes to change behavior for the sheer joy of changing behavior. We are natural creatures of habit and changing behavior takes more than just a short value add to do it," Lauren says. "A study came out a couple of years ago in a training magazine that said that the top two influences on training success are not the technology, not the modality, not the interface, not the content. It's what the manager says before the rep goes into training. And it's what the manager says when the rep comes out of training." Any behavior change at work starts with your leaders and managers.

Virtual Environments Make Change Harder

When everyone was in the office together, a manager could hear and even feel what was happening within a team. You could sit together with team members. You could increase energy and provide motivation in team huddles and one-on-one meetings. You could deliver feedback live and in the moment. These days, we don't have those privileges as often.

Whether you're onboarding a new team member or you're getting the entire team to do something new, "video is critical" in Lauren's view. Again, to provide training is to empower human development. Live video calls and recorded video feedback allow you to reach people more personally. They allow you to provide reinforcement or correction with subtlety, nuance, and emotion.

The Manager Must Model the Change

It's not enough to inspire and inform the team. For successful change, managers must model it themselves. "It's the manager's job to make sure that we don't see the unmade bed and the shower curtain in the background," Lauren says of modeling good video behavior. "We have to help them make smart decisions about what's okay and what's not okay on camera. Our job is to lead the way for them. And if they're scared to death to do video emails, just having our one-on-ones and our team calls on videos helps warm the water, if you will."

These calls and meetings are also opportunities to provide feedback. For example: "Hey, Steve, you've been multitasking on the other screen the entire time. We can't do that during customer calls."

Anticipated benefits, like the promise of increased reply rates, aren't always enough to open someone up to a new habit. "There's risk in that behavior change. But when your leader says, 'You're going to do it whether you like it or not,' there's some buy-in," observes Lauren. Better yet, "the leader or a team leader demonstrates that behavior by sending his or her own videos. When you've got that brave soul and when somebody in your clique makes it cool, then the rest of the people follow."

Model the behavior. Incentivize people with gift cards and contests. Make video the cool thing to do. Create friendly competition to bring people along. Try starting with video later in the sales process and then moving it forward to prospecting. Consider starting with internal communication before sending videos externally. No matter the path, realize it will be a process and that with each change you're making an important step toward human-centered communication.

For more ways to **get your team on board,**
get The Video Adoption Guide free at
BombBomb.com/BookBonus

SCRIPTS, SWIIFT℠, AND PERSONALITY

"Be human. Make fun of yourself. Don't do 27 retakes. Just let it fly," advises Lauren. Here in this section, we'll share things she's learned herself and taught others about connecting and communicating more effectively on camera.

Ditch the Scripts

"I hate scripts because you sound like a robot when you're reading a script. It's even worse if you write a script for somebody else because it's such a confidence killer," says Lauren. She's tried to read scripts from her computer screen but "it was awful. It was just totally the wrong message."

Instead of reading a script, she recommends talking to people like they're friends or neighbors. If you feel like you need a script, make a list of bullet points instead. Look at those points whenever you need to. "I don't hide behind a 'professional salesperson' mask. I don't try to be perfect."

Get SWIIFT℠

We introduced SWIIFT℠ (So What's In It For Them?) back in Chapter 2. Here's more detail so you can put it into play. Lauren typically teaches it in the context of a video call or a phone call, but it applies to a video message, too.

When reaching out to people, we typically open our videos in a "me-focused" way. We make it about ourselves or about what we need. But the goal is to get people engaged as quickly as possible in order to generate a reply. A human-centered approach can make this happen.

"I show that I know something about you and that I want to add value for you. Then, I pose one quick question that gets them talking," Lauren advises. We need to make clear right off the top and as quickly as possible what's in it for the other person, then ask a question, and then offer a call to action. It's as simple as this:

> Hey, I noticed you were doing (such-and-such) online. I thought it was super cool. I think maybe I can help. Can you tell me, would you prefer (this or that)? Just pop me a quick reply. Thanks! Hope we can talk live sometime soon.

In the body of the message, reinforce the question in your typed-out text: "Would you prefer (this or that)?" You're recognizing the other person, starting a conversation, and asking for a reply. You're also making it easy for them to quickly assess, decide, and respond. This is key to creating engagement.

Add Personality, Eliminate Distraction

"I think of my background as an opportunity to show personality. Because the number one goal is to connect with me as a human," Lauren reminds us. "And that's my approach, whether it's sales or training. Truth is, I probably win deals on personality even more than on competence. Because people think I'm real."

In setting up your camera shot for your videos, say "yes" to personality, but "no" to clutter. Give yourself a head and shoulders shot that's not too wide or too tight. Make sure there's lighting in front of you (even an inexpensive lamp will do). Eliminate distracting movement, like ceiling fans. And consider adding a logo in the background if you can.

Some of the things she'll include when she frames up her video shot include the Factor 8 or #GirlsClub logo, depending on who's joining the call or receiving the message. She may display an inspirational quote or books from friends that she hopes someone will ask her about. Greenery and an essential oil diffuser add to the environment. And Lauren's got a funny little pewter f-bomb, because . . . that's her.

As for virtual backgrounds, she's found that they never quite work properly. Something breaks through. Choppy artifacts violate the head and body. It takes people's attention away from eye contact and facial expressions. But she understands; some people don't have ideal spaces, so virtual backgrounds may make sense.

The key is to show a bit of yourself without compromising your professionalism. If you have to err one way or the other, favor what's personal over what's professional. "There's no reason we need to make sales more robotic and less human. We've got to swing the pendulum to the other side. And video gives us our opportunity."

Be a Bully

Years ago, it worked for her on one side of the screen after her client bullied her into turning on her camera. Today, it works for her on the other side of the screen, as she gets others to do the same. She uses the word "bully" playfully, but the consequences are serious. When everyone turns their cameras on, "it allows us to work with more people in a better way more often—in a more engaging and effective way."

Among the benefits of getting cameras turned on:

"You're going to get more interaction from the group."

"They're going to see body language and everything else going on."

"They're more likely to keep their attention throughout instead of multitasking."

Some lines she's used to get cameras turned on:

"Are you comfortable sharing video today so we can meet face-to-face?"

"Hey, I'm definitely going to be a camera bully today. I really want to see everybody's faces and have you present with us."

"Listen, no judgment if you're not sharing video because you haven't done hair and makeup. I will show you my yoga pants and slippers right now if it helps!"

"Hey, if you're not sharing video because you're new to this platform, grab your mouse, go to the bottom left, find the camera icon, and click on it. I would love to see you today!"

"Are you okay sharing video? I miss your face!"

Create Conversation

Here are some additional tips and ideas to turn virtual presentations into interactive conversations.

+ Face the camera and try to keep eye contact with the camera.

+ Dial the energy up, not down. Low energy immediately feels robotic.

+ Make it personal by, say, joking about yourself or commenting on others' backgrounds.

+ Don't multitask, except to take notes. Also: Make sure you ask permission to do so, so you don't appear disengaged.

+ Actively listen and personally engage people.

+ Provide visual and verbal affirmation, like head nods, lean ins, and hand gestures.

+ Demonstrate interest in others. Give attention back to them.

+ Pause periodically to check in with the entire group, especially if you pick up a visual cue that you've lost someone. For example: "Hey, let's pause. Can we just do a quick check-in, Kate? What are you thinking? What questions do you have?"

+ Call on people and ask questions to create interaction.

+ Be warm and be honest.

20% MORE HUMAN

Twenty years ago, Lauren taught a group of people at IBM how to sell directly as inside sales representatives. Some pushed back by saying that no one would ever buy a computer over the phone.

Ten years ago, Lauren taught a group of people at SAP how to sell directly as inside sales representatives. Some pushed back by saying that no one would ever buy software over the phone.

Five years ago, when video emails and video messages gained familiarity and early usage, people asked Lauren if it would work. She predicted the practice would only last a year or two, based on the gimmicky way they were being sold and used. But she's since developed a longer view.

"I understand now that if we use video correctly to add value and to connect as humans, it can and should be around forever."

Today, we must resist our comfort with the status quo and open ourselves to change. We must be both authentic and confident. To succeed in serving and supporting buyers, we must take a human-centered approach and turn our cameras on. And, as Lauren says, "Just being 20% more human is a massive differentiator."

FOUNDER, CEO, & MODERN SALES EVANGELIST at VENGRESO

"Sales is the art of helping."

A KEY IDEA IN THIS CHAPTER

Improving internal culture with video and vulnerability.

CHAPTER 9

The Art (and Science) of Helping

Featuring Mario Martinez Jr.

"Dude, we're in the heart of San Francisco," protested Mario Martinez Jr. "That's not going to happen. You can't even get into any of these buildings."

There was a time, much more recently than you might think, when Mario was expected by some leaders to send his team to office buildings and office parks to sell by door-knocking. And he wasn't alone; the company employed 120 other domestic salespeople and 350 globally. Yes, face-to-face, in-person experiences are the best way to connect. And yes, pounding the pavement can produce results. But this approach was inefficient and impractical. He knew there was a better way to reach potential customers. While many still clung to traditional methods, Mario had a vision for the sales organization staying personal, but going digital—with video and social media.

Soon after, as a Regional Vice President of Sales at PGi, he was asked to help launch a new video messaging tool competing with services like BombBomb. And the company already offered a live video meeting tool competing with Cisco, Zoom, and others. "One of the reasons why I was asked to be part of the launch team was because of my belief in what video could potentially do," he explains.

Mario observed that video had quickly become a top-tier marketing medium but that salespeople weren't leveraging it in their sales prospecting or cadences. Additionally, his organization's initial video messaging experiments yielded positive responses and improved engagement. As part of the launch, he turned his learnings and insights into an internal training program that combined the power of social media and video communication to start more sales conversations and build a more robust sales pipeline.

The result: an invitation to present at LinkedIn Sales Connect in October 2015. With 48 minutes on the main stage, he had the privilege of sharing the story of "how to launch a digital sales training program that drove 100% sales rep adoption and with 100% of reps attributing a sales opportunity to the open pipeline." Just by bringing video and social selling together to connect with buyers. The program and, more importantly, the underlying execution of the ideas were a huge success.

So was Mario's presentation. The exposure it generated shot up his personal brand equity; he went out on his own a few months later. "I started training and consulting and helping customers to launch their own digital sales training programs," he explains. Most pundits advised that he write a book to build his reputation and his business. Like Adam Contos, Mario opted instead to double-down on video and to start a podcast, neither of which was common at the time.

Mario's business has since evolved into digital sales training and technology company Vengreso, where he serves as CEO and Modern Sales Evangelist. A core tenet at Vengreso: "Today's buyer is digitally connected, socially engaged, mobile attached, and video hungry. And with those four components, by the time that a salesperson gets to that buyer, they already know what their problem is." Because buyers have done their research, know the solutions in the market, and often seek validation through the sales process, "now it comes down to who can build the best relationship through a digital engagement."

If you manage a remote team, this chapter will be especially helpful for you, as we go inside Mario's leadership and management approach and learn how to cultivate a workplace that's fully remote. We'll also weigh the art and the science of sales, learn more than a dozen ways to use video messages, and move past generalized personas to focus on individual people. And in the next chapter, we'll learn from Vengreso Co-Founder and Chief Visibility Officer Viveka von Rosen. The mantra that drives Mario, Viveka, and their team: Sales is the art of helping.

CREATING A VIDEO CULTURE

They've never met in person. They've never hugged or even shaken hands. "But I'll tell you this much," Mario says. "We love each other. We call each other. We've built a relationship." Her marriage. Her daughter's marriage. An illness. The sale of her house. Mario's been alongside this remote team member through years of the personal and professional ups and downs that life gives us. You can be personal, even when virtual. And you can build real relationships even when you're physically distant.

> You can build **real relationships**
> even when you're **physically distant**.

Vengreso was designed and built as a completely remote company. What Mario and his team have learned is instructive for us all. Once a month, he holds a virtual all-hands meeting. He also regularly sends all-company video messages. Typically they're less than five minutes long and include big announcements, notable new clients, and recognition of individuals' efforts and accomplishments. Occasionally he'll go longer, as in a recent 17-minute corporate strategy video. Mario "asked everybody to watch that message and make sure that they understood where we were going and what was happening."

Remote or not, every leader can and should be doing something similar with live and recorded videos. With recorded videos, in particular, you're able to provide updates with emotion, clarity, and a personal touch in a way that everyone can access at their own convenience.

Mario isn't just transparent with the business. He also invites people into his life. He stays engaged in employee social chats, interacting daily and sharing personal photos and stories. Through honesty and vulnerability, he's giving permission for others to be open, too. "I need to be a real person," he says about his openness. "I'm showcasing that it's okay to be a human and to be out there doing what you need to do." Along with live and recorded video communication, this helps him convey warmth, build connection, maintain trust, and enhance understanding within the team.

"As one of the founding members of our company and as CEO, a lot of people are trusting that we're making the right decisions for the corporation," explains Mario. "In the absence of being able to walk into my office, see me in the break room, or walk down the hallway and hear me say, 'Hey John, Hey Susie, Hey Mary, how's everything going?', we as leaders must be thinking of ways to build trust. The main ways to make that happen are one, you have a voice. And two, you allow the human connection through visuals and audio."

A little extra thought, a little extra care, and a lot more exposure through video. One-to-one and one-to-many. Live and recorded. Internally with employees and externally with customers. What Mario's known for years, he and his entire team bring to life every day.

Hiring and Expectations

How suited to today's world is your hiring process? Sure, it's likely a bit more remote and virtual. But are you just putting more cameras and screens into the processes of interviewing, selecting, hiring, and onboarding new team members? Or are you fully adapting and integrating them? Mario and his team have done the latter; here are some of the details.

To be a virtual company, you must build in video interaction. But how do you get everyone on board? How do you make being on camera the norm? The answer is easier than you think. The answer is like a human-centered design. You start with the end in mind. You plan it in from the beginning.

"Part of the requirement to be hired at Vengreso is that you agree verbally that you will have your video camera on 100% of the time," explains Mario. "And if someone's not comfortable with that, we need to know that upfront because that means we're not going to hire that person. Literally."

Vengreso's job interviews are by video. If a potential hire ignores instructions and shows up unprepared or with their camera off, they don't get hired. "If they do that in an interview, then they will do that with a customer," cautions Mario. "And that's not okay." The process continues with a panel interview, including role-play of a group sales call to assess how they interact with a buying committee remotely. Because we're going to be working more this way, not less, developing the skills of virtual connection is becoming more important. Hiring these skills into your organization becomes more valuable.

Learn more about Vengreso's **remote culture**
and see video examples at
BombBomb.com/BookBonus

Once someone is hired, "we do what's called virtual receiving lines." Everyone in the company is invited to this 20- to 30-minute live video call to welcome the new team member, give virtual high fives, and learn something about the new person. To transfer culture and tribal knowledge, they also do a few rounds in which newer employees and longer-term employees alike share something that a new hire should understand about the company and its culture.

Think back to Chapter 3 with Jacco van der Kooij. From the pre-hire Awareness and Education phases of The Bow Tie Funnel all the way through the on-going employee Growth Loop, Mario and his team create engagement, trust, and relationships through synchronous and asynchronous video communication. They demand of their team what they teach to their clients—connecting in meaningful ways even in virtual environments.

The ability to do so becomes more important with each passing month, quarter, and year. To understand why, we'll dive into Mario's driving philosophy and the role of meaningful connection.

THE ART OF HELPING

"Our philosophy in terms of selling, simply put, is 'sales is the art of helping,'" Mario shares. "The media by which we engage our buyers now include digital channels. And that includes both asynchronous and synchronous video communication." To truly help, we must use all channels and methods available, not just those with which we're most comfortable and familiar. And we must use them to connect with people, build trust with them, and guide them to solutions.

> Sales is **the art of helping**.

As we've established, customers are in control. They have access to information and they engage us in ways today that differ dramatically from just 5 or 10 years ago. "They know some of the solutions in the marketplace that can solve their particular problem. And they've already done oodles and oodles of research that indicate to them what they think they should be doing," Mario explains. "And now they're looking for validation through the sales process."

Validation is one of the most important social skills we can develop. It provides a form of acceptance that each of us needs. Validation lets people know they're heard and understood. It doesn't require agreement, but it does require that we acknowledge and justify the emotional aspect of what someone shares with us. Validation sounds like: "Wow, that sounds challenging" or "Great, that seems like an exciting opportunity for you." And it pairs nicely with good follow-up questions.

Art and Science

When pressed, Mario describes sales as 51% science and 49% art. On any given day, it might flip to 49% science and 51% art. The science is "a methodical approach to how I go about engaging and finding information." Do they have the budget? Who is the signer? When is that person on vacation? It's all about what you need to know. But to come straight out and ask these questions directly may feel blunt or invasive.

The art is how to get that information in the context of a conversation. In a human-centered way. In a way that benefits both people involved. In Mario's words, "If science says, 'Ask the question,' then art says, 'Ask the question and allow it to be human.'" The science holds the process of what. The art gets into the nuance of how and why.

Here's the difference:

You fall down.

Someone yells, "Are you OK?"

You say, "Yeah . . . I think so."

They move on.

You fall down.

Someone yells, "Are you OK?"

You say, "Yeah . . . I think so."

They respond, "Hold on, let me help you."

The former is the science. The latter is the art. "That is why, from my perspective, video is so critical—so that when we're having synchronous conversations, you can see facial expressions. You can see non-verbal cues. You can hear modulation," Mario explains. "You can see and hear all those things that make the human brain say, 'Yay, I trust this person' or 'No, this is not going to work.'" The art speaks to the visual, emotional, and subconscious decision-maker inside us.

Automation Cautions

Given what Mario's shared with us, you should start to understand the trouble with giving 75% to science and 25% to art, rather than 51% and 49%. The way Mario sees it, people are already working more hours as a workforce than ever before and they're already inundated in every communication channel. Therefore, continuing an overreliance on mechanics and automations won't reach people the way they need to be reached. Without an artful approach, we're far more likely to produce pollution than conversation. And we hurt our employees, customers, and reputation in the process.

"Unfortunately, automation has created a situation where sellers believe that the right course of action is to 'spray and pray' because sales leaders are managing an activity-based key performance indicator [KPI]," explains Mario.

The average sales development representative shoots for 50 or 60 "touches" per day. He expects less than half of that activity from his reps, but each of those activities is better-researched, data-informed, and more personal. By spending just a little more time up front, his team gets to their outcomes—booked meetings, sales conversations, new revenue—with fewer activities. This helps their employees, customers, and reputation in the process.

Few would disagree: The outcome matters more than the activity. But, over time, one may wind up confused for the other. The measurement, metric, or KPI can be mistaken for the goal itself. What gets lost isn't just the real goal, but also how we're treating our prospective customers. When we research, think about, and get personal with prospective customers, we produce empathy. This human-centered approach respects individuals much more than pointing a machine at them and setting it to blast.

"Is there a place for automation? Yes, absolutely. Is there a place for us to use certain sequences? Yes, absolutely," says Mario. "Should I just load a prospect into my sales sequence or cadence tool because they are now a 'target' and I found their email from ZoomInfo or Seamless.ai? No." Doing the latter burns through your list of prospective customers and through your salespeople, whose roles are already hard enough. Making their jobs more activity-based and bot-like is dehumanizing.

> "Making sales roles more activity-based and bot-like is **dehumanizing**.

Mario offers two specific improvements. First, "we should always attempt to warm up that particular buyer first with hyper-personalization even if you have them in a sequence. Social touch, interaction, connection, a possible one-to-one email message, a one-to-one video message, text, then a phone call," he says. "Don't just hit 'go' on the sales sequence; ensure each touchpoint is personalized."

Second, Vengreso's turned their frontline business development representatives (BDRs) into market development managers (MDMs). They get one-on-one training with the regional vice president. "They're going to join all of the sales calls. They're going to follow the sales opportunity through to close. They're also going to be prospecting and using the prospecting tools and mechanisms. But at the same time, we're training them to eventually take over their own territory." They're designing the experience with the employee Growth Loop in mind.

Script Cautions

Mario warns that scripts are like automations. They have their place, but they're often misused. When deployed improperly, they degrade both the employee experience and the customer experience. "We love scripts. We believe in scripts," Mario tells us. "But there's context." The script is the baseline. It's written for a persona—a generalized, fictional character created to represent a group of people who share specific attributes like job title, industry, age, or location. From there, we should allow our team members to artfully add context, color, and personality. A sales script written for a persona should be personalized for an actual person.

"We didn't go to school to learn how to write customer-centric messaging that attracts our buyer," Mario reminds us, adding that most companies don't train salespeople on this, either. This is why providing people with a baseline is so helpful. It's easier and more efficient to start from a script written for a specific group of people and refine it for someone within that group than it is to start with a blank screen.

To further drive the point that we're communicating with humans and not with customer segments, it's important to note that less than 20% of the video messaging use cases that Vengreso teaches their clients come with scripts. Mario kindly shares all 16 of those video messaging use cases in the next section. The three that include scripts are all persona-based by necessity: out of office response, prospecting to a persona, and new LinkedIn connection by persona.

The caution about using scripts appropriately is especially important in video because it's not faceless text. Text can be written by anyone and sent by anyone. It can even be written by machines and sent by machines. In the recipient's experience, it was written and sent by no one in particular. In contrast, video is far more personal than mechanical. It can be used in a scientific way, but it's more art than science. Video is just as much about *how* you communicate something as it is about what you're communicating.

Selling is the art of helping people. Not of closing people. Not of helping yourself. Not of hitting numbers. Again, when we treat people like people, the outcomes follow.

16 WAYS TO USE VIDEO MESSAGES

As promised, Mario shares more than a dozen ways his team teaches clients to use videos in emails, text messages, and social media messages. With video, you can augment the other ways you're connecting and communicating "to continue building that relationship of trust as a result of seeing our face through asynchronous communication."

We've ordered these to match The Bow Tie Funnel shared in Chapter 3 and included again in Figure 9.1. Because these use cases are primarily for salespeople, most fall on the Acquisition side. Most of the Education examples, however, would benefit an account manager working to create Impact and Growth on the Expansion side, as well. Further, these concepts are adaptable to other roles and situations, so read through them no matter your role or responsibilities.

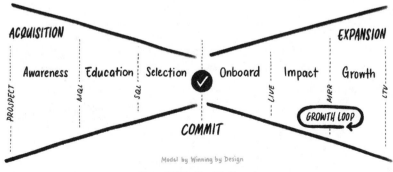

Figure 9.1 The Bow Tie Funnel

These videos may be created as truly personal (one video made for one specific person at one specific time) or as evergreen (made for a general persona or a common situation and sent as needed). A personal video requires more time and effort, of course, but tends to produce more and better replies.

Customer Acquisition—Awareness

1. Send a prospecting message to a particular buyer via email, LinkedIn message, or InMail.

    • Refer to other messages you've sent and put a face with your name.

2. Reach out when you've connected to a new connection on LinkedIn.

    • Introduce yourself. Start a real conversation. Create a true connection.

3. Re-engage prospects who've gone dark.

    • Remind people where the conversation left off and why they were interested. Provide a clear call to action.

4. Introduce yourself to someone who's been referred to you.

    • Make a warm introduction even warmer. And send a "thank you" video to the person who referred you.

Customer Acquisition—Education

5. Demonstrate your product or service.

    • Provide more clarity and understanding with a show-and-tell video than typed-out text and static images ever could.

6. Invite prospects to a webinar or an event.

    • "Hey, Steve. I was reaching out to you because I know we've talked in the past about digital selling. I thought this webinar that we're hosting would be great for you and your sales team. Why don't you register yourself and tell your team about it at your next sales team meeting?"

7. Send the latest blog or video post or share relevant content that your marketing team or another team produces.

   • Include a synopsis and speak to the benefits of watching the video or reading the article. Keep your channel partners updated with this type of video message.

8. Send a monthly video newsletter and content roll-up.

   • Reach out to your top 5 or 10 prospects to offer this personally.

9. Share a success story, video testimonial, case study, or LinkedIn recommendation.

   • What others say about you is more meaningful than what you say about yourself.

10. Provide a relevant feature insight or thought leadership piece on a one-to-one basis to a specific prospect.

   • Support the buying journey and let them know you're thinking about them.

Customer Acquisition—Selection

11. Send a personal "thank you" message when someone engages on a deal, moves it forward, or makes a commitment.

   • None of us hears or says "thank you" often enough. Send sincere gratitude whenever you feel it in a way that others can feel it, too—in video.

12. Send a message from the sales leader.

   • "Hey, Steve. I know my sales account executive, John Smith, wanted to reach out to talk to you because . . ." Leverage the leader's title, but send it from the seller (in this example, John Smith) on behalf of her or him.

13. Provide a guided overview of a proposal after the call.

   • Show the document on-screen and walk-through it.

   • Know that you're providing something that can be easily shared with other decision-makers.

For Any/Every Stage

14. Humanize your out of office message.

    - Make your automated email reply or LinkedIn message reply unique and different.

15. Humanize your email signature.

    - Add a video thumbnail or animated preview to your email signature.

    - Introduce yourself and provide a valuable resource.

16. Respond to any email or answer any question.

    - Save time, increase clarity, and create connection by sending a video instead of typing out the answer or response.

As a reminder, selling is the art of helping. Timeliness and relevance are key. Simply sending out more information to more people isn't necessarily helpful. In fact, it may pollute. Human-centered communication challenges us to think first about specific people and their specific needs.

As a caution, do not try to implement all of these at once. Choose one or two. Get some practice in. Build some confidence. Train your team. Then start to add more into your daily, weekly, and monthly workflows.

VIRTUAL BACKGROUNDS TO DRAW PEOPLE IN

For video calls or video messages, especially from home, you may be thinking about virtual backgrounds. Some people find them distracting or inauthentic. And they can be when they're poorly executed or irrelevant to the message. Mario advises that you find a way to make them work for you, your recipient, and your message, because "what you're looking for is how to stand out from the crowd." And virtual backgrounds can help.

"For all those influencers that say that virtual backgrounds are inauthentic or that you shouldn't use them, you can mark my words—they are 100% wrong," Mario makes clear. "Because as a seller, our job is to figure out how to draw our buyer into our message and the only way that you're going to draw a buyer into that message is if you can touch them with something that is valuable or meaningful to them."

Your background is another way to add value and meaning. You can match it to a theme or bring an idea to life. "Show me that you know me" is an unspoken demand most potential customers have. Every one of us wants to feel seen, heard, and understood. A virtual background can show that you "know thy buyer" and generate responses as a result.

Imagine that you're going to send a prospecting video to a trucking and logistics company. Which do you think would make a better impression: you sitting in your home office or you sitting in the cabin of a truck alongside one of the company's drivers? One of Mario's team members opted for the latter. He downloaded one of the company's video clips from YouTube and put himself into the frame of "driving a truck" virtually. This inexpensive creativity proved that he did his research and landed him the meeting.

Or simply use virtual backgrounds to add some light-hearted fun to your messages. For example, Mario uses a beach scene or a forest in his out of office video when he's on vacation.

Whether here in these pages, out on LinkedIn, or elsewhere, you'll encounter resistance to virtual backgrounds. Most of the criticism falls into two categories: poor technical execution or irrelevance to the message. They benefit significantly from a green screen and great lighting and typically require editing. If you can't execute it cleanly for lack of time, expense, or skills, it's probably best to avoid virtual backgrounds for now.

Irrelevance to the message can make virtual backgrounds as distracting as poor execution can. From the perspective of human-centered communication, the additional personalization and interest a virtual background provides can be beneficial. Your choice of background should enhance the message, rather than distract from it. Your creative choices should be for the recipient's understanding or entertainment, not for your own.

As for the argument of inauthenticity . . . it depends. The judgment is subjective and will be made person-by-person. A well-chosen and well-executed background brings people into the message. A poorly chosen or poorly executed background distracts. It begs questions. One of those might be a version of: What's back there? What are you hiding? This is when thoughts of inauthenticity creep in.

If you are prepared to take on virtual backgrounds in a human-centered way, Mario encourages you to do so. Vengreso co-founder Viveka von Rosen does, too. Look for additional background ideas from her next in Chapter 10.

THE MOST SUCCESSFUL SELLER

If sales is the art of helping, then the most successful sellers will find ways to balance art and science in service of others. Mario's vision is one that aligns with human-centered communication. It drove him to start his own company. It drives his recruiting and hiring. It's foundational to his teaching and training. It allows us to be virtual, yet personal.

"The most successful seller, in my opinion, is going to be the one who understands how to create trust-building opportunities through digital communication," Mario predicts. "And the ones who are using asynchronous video communications will have a leg up. Because now I can not only hear the follow-up message, the pitch, or the proposal review, but I can see it as well. And that's human connection."

Creating connection, rather than pollution, in digital environments. Building trust, rather than diminishing it, through virtual experiences. As Mario predicts, any informed look to the future sees these skills growing in value.

CO-FOUNDER, CHIEF VISIBILITY OFFICER & MASTER TRAINER at VENGRESO

"The thing we all have in common is we're all human beings."

A KEY IDEA IN THIS CHAPTER

Achieving a 70% response rate from C-suite executives.

CHAPTER 10

The Teacher's Take on Connection

Featuring Viveka von Rosen

Viveka von Rosen isn't just a LinkedIn expert. She's *the* LinkedIn Expert. It's in her LinkedIn profile address. It is her Twitter handle. It was her original YouTube channel. She's created a half dozen LinkedIn Learning courses. She contributes to LinkedIn's official Sales and Marketing blogs and "Sophisticated Marketer's" guides. She authored *LinkedIn Marketing: An Hour a Day* and *LinkedIn: 101 Ways to Rock Your Personal Brand.* And she's taught and trained LinkedIn strategy and tactics in pretty much every content format for more than a decade.

Co-founder, Chief Visibility Officer, and Master Trainer at Vengreso, Viveka is focused on the art of helping. She's helped all kinds of people become more known, liked, and trusted through personal branding and LinkedIn engagement. And she's done a lot of it through live and recorded videos—native uploads to social media, live streams, training courses, and personal messages. She's been on camera consistently since 2006 as a teacher. Creating engaged learners is her art.

"I want to teach and train. Whether it's native video, whether it's my live streams, whether it's sharing a one-on-one video through LinkedIn Messenger, I want to come from a place of teaching and training," she explains. "We want to set ourselves up as trusted advisors instead of coming across as sleazy, scammy salespeople. For me that comes easily and naturally because I'm just here to train."

Whether you lead, manage, sell, serve, or support, your success is based on your ability to teach, train, and help people transform. Here in this chapter, Viveka educates us on enhancing the customer journey with video, creating more engagement through the screen, and building our confidence on camera. Throughout, you'll experience a human-first philosophy consistent with human-centered communication.

THE GOLDEN RULE AND REAL RELATIONSHIPS

Tools and tech stacks vary. Team and company sizes vary. Roles and responsibilities vary, along with industries, strategies, and budgets. In the face of all of our differences, Viveka approaches her work by focusing on the most important factor. "The thing we all have in common is we're all human beings." Unless you're selling undifferentiated products at race-to-the-bottom prices, the most essential aspects of your business are based on human-to-human interaction.

"If you're looking for a job, be human. If you're trying to sell something, be human. If you're trying to create awareness, be human. I mean, it's not rocket science," Viveka reminds us. Despite all of our activity, technology, and sophistication, "all we have to do is be human and create real relationships." Our success is enabled when we work with and for our fellow humans.

> Our **success** is enabled when we work
> **with** and **for** our fellow humans.

So what does it mean to "be human"? Viveka points to The Golden Rule. To be human is to think of others first. To do no harm. To treat others with the same respect you'd like to be treated with. Any concept or philosophy worthy of applying in our personal lives is worth applying in our professional lives, and this rule is no exception. That's why we opened Chapter 2 with The Golden Rule.

What is a real relationship? Viveka points to something that's been a theme throughout the book—authenticity. Too often, she's experienced a gap between the person you see on a stage, in a video, on a social network, or in a blog post . . . and who they really are. You enjoy and engage with their content, but then "you hit this weird glass wall when you try to engage with them as people." This divide can be costly. Meaningful relationships are only possible when we have the confidence to be our authentic selves personally and professionally.

In an article for Booz & Company's *strategy+business*, LinkedIn co-founder Reid Hoffman defined four categories of attitudes about business relationships.

They range from the first transaction-based attitude ("I'll do something for you, if you'll do something for me.") to the fourth values-based attitude ("I'll invest in this relationship because it is the right thing to do."). "Usually people in this fourth category have deep personal integrity," he wrote. "In the long run those alliances built on trust and integrity are the most valuable."[1]

Our integrity across the roles we play, the relationships we develop, and the environments we occupy is foundational to our success. It's a matter of bringing the inner you to the outer world with honesty, consistency, and respect.[2] We can exemplify these not just in person, but also on screen. We've all been forced into video calls. They've become a regular, frequent part of our work lives. But that doesn't mean we're our true selves or our best selves on camera.

"If you have enough confidence in who you are, what your product or service is, and what you're 'selling,' whatever that is, a piece of technology shouldn't matter very much once you get used to it," Viveka adds, echoing Julie Hansen's call for alignment in Chapter 6.

"If we're doing synchronous or asynchronous video, whether we're doing a live Zoom meeting or a BombBomb video message, we must practice, practice, practice until we get more confident." Fortunately for us, she's taught all kinds of business professionals when, how, and why to be more effective and authentic in video—and shares some of that with us here.

LEARNING TO SELL WITH VIDEO

"I think there's a place for video across the entire buyer's journey," Viveka says. Hopefully, you share her vision. We covered it in Chapter 3 with Jacco van der Kooij and The Bow Tie Funnel. Her fellow Vengresonian Mario Martinez Jr. provided 16 ways to use video messages in the previous chapter. From "earning the right to the conversation" in the Awareness phase to sharing resources and differentiating yourself in the Selection phase, you'll benefit from being more human-centered in your communication. Here, she explains why, provides a message framework to help, and shares results from a person she's trained.

KLT and PVC

All other things equal, we prefer to do business with people we know, like, and trust (KLT). You've heard this truism before and you'll hear it again. Viveka became attuned to the value of building know, like, and trust from an early mentor of hers, Bob Burg, best-selling co-author of *The Go-Giver* book series. But people can't know you unless you open up and make yourself available. The more others get to know you, the more similarities you'll discover. Similarity increases liking, as do familiarity, positivity, imperfection, smiling, shared values, and listening.[3,4] The more consistently and authentically we demonstrate and convey these, the more trust we build with others.

The know, like, and trust dynamic is as valuable today as it was before Viveka was on social media. Over the years, she gave out many copies of *The Go-Giver* in order to help people, to spark conversations, and to build trust. Now she does this through her online presence, which provides a unique opportunity to create a sense of familiarity. These platforms allow people to feel like they know, like, and trust you, even before they ever meet you. In her experience, adding videos to the social media mix can be explosive.

To help people connect virtually, Viveka and the Vengreso team teach the PVC method—Personalize, Value, Call to Action. "Any time that we teach people to reach out, whether it's on LinkedIn, through a voicemail, in a video, or even in a written message, we teach them to use the PVC method," she says.

Personalize the message.

Add value for the person.

Provide a clear call to action.

This simple, memorable framework helps you avoid being a digital polluter. Creating the message specifically about them, helping them, and making it easy to take the next step are efforts in service of the other person. Share an article. Provide an insight. Answer a question. Do it with video to add familiarity and psychological proximity. Use this framework to help people feel like they know, like, and trust you and to begin a conversation.

Truly personal videos recorded and sent in a human-to-human way are especially effective. Doing this requires time and effort; it's not automated and it doesn't scale. This is where its value lies. This type of video requires a level of sincerity, intention, and commitment that many competitors won't demonstrate.

Personal videos are extremely differentiating, in part because "everyone thinks quantity, not quality." If it takes five good opportunities to generate two closed deals, why blast a potentially polluting message to 5,000 people? Instead, Viveka recommends reaching out to 15 or 20 people in a high-quality way to create those five opportunities.

A 70% Response Rate from the C-Suite

To illustrate the power of human-to-human video messages as high-quality outreach, Viveka shared some results from a "Selling With Video" class she teaches. She's seen open rates and response rates dramatically improve with video, especially in LinkedIn messages. She's seen a single video get played dozens of times, including by every member of a buying committee.

One of her favorite results came through teaching a team that sells insurance directly to companies. One of the women in the class reached out cold to 50 C-suite executives with video messages. She received 35 responses (70% response rate), got 10 meetings (28.6% set and hold rate), and closed 3 deals (33% close rate) . . . in the first 30 days alone.

The videos were unique to each person. There was no hard sell. Rather, she acknowledged that people in their position seem to share a particular challenge, affirmed that she understood the frustration it causes, provided resources they might find helpful, and invited them to connect.

This account executive didn't drag her feet or dip her toe in the water. She jumped right into video, confident that she could help these executives. She's since adopted Viveka's more advanced strategy of recording and uploading videos to her LinkedIn feed. These videos demonstrate her expertise, establish her credibility as a trusted advisor, and build know, like, and trust with people she's never reached out to or met.

What is Viveka teaching in these sessions? Of course, she's teaching the PVC method as a framework for better outreach. Here are four things students work on until they pass the pass/fail test:

1. Video technology. Get hands-on. Learn it. Get familiar with it. Know what's in frame.

2. Nonverbal cues. Learn from the best TED Talks. Smile more often to increase perceived intelligence and use your hands to seem more charismatic.[5] Practice until it feels natural, rather than forced or robotic.

3. Verbal cues. Turn yourself "up" a little. Modulate your voice. Vary your pace and tone. More vocal variety enhances perceived charisma and credibility.[5]

4. Scripts. Get familiar with the script. Internalize the message. Then alter and "own" it so it's in your voice and style.

No matter your level of experience, you can improve by practicing these four things. Consider starting by recording a video for new LinkedIn connections. You can record one and use it over and over again for each new connection. Or, better yet, you can record a personal video for each new connection. As with all cold or initial outreach, saying someone's first name isn't enough. Really personalize it with a level of detail that "shows them that you know them."

See our **interview** with Viveka, and see
some of our favorite **TED Talks** at
BombBomb.com/BookBonus

SEVEN LESSONS TO IMPROVE RESULTS

In this section, Viveka provides tips to improve your live, synchronous videos and your recorded, asynchronous videos. The first four tips apply to videos in any channel or format. The final three tips apply to specific types of videos.

1. Practice

Practice is the key to success. Practice is how you build confidence. Practice is where you develop your voice and discover your strengths. Practice gets you familiar with your software, equipment, and setting. There is no substitute.

2. Lighting

More light is always better than less, as long as it's not coming from behind you. Overhead lights. Windows. Lamps. Professional lights. Whatever you've got, open it up and turn it on. More light tends to improve video clarity and provides a better read on your facial expressions.

3. Headphones

To wear or not to wear a headset or headphones is a running debate. Viveka's tip sidesteps that debate. Yes, they can distract a little, but she will wear headphones on a bad hair day. They're more contextually appropriate than a baseball cap but provide more confidence and cover for her hair. You might also wear them if you need noise cancelling.

4. Super

Viveka recommends being "a little bit extra." Not inauthentic, but just a little bigger. More expression. More personality. More energy. Whether on stage or on camera, she takes on the role of "Super Viv." Confidence in your material provides an energy boost, as does standing up. Creating action helps, too—by using your hands and body or by drawing or writing on a board.

5. Interact

On your live video calls and presentations, ask for responses. In an hour-long session, ask 10 times for people to, "Let me know in the chat." Respond to what people provide in chat to show you're listening and to create engagement, so people aren't just sitting there. Introduce polls. Play music. Play videos. Drop out of the slide presentation and invite people into conversation. And ask people to turn their cameras on.

6. Identify

When uploading videos to LinkedIn, YouTube, or other channels, use text to help people self-identify as someone who should watch it. Let people scrolling and browsing know that the video is relevant to them before they play it. Be clear about who the video is for and what problem, opportunity, or question it helps them with. Ask people to comment on or share the video to reach others who might identify with it.

7. Prepare

"Going live" or live streaming on social media requires more work than you might expect. Don't just show up and wing it. Remember, every message or experience you create trains people to engage with or ignore the next one. Viveka loves—and prepares for—live videos. "It really gives people a feeling of who you are more than anything else because you can't edit it. It's live. And it really shows people your capacity to deal with what life throws at you and what the internet throws at you."

PRODUCTION QUALITY AND YOUR CONFIDENCE

Should you invest in expensive lights and cameras? Should you use a green screen or virtual background? Viveka answers questions like these with a question. Does it give you confidence? If so, do it. Your self-confidence is a primary driver of video engagement; your confidence is transferable to the viewer. If spending extra time or money buys you some confidence, it very well may be worth it.

Viveka describes a "love/hate relationship" with green screens and virtual backgrounds. Most people use them to hide their actual background. Many feel that they're inauthentic. But she appreciates what they allow: She adds people's logos to her background to show partnership and to let people know "I was thinking about you" in advance. She'll also put herself over graphics she creates in Canva or Easil. Editing training videos in Camtasia is also easier when she's shot over a green screen because she can move herself around.

In the previous chapter, Vengreso CEO Mario Martinez Jr. shared the story of a salesperson putting himself next to a truck driver in a virtual background. Here, Viveka adds a couple more examples of smart uses of green screens to personalize videos. To invite sales leaders to a retreat in Lake Tahoe, Vengreso's Chief Sales Officer, Kurt Shaver, recorded himself in a ski jacket and goggles and put himself over video of a downhill run. To get a potential customer's attention, Kurt grabbed a video clip of the exterior of the customer's office building and put himself in front of it. As long as it's relevant to the message and technically well-executed, a virtual background can enhance your message.

As for production quality overall, "I'd rather see someone put a video out there than not have it at all," Viveka says. But if the production quality is so bad that you're not listening to the person, "then it becomes an issue." Anything that distracts from the message should be avoided or eliminated.

Here's an extra step that can be of benefit to video viewers: "If you can get it transcribed or get it captioned, I think it's a really, really good idea." Adding the words being said over your video or adjacent to your video helps in a variety of ways. It provides greater accessibility. It supports multiple learning styles. It helps people who don't want to turn the sound up for a variety of reasons. Captions and transcriptions help humans.

In short: If it gives you confidence and it makes things easier, clearer, or better for the other person, do it.

CONNECTION, NOT SOPHISTICATION

Viveka shares our vision that communication must get more personal and human in the years ahead. Video will become easier to create and consume on more and more devices. But its effectiveness is up to us. And it's not about sophistication. It's about connection.

Sophistication may take the form of augmented reality, holograms, and 3D televisions. If they help us communicate more effectively, then they may be a benefit to others. Sophistication may take the form of hair, makeup, or skin-smoothing filters. If they give you confidence, then they may be a benefit to others.

Teaching, training, and helping people transform requires human connection and real relationships. Think of others' needs, seek to serve, and use the most appropriate technology available.

SHEP HYKEN

CUSTOMER SERVICE & CUSTOMER EXPERIERENCE EXPERT

"You can't automate a relationship."

A KEY IDEA IN THIS CHAPTER

Understanding and applying the elements of engaging presentations.

CHAPTER 11

Always Be Amazing

Featuring Shep Hyken

Near the conclusion of every episode of The Customer Experience Podcast, I give every guest the opportunity to thank someone who's had a positive impact on their life or career. Family, friends, teachers, mentors—I've heard so many wonderful responses and stories. In more than 150 episodes, though, only one person has been mentioned twice.

That person is Shep Hyken. Customer experience leaders Dan Gingiss and Stacy Sherman both thanked him for his generosity, time, and guidance. They both describe him as Steve and I would: amazing.

Amazing is a powerful word that connotes feelings of astonishment, bewilderment, or even magic. But it's much more approachable than you might think. "To be consistently amazing, you need to be better than average all of the time," Shep explains. "On a scale of one to five, one is bad, five is great, and three is average. To be amazing for your customers, be a little bit better than a three, consistently and predictably."

How do you know you're delivering this for people? Yes, you can see it in customer satisfaction scores and online ratings. But Shep also knows it when he hears it. He listens for the word "always" followed by something positive:

"I love doing business with them because they are *always* so knowledgeable."

"They *always* get back to me quickly."

"They're *always* friendly."

"They're *always* helpful."

"I know I can *always* count on them if there's a problem."

"Always Be Amazing" is his mantra. And it's his challenge for each of us. A customer service and customer experience expert, Shep is Chief Amazement Officer at Shepard Presentations. With a background in radio and a passion for magic, he's been inducted into the National Speakers Association Hall of Fame for lifetime achievement. He hosts the Amazing Business Radio podcast. He's a *New York Times*, *Wall Street Journal*, and *USA Today* best-selling author with book titles like:

The Amazement Revolution

The Convenience Revolution

Be Amazing or Go Home

The Loyal Customer

Amaze Every Customer Every Time

Moments of Magic

For nearly four decades, clients ranging from small businesses to Fortune 100 companies have hired him to develop a loyalty mindset, a customer-centric culture, and consistently remarkable experiences. Shep believes that when you are amazing for your customer, you remind them of their healthiest personal relationships—ones in which they can always rely on the other person.

Something that's helped Shep create this level of emotional connection with his clients and community is his human-centered approach to video. He's taught and trained through video for more than a dozen years. He used to do 15 virtual presentations per year. He's currently doing 15 *per month*. More than 10,000 people subscribe to Shep's YouTube channel, which has earned more than 1.5 million views and counting. He's sent more than 500 personal video messages. Production values range from casual smartphone videos to professional studios and television broadcasts.

Regardless of the video style or channel, Shep always keeps the other person top of mind with sincerity and gratitude. That's why people call him amazing. And that's why he's an important part of this conversation. Look for insights here in balancing automation and personal touch, using video messages in two specific ways, becoming more effective on camera, and creating more engagement in virtual presentations.

BALANCING HUMANS AND TECH

"We're in a wonderful era of technology. With all the great tech that's out there, though, the thing we have to be careful about is trying to do too much of it," Shep advises. "The best companies are finding the balance between technology and human-to-human interaction. You can't automate a relationship. You can't digitize a relationship."

> You can't automate a **relationship**.

Shep acknowledges rare exceptions like Amazon. He acknowledges specific benefits like enhancing self-service and reducing friction. But he also acknowledges that Zappos, an ecommerce company acquired by Amazon for more than $1 billion more than a dozen years ago, offers its phone number as the number one "contact us" option. Shep notes that as many as 20% of their transactions involve direct human contact and says that the best companies "recognize the balance" and "use technology to generate a better personal experience."

Our technology, then, should augment our people. Our people should have autonomy to help and serve our customers. Why? Because loyalty comes from the emotional connections we make. "Repeat business is not loyal business. Loyalty isn't going to come from the fact that you give me a punch card and every time I buy a sandwich, you punch my card and the sixth one is free," Shep says. "When you take away the punch card, I'm not coming back." Repeat business that's more mechanical than emotional isn't sustainable.

Another example he offers is the airline industry. The website or mobile app must make it easy to research flight options, compare prices by day and time, book our reservation, and check in for our flight. If the technology removes friction or adds personalization throughout those steps, we're especially pleased. But what makes us feel, think, and say, "I love this airline" isn't the app. It's that amazing employee we interacted with at the airport or in flight.

This is why Shep advocates for doing more customer service calls via video. "If I'm going to do a video customer support call, you're going to know that I'm 100% focused on you, not on two or three other conversations going on at the same time," he says, referring to the fact that one agent typically engages in several text-based chats all at the same time. Video adds a layer of identity and verification; the customer gets clear, tangible evidence that they're worth your time and attention and that you're actively solving their problem.

Loyalty may have rational components, but it's fundamentally emotional in nature. When we consistently feel seen, heard, and appreciated, we feel amazing... and amazed.

TWO AMAZING VIDEO MESSAGES

Shep has sent hundreds of video messages. He has the ability to send them to hundreds of people all at one time. And sometimes, he will. For example, he might offer to send to audience members a video email with presentation notes and related resources. But it's the exact same video for all of them. Yes, it's more personal than text alone. It's also more efficient than sending hundreds of unique videos. This is an example of an effective evergreen video—a video that's recorded once and used over and over for everyone who fits a particular set of criteria. In this case, the criteria are: attended this particular event and requested additional resources. It's highly relevant and feels somewhat personal.

Shep's more powerful use of video is truly personal.

"I just love to say 'thank you' to people," Shep says. "I want them to know how much I appreciate them." His most common video: a human-to-human "thank you" video to a client who hosted him with a few specific details about his experience. These videos often get played again and again as clients forward them to other people.

Making a habit of saying "thank you" in video messages makes you amazing to others—slightly better than average, every single time. The physical and psychological benefits of consistently expressing your gratitude are amazing for you, too. People who are regularly grateful sleep better, experience fewer aches and pains, and have higher self-esteem, to name just a few.[1] "Thank you" is the first of Shep's two favorite video messages.

The second is based on something Shep learned from Dan Sullivan, Founder and President of The Strategic Coach Inc. This message ties together a potential client's danger, opportunity, strengths, and future.

On a discovery call with a client interested in booking Shep for a speech or training project, he seeks the answers to these four sets of questions:

1. Danger: What's the danger? Why are you researching and interested in this right now? What happens if you don't do it?

2. Opportunity: What's the opportunity for you if we do this right?

3. Strengths: What are you doing right now that's working or not working?

4. Future: If we were to get together a year from now after deciding to work together, what would have to happen for you to say this was the best investment you've ever made?

Asking these (or similar) questions during your initial conversations and then actively listening creates a powerful experience for you and for the other person. The future question, in particular, gets clients thinking strategically. Sometimes they can't give Shep an answer at that moment. They have to think about it and get back to him. When they do, they know that the answer is for their benefit, not just his.

With the insight and understanding he gains from this initial meeting, Shep records a video that is warm and conversational, telling the story back to them in his own words. He demonstrates that he understands their situation. He reiterates the danger—the reason they reached out. He describes the opportunity of getting it right and achieving a great outcome. He acknowledges the strengths they have in play. And he looks back from a year in the future at the situation they're in today.

He used to type all of this up in an email. But using video helps him avoid grammar and punctuation issues. And it allows him to present "in a way that they can really hear me." They get the sense that he's in complete alignment with them. This isn't easy to do with text, plus "it's a lot quicker to do it on video than it is to write this whole thing out." The video becomes, in a way, a humanized proposal.

Done consistently, recording and sending this video message can make you better than most competitors. A few additional tips to support it:

+   Offer to send it in writing, too.

+   Don't talk pricing on video. Reserve that for a more formal proposal.

+   Include typed-out bullet points with the video so people can easily follow along.

Does it always win Shep the deal? No. But it's still amazing. Recently he was in consideration for a "brilliant, seven-figure project." He presented everything in a written format and included a short video summary. The client's response: "You know what? You didn't get it, but your presentation with that video was the best presentation of all of them. What we got in your proposal, though, wasn't exactly what we wanted." But what if the proposal *had* included more of what the client wanted? That video would have separated Shep's proposal from his competition. It would have been what tipped the scale in his favor and earned him the business.

The format of danger, opportunity, strengths, and future has roots in human-centered design. It considers the human first. It requires you to immerse yourself in their experience and understand their situation. Communicating this back to them in video demonstrates your clarity and alignment.

Here at the Selection phase of The Bow Tie Funnel, you won't win the Commitment every time, but you can create remarkable experiences and increase your chances in the present, keep the door open for the future, and often earn yourself referrals.

CONNECTING ON CAMERA

From a professional production in a fully equipped studio to handheld smartphone videos, Shep's done it all. Here are some tips and cautions he's learned along the way to help you and your team members create amazing videos.

A Shorter Video

"If I had more time, I would have written a shorter letter." This famous quote is best attributed to Blaise Pascal, but has connections to Benjamin Franklin, Henry David Thoreau, Cicero, and Mark Twain, among others.[2] Regardless, Shep suggests you apply it to your videos. "If I have more time, I will record a video that's short and concise," he says.

Before you turn your camera on, think about the other person. Think about what you're going to say. Be purposeful. Be brief. This shows respect to other people and reflects favorably on you. Shep feels that a video message should be two minutes or less, unless it's a summary or recap video as described in the previous section of this chapter. Those may take a little longer.

Appropriate Attire

Especially for a video call or a video presentation, dress appropriately. If you're not clear, ask in advance. Match your audience or take one step up in formality. Shep's been embarrassed both ways. He's been overdressed by showing up in a suit on a "casual Friday" that he didn't know was casual. He's been underdressed showing up in a sport jacket without a tie at a dinner with people in full business suits. You can't always get it right, but giving it forethought shows that you care.

We've also got this wrong before, but getting it right most of the time is a worthwhile effort. One of Steve's and my team members at BombBomb won a six-figure deal in part by showing up on video calls and video messages in a suit jacket, which was consistent with the customer's company culture. By dressing appropriately, our team member showed that he understood and valued them.

Body Language

"If you want to really make an impact, lean in and get really serious," advises Shep. "If it's lighter, lean out. Those are stage techniques. If you want to make a point on stage, you walk toward the audience and lean forward. Your body language is going to help support your point. And it's the same thing on video."

You may not need to be this formal in casual video messages, like a brief "thank you" message. But Shep suggests that we "give time, thought, and consideration" to our body language in order to enhance our communication on screen.

Good Audio

"People forgive poor quality video, but they won't forgive poor quality audio," Shep says. "A big mistake is allowing so much background noise that people can't hear you well. Or it could be just a lousy microphone." As you might expect, he's an incredibly busy person, which means he sometimes has to record whenever (and wherever) he has a few spare minutes. He's even recorded videos for big clients from the back of a cab. You don't necessarily need anything expensive. Shep says a good set of earbuds may be just fine in the right environment. Try to minimize background noise and be as close to your microphone as possible.

Eye Contact

Whether you're making direct eye contact or you're looking around, your eyes are communicating with others. Among more than 200 species of primates, humans are unique in that we have whites in our eyes, which allow people to track where we're looking. "Thanks to the whites surrounding our irises, we can follow the direction of one another's gazes," writes Rutger Bregman in *Humankind*. "The glimpse this gives us into other people's minds is vital to forging bonds of trust."[3]

What does this mean for our videos? "Look in that camera lens. Look at it like you're looking people right in the eye," Shep advises. "It's okay, once in a while, if you want to look around. But when it comes to what you're really trying to say—and you want to make the message connect—look at the camera." By making that direct eye contact when making your important points, you're further reinforcing their importance.

You don't stare people down when you're in a conference room, so you don't have to stare people down in your videos, either. Try to maintain eye contact at least half of the time when speaking. Look into the lens for four to five seconds at a time. When you look away, do it slowly so that you don't appear too nervous or shy.[4] Remember, your gaze is part of your message.

A Caution about Teleprompters

For years, people have asked Steve and I which teleprompter they should use for their videos. Our recommendation: no teleprompter at all. Generally, Shep agrees. But there's nuance.

For YouTube videos, Shep writes an article or blog post first, then records a video on the topic. When we go to the camera first, we're more likely to ramble. In contrast, the process of writing forces us to organize our thoughts. Also helpful is that Shep always writes like he speaks. Being conversational makes the information more approachable and creates consistency between his written and spoken words.

Some of Shep's videos are recorded for television, which require him to time them down to the second. For these videos, he uses a voice-activated teleprompter that advances automatically as he reads the words aloud. "The art of being on a teleprompter is a practiced art. It's like anything. If you practice it, you get better," Shep says. But he cautions that if you haven't practiced extensively with a teleprompter, you're likely to lack emotion and come across as a robot.

This is why we've advised against it, too. Of all the skills you can practice and develop, reading from a teleprompter isn't nearly as useful as speaking to people clearly, naturally, and confidently. Unlike reading from a teleprompter, the ability to articulate your ideas aloud helps you in almost any personal or professional role you find yourself in.

In addition, writing scripted words and reading them from a teleprompter puts the focus on the wrong thing. Because reading is a conscious activity, you're doing more thinking than feeling. And the way you say something is more important than what, exactly, you say. Yes, you need to speak accurately. But saying the exact "right" words in the exact "right" order isn't necessary. Focus on expressing your message, not just saying the words.

Before you turn on your camera, be familiar with what you want to say. Internalize the message. Then say it with your whole self. It requires less practice than reading from a teleprompter and provides a broader array of benefits to you and to other people.

Confidence Within Teams

We've noticed it. Shep's noticed it. You probably have, too. Most people are initially uncomfortable on camera. "The camera causes people to freeze. It causes people to act differently," observes Shep.

One way to normalize interaction with the camera is to put people on camera in more situations. We become more confident through exposure. When you're doing coaching or training, for example, put it on camera. Have people ask and answer questions on camera. Get people talking to the camera every day. Make it fun. Consider a contest.

"If I'm a manager talking to my employees and saying, 'We're going to start doing more and more video interaction,' I just want it to be real. I want them to be genuine," Shep says. "And so I'm going to work with them and make sure they get comfortable." You don't need to coddle people, but you also need to take care not to destroy confidence early on. A lack of confidence on camera creates a lack of confidence in viewers.

We can also build people up by watching their videos and providing small tips to enhance their presence. Provide coaching around pace, tone, eye contact, body language, video length, opens and closes, lighting, and other details. If you're using a message framework like Vengreso's PVC, speak to that. You may see things that they don't see. You might be fairer and more objective with them than they would be to themselves.

ELEMENTS OF ENGAGING PRESENTATIONS

Presenting information in a visual, virtual format is something most of us have the opportunity or obligation to do. It's helpful across the entire customer lifecycle and throughout the entire employee journey. This time is wasted if we make it about ourselves or about the material. We must make it about other people.

Shep's built his career around engaging audiences in a way that transforms behavior. He's adapted his expertise on stage into virtual environments, where attention spans are short and people check out sooner than ever before.

Shep's tips on energy, structure, texture, engagement, and equipment will teach you to masterfully keep your audiences engaged.

Energy

Energy level is crucial. And it's harder to transfer energy virtually than it is from the stage.

"The concentration factor required for me to look into that lens for the 30 or 40 minutes I'm speaking is so much more draining," Shep admits. "And on the other side, how long can somebody look at a video? Especially a talking head!"

Viveka von Rosen brings Super Viv to the screen. Julie Hansen advises us to turn everything up a little. Shep agrees and suggests that you provide alternative structures and styles. Doing so will allow you to sustain your energy for your own benefit and for that of your audience.

Structure

Most presentations start with a host, who introduces a guest, who then puts up a slide presentation, which takes up 90% to 95% of the time. If the audience is lucky, one or two questions get answered in the closing minute. You already know the problem with this. And you've already received some good alternatives. Shep has more.

He's found success taking all of the information from a typical presentation and restructuring it as a fireside chat. An executive, a leader, or another respected member of the host organization leads Shep through a series of questions. He tells the same stories, lessons, and learnings, but in a more personal and customized format. It can still be supported with some visuals. If your presenter or speaker isn't as talented as Shep, this format works especially well because they don't have to carry the entire session alone and the host can control the cadence and speed.

Shep's also delivered a hybrid version of a traditional presentation and a fireside chat. It starts with a traditional 20- to 30-minute presentation, then transitions to a sit-down with a leader from the host organization. Together, they break down the information, customize it for the audience, and answer questions from those in attendance.

A variation of this hybrid approach starts with a pre-recorded presentation. That traditional 20- to 30-minute segment is recorded in advance and played at the scheduled time. This allows the benefit of video editing, including more and better visual support. Once it's done, Shep shows up live with the host in the same clothes he wore in the recording. From there, they conduct the chat and Q&A. One client enjoyed this format so much that they've made it their model for all of their presentations.

Texture

For some presentations, Shep takes his preparation even further. He weaves his speeches together by visually mapping out the topics he wants to address and the tone he wants to set. He uses a 2-foot by 4-foot piece of sheet metal that's wrapped in felt and mounted to his wall in his office. To style it up, he had it framed so that it's nice and neat, and he uses magnets to pin up index cards.

He writes out each point or topic on a separate index card, then lines them out in sequence from left to right. If he's going to make the point with high energy, humor, or a motivational story, he moves it higher up on the board. If it's a more serious point or an emotional story, he moves it down lower. See an example in Figure 11.1.

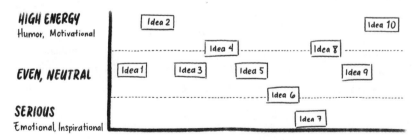

Figure 11.1 A Texture Map

Once mapped, he can step back and see the texture of the presentation. How does it feel? Does something need more build up? Or a longer pause? Is there a stretch that needs a laugh or smile?

By visualizing both information and emotion, Shep intentionally designs a presentation to engage, serve, and move the people who experience it. He maps texture as he's outlining the chapters of his books, scripting and storyboarding produced videos, and creating speeches.

Engagement

Audiences are checking out faster than ever. So if you want engagement, you can't just be a face in a postage stamp-sized window sitting on top of slides for your entire presentation.

After 15 or 20 minutes, Shep gets people to stand up, look around, and move their shoulders. He may even engage them with a synchronized clap. This breaks up the session, gets the blood flowing, and earns more attention for the information that follows.

Over the years, he's tried to include a smile or a laugh for the audience every two to three minutes. "On video, it becomes harder because you don't know how to time the laugh. You're doing it by gut feel." Since he's been doing it for years, it's not as challenging for him as it may be for you or me.

Do you have to create smiles and laughs? Not necessarily. "You don't need to be funny, but you need to be engaging. You need to have some level of entertainment," says Shep. What he means by entertainment, though, may not be what first comes to your mind. "I'm talking about getting people to feel engaged and feel as if they've not only learned, but also been fulfilled by the actual presentation. That's entertainment."

A magic aficionado himself, Shep's attended virtual shows by magicians. One sent a box to each audience member in advance with instructions not to open it until the event. Throughout the show, the magician engaged the audience with interactive elements from inside the box. These were literal "moments of magic," but you can create your own engaging experience for people with some planning and creativity.

Near the start of a presentation, Shep challenges the audience to keep track of their top takeaway and to type it into the chat as soon as they have it. Not only does this engage the audience, but the responses give him questions and ideas to further customize the presentation for the specific people in attendance. Most online meeting platforms allow you to create and run polls. These also create engagement, help you understand your audience, and provide more information to teach from.

Shep uses slides, but not the entire time. To make some of his points or to answer questions, he'll go full screen in a normal head and shoulders shot. To help people remember key ideas, he displays some of the information that typically goes up on a slide in unique ways. "Put some of your visuals on a note card and just hold them up. It sounds so prehistoric, so non-techie," Shep says. "But that is actually what makes it intriguing for the audience. They don't expect that when it comes time for the next slide that you're just going to hold up a piece of paper."

Getting creative and increasing engagement doesn't have to be complicated or expensive. Start by thinking about the people for whom you're designing the experience.

Equipment

In his office, Shep's developed a full, 16-foot by 10-foot production studio. It's got a green wall for virtual backgrounds. It's got a white wall for a clean shot. It's got an over-sized monitor for visual support. And it's got multiple cameras and multiple camera angles. He uses this space for all of his television work, many of his YouTube videos, and some of his client presentations.

Increasingly, though, he's staying at his desk. He describes the scene as a "Saturday Night Live" or "TGI Fridays" type of set. It's a fully functional office space with a home-like feel. This look has become much more acceptable and normal, but he always gives his clients a choice of the professional studio or the approachable office.

See Shep's office and watch our interview
at **BombBomb.com/BookBonus**

The client's choice comes with some sacrifice in production quality, but a lot less sacrifice than just a few years ago. Video equipment has become much less expensive and much more powerful. From his desk, Shep still switches between visual sources with a single touch using his ATEM Mini from Blackmagic Design, which has up to four cameras hooked to it and plugs into his computer by USB. It allows him to do basic programming so he can easily cut, fade, and transition between sources while he's presenting.

One of the cameras hooked up to the switcher is behind him. When he activates this camera, he swivels around in his chair and has all of the meeting participants on the screen behind him. This allows him to interact with people in a different way.

Other equipment he uses includes the Logitech Brio webcam, the Sony A6400 mirrorless digital camera, a Yeti microphone, the Elgato Stream Deck, OBS (Open Broadcaster Studio), and Ecamm Live, which is a Mac-based program that allows him to overlay slides, photos, graphics, text, and other images over his video. He also uses an ATEM Mini Pro in his studio space.

Shep is a professional. His clients pay for and expect a high-quality presentation. He seeks to amaze every customer every time. That's to say: You may not need to make these types of investments. We share this to open you up to the possibilities.

OFF TO COLLEGE

The trend of increasingly powerful equipment getting less expensive and easier to use is one Shep expects to continue. When asked about the future of video communication, he likens it to the growth and development of a human:

> I think that a few years ago we were toddlers. Last year, we were probably still in kindergarten. I think the pandemic pushed us into high school. It jumped us several years into the future. Whether we know it or not, we would all be doing what we're doing right now five years from now without a pandemic. We're going to college next. We're not in the true infancy of it all, but I think that we have so much further to go.

Most of the adoption has been in live, synchronous video calls, meetings, and presentations. Shep feels that it's still early for video email and video messaging. But he's confident that it'll become normalized in the near future.

"You can't afford to wait until then, just because it'll be a little bit easier," Shep advises. "You need to do it right now."

MORGAN J INGRAM

SALES TRAINER, PODCASTER, LIVESTREAMER, SPEAKER & GAMER

"We should add humanity into our prospecting outreach and stop being robots."

A KEY IDEA IN THIS CHAPTER

Making and honoring your daily commitment to improving.

CHAPTER 12

People-First Prospecting

Featuring Morgan J Ingram

Morgan J Ingram is part of an exclusive club—though we expect membership to grow in the years ahead. Entry requires just one qualification: creating more than 10,000 videos for the purpose of building relationships and growing your business. Membership in this club is one of several things Steve and I have in common with Morgan, Director of Sales Execution and Evolution at JB Sales Training and a LinkedIn Top Sales Voice for three years running. To reach that milestone, he consistently sends video messages, goes live across several social networks, and created several series, like The SDR Chronicles and Muffins with Morgan.

"Humanity in the sales process is extremely valuable, even though it should be normal," says Morgan. He believes that we've come to rely too much on automation and that text-based communication misses qualities like confidence, inflection, and tone. "People feel way more connected when they see you," he says. "They feel they know you more than if they were to read your blog or even read your book." As a result, Morgan's been using his webcam and smartphone, not just his keyboard, for years. Never fancy. Always personal.

His video origin story is similar to that of Adam Contos, which we shared in Chapter 7. Morgan got turned onto the power of video in a personal branding class in 2014. His first reaction was like most people's—a bit fearful of what others would think or say about him. But he understood that communicating his story and sharing his expertise through video could help other people. When you hold back, "you could be preventing someone from hitting their goals or reaching as high as they can reach. Your voice could help them get to that next level."

Compared to what he'd experienced using other digital media, the benefits he enjoyed from adopting video communication were immediate and significant, including:

+ Telling stories in more verbal, visual, and creative ways.

+ Helping people better understand and remember the information he shared.

+ Getting approached by people as a good friend, even though they'd never met.

+ Creating emotional experiences and making deeper connections.

Rather than wait for the umpteenth case study proving video's efficacy or the complete, fool-proof plan to avoid any missteps, Morgan got started and kept experimenting. And he'll continue to do so. "As humans—and especially in sales—people are always looking for the silver bullet or the magic template." But Morgan points out the answers are never as easy as we want them to be. In video and in other efforts, he encourages us to be agile, experimental, and curious. To try things, figure out what's working, and continue to iterate.

With a pro-human philosophy, Morgan's been on the leading edge of video in sales for years. In this chapter, you'll learn specific tactics that have worked for him. More important, though, are the strategies behind them. You'll get those here, too.

His expertise is in prospecting—in the Awareness phase on the Acquisition side of The Bow Tie Funnel. But what he teaches is applicable to anyone for two reasons. First, each of us must reach out to people we don't know and make meaningful connections; we all "prospect" from time to time. Second, many of the ideas transcend any single application; lessons learned in prospecting can be useful across the entire customer or employee lifecycle.

Morgan is a master of sales development and kindly shares his expertise in this chapter so you can join him in connecting, training, and selling in a personal way, even in virtual environments.

THE DAILY COMMITMENT

Kobe Bryant was blessed with natural talent and athleticism, which made him a very good basketball player. But he wasn't just very good. He was one of the greatest basketball players the world had ever seen. What separated him from the pack and made him truly elite? His daily commitment.

In his conversation with Lewis Howes on The School of Greatness podcast,

Kobe shared the story of playing basketball as a child in a summer league.[1] That summer, he was totally shut out—he didn't score a single point. Though frustrated and embarrassed, he didn't quit. Instead, Kobe made a commitment. From a menu of fundamental basketball skills, like free throws and crossovers, Kobe focused on one skill at a time for a few hours every day. By his early teens, he'd caught up to his peers. Shortly thereafter, he'd surpassed them. And he kept on going, en route to being a 5-time NBA champion, 18-time NBA All-Star, 12-time All-Defensive Team selection, and 2-time NBA scoring champion, among many other accolades.

Several years into his professional career, Kobe added another commitment he learned from legendary coach Tex Winter: watching recordings of every game. Not isolated cameras. Not highlights. The whole game from start to finish. The same night it was played. The insights and perspective he gained helped him in several ways, including expanding the scope of what was in his control, slowing the game down, and changing how he communicated with his team members.

Why did Morgan share this with us? To remind you that frustration or embarrassment are not reasons to quit, but reasons to commit. As Mathew Sweezey recommended in Chapter 5, as Julie Hansen recommended in Chapter 6, and as Morgan recommends here, take the time to review some of the videos you've sent. Record and send. Build the habit. Then start playing them back. Identify areas for improvement and write them down. Work on those skills one at a time. Your goal isn't to be the best in the world or to be better than anyone else. It's only to make consistent progress by becoming a better version of yourself today than you were yesterday.

> After you send videos,
> watch some back to identify
> **specific areas for improvement**.

"You're not going to make your first video and have it be the best thing of all time. You have to make it a daily commitment," Morgan advises. He'd initially started using video on YouTube and found some success there. When he took what he'd learned and applied it to video messaging, he got frustrated, because it didn't work as well. The problem: Three- to five-minute videos are great on YouTube, but too long for prospecting messages. The solution: Make them shorter and keep tweaking.

Morgan committed to arrive at the office a half hour early and do five prospecting videos every single morning. As he got comfortable with the process, he was able to record 10, 15, or even 20 videos in the same amount of time. A couple of pro tips he picked up: 45 to 60 seconds (90 seconds max) is about the right length of videos for people who don't know you yet. Think of them like a movie trailer. Your goal is to spark interest and generate a reply, not provide the entire story.

Not every effort is going to deliver the result you want. But consistent effort produces consistent growth and consistent results. Take for example this reply Morgan received thanks to his daily commitment: "Morgan, I've never responded to an outbound email in my 20 years as a professional. This was creative, it was thoughtful, and it definitely stood out. I'm open to meeting with you all." This came from a C-level executive who's inundated with unsolicited calls and emails all day every day. And this executive became a customer.

This won't happen every time, but it reinforced Morgan's confidence in the approach. As for being creative, it doesn't have to be as expensive or time-consuming as you might think. All it took to land a meeting with an NBA franchise, the Atlanta Hawks, was an iPhone, a mini hoop, a foam basketball, and a few minutes, as Morgan describes:

> I was the passer and the rep dunked the alley-oop. I said, "Hey, my name is Morgan. I'm a manager here for the sales development team and one of my reps has a quick message for you." And I threw up the alley-oop, she dunked it, and said, "Hey, happy to meet you. My name is so and so. And we want to help you slam dunk your marketing efforts," and then made a short pitch.

They loved it. It produced a meeting. Simple, fun, and on-theme, their video delivered something that a typed-out email or a faceless voicemail never can. And if you never get started with the simplest videos, you'll never send a creative one.

THE FOUR 5s

In email, LinkedIn, and other channels, everyone's inboxes are getting blown up. And all the messages look the same. Spam, automation, and bots all turn up the noise level. Your messages often get lost in the crowd. To help people recognize the value and opportunity you represent, you must make a little extra effort and be a little more human.

Morgan's so passionate about this that he encourages you to take ownership over the human touch, even if your manager doesn't support it. The alternative is competing against pollution, swimming in the sea of noise, and appearing the same as a bot—a losing battle. Morgan's friend Kyle Coleman, a sales and marketing leader, created The Three 5s to break through and create conversations. Morgan adopted it and later evolved it to The Four 5s by adding video and voice notes to the mix.

It's a simple daily formula that anyone can use to create more meaningful connections:

5 personalized text emails

5 personalized video messages

5 personalized voice notes in LinkedIn

5 minutes for each of these three sets

That's 15 minutes and 15 touches per day. That's 75 per week and 300 per month. Because they're personalized, you should expect higher engagement rates. Even a 10% response would give you 30 replies per month. That's more than one new conversation every single weekday.

"I think what happens is that people feel overwhelmed because their managers and their leaders say, 'Go do all these activities.' This doesn't allow them to be human," Morgan cautions. Instead, he recommends you find 15 minutes somewhere in your day, time block The Four 5s, and get them done. And if you're worried about this time commitment, "you've just got to get rid of stuff that probably isn't worth your time, even if you think it is."

You must ask yourself: "What are the daily things that I'm going to do to be successful?" If you don't, Morgan fears that "you're going to become a robot. We talk about it all the time over here at JB Sales. You're going to die the death of an average salesperson because you're just going through the motions. You're going to get lapped." You may not have aspirations to be the absolute master of your craft like Kobe Bryant, but these are the types of commitments you need to make to be sustainably successful in the future.

THE FORMULA FOR VIDEO PROSPECTING

We promised tactics. Here they are. Morgan's been doing video prospecting for years; these are some things he's learned along the way.

Video Third or Fourth

Morgan doesn't lead with a video message. He always wants his first message to reach the prospect, but the extra image (the video thumbnails or animated preview) and the extra link (to the actual video) may inhibit that. He prefers video as his third or fourth touch.

His recommended sequence:

> Step 1: LinkedIn connection
>
> Step 2: Text-based email
>
> Step 3: Phone call/voicemail, plus a video email that refers to the voicemail

As an alternative:

> Step 1: LinkedIn connection
>
> Step 2: Text-based email
>
> Step 3: Phone call/voicemail
>
> Step 4: Text-based email
>
> Step 5: Video email

Along the way, if someone opens two of your emails, treat it as an indicator of interest. When that happens, he moves that person out of the sequence and follows up with a truly personal, human-to-human video.

10-30-10

What should you say in those video messages? Morgan prescribes a 10-30-10 formula, referring to the amount of time speaking to the reason for the video, the value proposition, and the call to action. This forces you to be clear and concise about who the message is for and why it's of value to that person.

First 10 seconds: The reason for your video

This could be a trigger for sending; a research point; an observation about their website, LinkedIn profile, or LinkedIn activity; or another point of personal relevance.

If delivered in email, say your name in the beginning of the video. If delivered by LinkedIn message, your name, face, and profile do that job for you, so you don't need to say it.

Next 30 seconds: The value proposition

Adapt this from your text-based emails or voicemails. Personalize it to the individual.

Final 10 seconds: An "interest" call to action

Based on Gong.io data, cold emails with an "interest" call to action are more than twice as successful as those with specific or open-ended calls to action (CTA).[2] An "interest" call to action seeks to create a conversation, whereas a specific one asks for a meeting or an appointment. An open-ended call to action is just too vague. Some interest-based CTAs that Morgan's had success with include:

"Would you be open to learning more?"

"Would it be crazy if we had a conversation around this?"

"Would you be curious to have a deeper dialogue on this topic?"

Formulas, Not Scripts

$0+4=4$

$1+3=4$

$2+2=4$

No, this isn't a basic arithmetic lesson. It's an illustration of the fact that there are multiple paths to any outcome. This concept is why Morgan strongly favors formulas over scripts. It's why he teaches the 10-30-10, rather than a tightly scripted, 50-second video. People don't need moment-by-moment handholding or over-the-shoulder micromanagement to get the job done. Following strict orders makes people feel and sound like robots. Restoring appropriate levels of autonomy and creativity to people's roles restores their ownership over the outcomes.

Formulas provide guidance, including some step-by-step recommendations based on what's worked in the past. Formulas also provide boundaries, defining a safe and successful area to operate within. But they allow for experimentation, learning, and growth. Give people best practices, guardrails, and feedback and they will deliver. When we have personal investment, we go the extra mile.

Along with several other people featured in this book, Morgan is firmly in the "no scripts" camp. And if you're not keeping score, don't worry. We'll round up recommendations like these in Chapters 14 and 15.

Well-Written Words

If you've already got an established relationship with the recipient, sending a video on its own can be effective. More effective, though, is supporting a video with well-written words. In the first sentence of your message, provide a reason to watch the video and make clear how long it is. Don't make people guess. Reduce any mystery about whether or not your recipient should click play. If your video's truly personal, mention that in the text, too.

For example: "I know you may think this is a mass-blast video, but click it and watch for five seconds. You'll see that it's actually just for you."

Just as a good thumbnail image increases plays of a YouTube video, a good thumbnail or animated preview can increase plays of your video messages. Use an app like Make It Big, or even something as low-tech as a sticky note or small dry-erase board. Write down the reason someone should watch your video. It could be that person's name, a sketch of their logo, or a note about why you recorded it for them. Also effective are doing screen recordings over a person's LinkedIn profile or website; this communicates that the video is about them even before they click play. It communicates that they're worthy of your time and attention.

The purpose of your subject line is to encourage someone to open your email. The purpose of your opening line of text and the image that represents your video is to motivate them to play your video. No matter the promise you're making, your video must deliver. When you create false expectations or misrepresent the contents, you reduce engagement and trust. Clickbait is a short-term play. Clarity and sincerity are the long-term play.

Keep It Simple

Record your videos in a well-lit area; people need to see your face in order to connect with and understand you.

Smile. You should feel and look excited; it's contagious to others and capitalizes on the power of the medium.

Keep it short. We already said this, but it's so important that we said it again.

Stop doing retakes. Morgan's approach is to put yourself out there and see what works. You'll never know what works if you keep re-recording yourself. You have to record and send, then track the results. Over and over again.

BEYOND PROSPECTING

Like everyone who's found success with video messages, Morgan's expanded far beyond his initial use case (prospecting and cold outbounding). Other ways he's using videos include:

Meeting Follow-Up

It's hard getting everyone together at the same time. It requires coordination and commitment. So after a meeting with a prospective customer, record a video thanking people for their time and recapping the most important points discussed. This is easily forwarded to other stakeholders or decision-makers who could not attend and allows them to meet you.

Objection Handling

Getting a reply is better than no reply. But many include objections. For example: "Reach out to me in six months," "We don't have the budget," or "I don't see the ROI." Morgan always tries to call and discuss the objection. If they don't answer the phone, however, he sends people a video rather than typing out his thoughts. This creates familiarity with you, helps you manage any emotions or complexity involved, demonstrates your expertise, and gives people something they can forward to others.

Warm Introduction

An internal influencer or champion can be your guide inside a new organization. Once you've established a relationship, he or she may direct you to someone else. Often the decision-maker, the someone else you're directed to is often someone busy. Morgan has found it effective to send a personal video introducing himself to that person. No selling, just a warm introduction and perhaps an open-ended offer to meet. You might even record the video with the influencer or champion, so the decision-maker sees a familiar face in the frame and you get a warmer welcome.

Proposal Walkthrough

When you send a proposal, offer, or contract, add some context by doing a show-and-tell screen recording with the document on the screen. You've worked hard to build a trusting relationship. Don't let them navigate a confusing contract on their own. And no need to schedule a 30-minute meeting to provide your guidance. Send the video to your primary point of contact and have that person share it with any other executive or decision-maker who should see it.

CONVERSATIONS, NOT PRESENTATIONS

Make it a conversation, not a presentation. Mentor, friend, and sales enablement pioneer Roderick Jefferson shared this advice with Morgan, who took it to heart. This advice informs his approach to sales calls, video meetings, webinars and presentations, and live videos.

Bring energy to all of these interactions. But create the feeling of a normal chat, even when you're delivering tips and tactics. Again, it's a conversation, not a presentation.

Sales Call

Don't just show up on the call and use the weather or something you learned from a 30-second visit to their LinkedIn profile as the basis of conversation. Go deeper. Before the call, go to their website, as well as their LinkedIn profile. Learn who their ideal customers are. See which markets they serve. Look at what roles they're hiring. Read online reviews from their customers. Seek to understand their business as if you're a consultant.

From there, start the call by walking through what you've learned and turn it into a question. For example: "(Several key things you learned). Is that accurate or am I missing something?" Then, lean in and prepare to take notes, because they've got information to share.

In this way, you're making it about the other person. You're starting the conversation with momentum. You're not wasting time on the call gathering information from that person that you could have gathered on your own. This is a sign of respect. It makes for a more effective and satisfying call. And it builds trust.

Prepare in advance and make your
sales calls all about the other person.

Webinars, Trainings, and Presentations

When you have a live event, reward people for attending. Otherwise, they might just as well have watched the recording. To set the scene and start with energy, Morgan welcomes people with music. He stops and takes questions throughout. Don't put up your slides, plow through them, and wait until the Q&A session to engage the audience. They'll feel long forgotten by that point. You've got to cover the necessary information, but think first about the experience you're creating for each attendee. Serving their wants and needs through conversation will likely meet the learning objectives more than running through a presentation will.

Live Videos

When you're streaming a live video, the webinar rules apply. Give live attendees something they can't get from a recording. Morgan welcomes people with music and greets specific viewers by name as they arrive. He gets people engaging with him and with each other in the chat. He recommends learning from musicians who know how to work a crowd at a concert. Travis Scott, a rapper, songwriter, and record producer whom Morgan respects, is a master at this—jumping into the crowd, bringing people on stage, getting people to sing the lyrics, and creating an experience that can't be felt by watching a replay.

Another way to respect the people who join live or watch the recording: Be clear on the theme and the structure. Whether it's an interview, a content review, a Q&A session, a product showcase, or a different format, be clear about where you're headed and be prepared to get everyone there. This is the equivalent of doing the work to be concise in your video messages. Even though the format is longer, don't wander or meander too much.

Finally, keep a consistent time frame when you go live. Consistently going live on the same day, at the same time, and for the same duration creates and honors a clear expectation for the people who join you.

YOU'RE NOT LATE

"If you think you're late, you're really not," Morgan says of the opportunities of video. "There are lots of people still trying to figure this out. And there are lots of people who maybe have tried it out, they gave up on it, and they're not doing it anymore." Even though the 10,000-video club is growing, even the 10-video or 100-video club awaits millions more members.

"Video is still in the early adopter phase because so many people are hesitant about it. But I think more buyers are going to prefer a video over another email or cold call," Morgan predicts. "And I think they're going to become a little bit warmer to it. They'll appreciate a video that they could watch between their meetings."

In Figure 12.1 is a standard technology adoption curve. Live, synchronous video calls through Zoom, Google Meet, Microsoft Teams, Cisco Webex, or another platform are certainly in the "Early Majority" or "Late Majority" phase. Recorded, asynchronous video messages, however, are still very early in the "Early Adopter" phase.

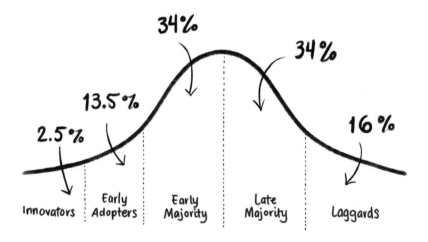

Figure 12.1 Tech Adoption Curve

Like Mario Martinez Jr., Morgan sees a growing demand for people who are ahead of the curve and who make video communication about other people, not about themselves. "If you can get really good at it, I think in the next five years, you're going to be more successful than most. If you can get really strong on video, you're going to stand out more than everybody else."

SALES EXECUTIVE & ORIGINAL TEAM MEMBER at HUBSPOT

"You help, not sell. You treat people like human beings."

A KEY IDEA IN THIS CHAPTER

Reaching out to people in ways they're most likely to appreciate.

CHAPTER 13

The Year of Video?

Featuring Dan Tyre

"My bold prediction for the past four years has been that you'll get three video emails every day," says Dan Tyre. "And it still doesn't happen. I am amazed."

For years, Dan had been encouraged by the data about the efficacy of adding videos to emails. He'd also been experiencing those benefits himself. "Over my first six or seven years at HubSpot, I got about a 50% response rate to my calls and my emails," he shares. After incorporating human-centric video messages, "it went up to 70% and then 80%. Now, I'm at about 85%."

Given the the obvious effectiveness of the format, Dan expected that business professionals would race toward video email "like a hungry man to a free buffet."[1] Instead, his prediction did not come to pass back in 2017—or in any of the years since. "I still don't get three a day. I don't even get three a week. I maybe get three a month and two of them are from you guys," he says, playfully referring to Steve and me.

Why is Dan so surprised and disappointed? Because he regards video messages as "the biggest transformation in prospecting in 30 years" and the biggest innovation since email started. And he should know. As the first salesperson and sixth employee, he joined HubSpot more than 14 years ago as an original member of the team. In that time, he's helped build the sales organization and trained thousands of salespeople around the world. Dan pioneered the concept of "Smarketing," the alignment of sales and marketing, and he co-authored *Inbound Organization: How to Build and Strengthen Your Company's Future Using Inbound Principles.* Prior to joining HubSpot, he spent a couple of decades founding and leading companies and building sales and marketing teams, primarily in the software industry.

Dan recognizes that the innovation and transformation of video messaging isn't about the technology. It's about what it enables—human expression and personal connection in digital channels. In the pages ahead, you'll learn what drives Dan's 85% response rate and why sales is no longer about closing. You'll also learn how the HubSpot team got turned on to video, how to improve your live video meetings, and whether or not Dan thinks his bold prediction will ever come true.

"ALWAYS BE CLOSING" IS DEAD

Dan's personal mission is to "do the most good for the universe." His mission aligns with HubSpot's inbound philosophy, which requires that "you help, not sell. You treat people like human beings." He trains salespeople to engage with buyers in the Awareness phase of The Bow Tie Funnel. He helps them identify best-fit customers and meaningfully connect with those people.

His human-centered approach is consistent with the trend toward customer control. Dan experienced firsthand the changes that the internet brought to the buying and selling processes years ago. He understood that "people no longer have to talk to me if they don't want to." They may ghost you. They can ignore you completely. They might even shame you publicly on social media if you're too selfish or aggressive. In the earliest stages of the transformation, he realized, "Oh, my goodness, it's a whole new ballgame."

In 2015, Dan conveyed the implications of this shift in a still-popular blog post "Always Be Closing Is Dead: How to Always Be Helping." The title plays on the old sales cliché that salespeople should "always be closing" deals. This aggressive strategy was best embodied by Alec Baldwin's character, Blake, in the film adaptation of David Mamet's Pulitzer Prize-winning play *Glengarry Glen Ross*. Blake commands that his sales team "always be closing." He asserts that it's not their sales leads that are weak, but them. He taunts them: "Coffee's for closers only."[2]

But people don't need or want to be closed. They need and want to be helped. So Dan laid out the five steps to always be helping instead:

1. Determine if the person has a problem you can solve.

2. Understand where your prospect is in the decision-making process.

3. Engage with key decision-makers early in the process.

4. Tailor your process to make it easy for the customer to buy.

5. Focus on educating.[3]

"That blog article is about being human and plays to the use of video at every stage of the sales process," Dan explains. "And this is why video is going to win."

Dan sends 10 to 15 videos every day and none of them are perfect. They don't have to be. He only has one low tech setup—his laptop and a basic microphone. Despite his conviction that he "can't live without video," he's never found the need to invest in upgraded equipment. Dan sends these videos to connect with people and to help them.

TRANSACTIONS AND RELATIONSHIPS

Dan's passion for video is based on the value of humans within a sales process. Not every process needs a person in it. "It depends on the nature of the transaction," he says. "If it's solely a transaction, the need is zero." When buying staples and commodities, we tend to favor price, availability, and convenience. When looking to schedule a flight, we tend to go to websites and apps rather than travel agents. In these cases, observes Dan, "there's very little that a human interaction will do" to improve the experience.

If there's any aspect of the experience that's value-added, however, "then the human part is *everything*." Humans bring conversation and differentiation to these exchanges.

"Our job is to make people feel heard and to understand how they're different from others," says Dan.

Then, as specialists, we must determine if they're extremely different from those we typically help, if they're a little bit different, or if they're not that different at all. This is the job of a responsive human. It requires curiosity, questioning, and recommending. It's all enabled by trust.

"If it's a pure transaction, I want a chatbot. I want a link. I want a mobile website. But if there's any opportunity for a nuanced conversation where I can add value, I want to be the best human being I can be," summarizes Dan. "That means I want to be attentive. I want to do my research. I want to be responsive." Within our areas of expertise, we need to be able to say, "Yes, I can help you, and this is how" or "No, I can't really help you," and refer that person to someone who can.

Unfortunately, not everyone understands this divide between transactions and relationships as clearly as Dan does. He points to those polluting LinkedIn with bots, automation, and spam.

"Do you know what they're doing? They're destroying their potential to work with you. They're crushing their brand," he cautions. He even compares them to poorly behaved dogs, saying, "They are worse than spammers, because they asked you to invite them into your trusted circle, and then they peed all over your leg. They threw up in your lap." No one wants that.

We must be clear about this difference. We must commit to human-centered communication. Finding the right spots to add video messages benefits and differentiates us because "you can't be human in a text email." In Dan's experience, adding video in place of some of the typed-out text in our messages allows us to offer help in a nuanced and personal way. And it helps us do things that are hard to do in exchanges of written words, like negotiating, solving problems, and building teams.

A PROSPECTING SEQUENCE AND STRUCTURE

It's one thing to call out impersonal and aggressive engagement tactics on LinkedIn. It's another thing to recommend a better way. Dan's got one.

An important part of his role is training sales professionals to improve the Awareness stage of The Bow Tie Funnel. Here, you're helping people you don't yet know by informing them about a problem or opportunity they're likely facing. To turn your prospecting into helping, adapt and apply his insights. If you ever reach out to people you don't know well to initiate a conversation or make a request, you'll also find these ideas helpful.

Done well, prospecting videos are "respectful, human, and smart."

Sequence

Here's a general framework for a series of activities over about one week's time:

1. Send an email. Make a phone call. Leave a voicemail if you don't connect.

2. Wait two days.

   - Call a second time. Leave another voicemail if you don't connect.

   - Make the email a little different and send it again.

3. Wait two or three days.

   - Call a third time. Leave another voicemail if you don't connect.

   - Send a third email.

4. Wait two more days.

- Send a "breakup" email. Let them know you won't be reaching out again unless they reply to this message.

- At least two of these four emails should have a video in it. Dan recommends a personal, human-to-human video in all four, but your schedule may not permit it. By including at least two videos, they get the chance to meet you and you get to demonstrate that you're doing your research. The goal of the videos is "to make sure they know you really care."

Structure

"These videos should always be less than 60 seconds long," says Dan. He uses the person's name at the start of the video and follows this structure:

Introduction: Show the research you've done by explaining why you're engaging this specific person on this specific topic.

Bullet points: Provide two or three supporting ideas about the problem or the opportunity that are relevant to this person.

Call to action: Make it clear what the next steps are. Name yourself and your company.

To reiterate, Dan tends not to refer to himself at the beginning of his videos. Instead, he uses the valuable attention at the top to engage the other person. Additionally, most contexts in which people are watching your video include your name and often a picture of you.

Evergreens

Dan defaults to truly personal, human-to-human messages recorded for one specific person. That's why he averages 10 to 15 per day. At times, though, he'll fall back to evergreen videos—recorded once and used over and over again as necessary or appropriate. "You can't treat all your sales pursuits the same way," Dan explains.

We must find the balance between volume and value. When communicating with an executive, for example, always send a human-to-human video. And take care to do your research first. As Dan reminds us, "When you call him Fred, rather than Frederick, that is not a good look." Time and circumstance may produce a situation in which an evergreen video is as personal as you can afford to get. These videos "have their place," according to Dan.

In these cases, make it as warm and relevant as you can. Imagine one person and speak to one person. Make the evergreen video as specific to the circumstance as possible. And personalize the text that supports your video—type in the person's name and other details specific to her or him.

VIDEO AT HUBSPOT

Dan's journey into video emails and video messaging was inspired by his pro-human business philosophy. It was also informed and inspired by his team members at HubSpot. In our conversation, Dan mentioned three specific people who experienced many of the same early wins that he did. Here, we share some of their learnings.

Starting in 2017, Adam Rataj, Senior Sales Manager Mid-Market, was one of the first HubSpot team members to use video messages. His primary approach is more evergreen than truly personal; he most often records a video once and uses it over and over as necessary. For example, dentists were one of his first customer segments, so he recorded one video with a toothbrush in hand and spoke to how he could help a dentist. Even though that one video was recorded for many different people, it felt personal as he sent it out on a one-to-one basis.

As one of the highest producers of revenue from current customers, Adam also created more than a dozen videos answering their frequently asked questions. These videos tend to be show-and-tell screen recordings that save him time and create happier customers. He also uses video to reach out to his team members to explain things like how to update their forecasts in the sales system. As he told me in a personal video, this "makes things more human for everybody."

In early 2019, Nick Saltzman was a new HubSpot team member who realized that he'd "stepped into a territory that had been hammered by cold email and phone outreach."[4] He knew there was a better way to engage people than doing more of the same emailing and calling. In his onboarding and ramping period, Nick made the bold choice to dedicate an entire month to prospecting exclusively through video. His opportunity creation rate of 27% was remarkable, as were the quality and quantity of replies he received to his videos. Now the Principal Channel Partner Manager, he continues to connect and communicate daily using video messages.

A HubSpot team member for more than 13 years, Senior SaaS Sales Manager Katharine Fischer was trying to break into a target account by connecting with their Chief Revenue Officer through video. Though he wasn't responding, the tracking and analytics showed that he was watching her videos. When she paused the outreach, an internal champion within the account reached out to Katharine on behalf of the CRO to ask why she stopped sending the videos. Her outreach was so exceptional that the recipient missed it when it was gone!

When she finally connected directly with the CRO, he talked specifically about the contents of her videos; she'd established familiarity and built credibility. What is she sending to people like him? It's simple: She sends help. Katharine led with value in her videos and supported it with additional links and resources. Rather than asking for time, she gives them an idea or insight they can act upon same day.

At the end of her prospecting sequences, she always does what Dan suggests— sending a "breakup video email." Its purpose is to generate a response—a "yes, let's talk" or a "no, thank you, goodbye." Because the preceding video emails are so useful, her breakup video letting them know it's her last is delivering a "huge overperformance" in reply rate.

Because time is our most valuable resource, we have to find that balance between personal videos and evergreen videos. Many of the videos in Katharine's sequences are evergreen, but the context makes them feel somewhat personal. For high-value accounts, she always sends truly personal videos.

No matter the recording style, Katharine takes care to mention the other person or use "you" at least twice as often as she mentions herself or uses words like I, me, or my. She prefers "scrappier" recordings to those that are polished and produced. Videos have given her and her team members "more of a natural way" to communicate with their fellow humans.

> Mention or refer to the other person
> at least **twice as often** as yourself.

The HubSpot team uses video across the entire customer lifecycle. In addition to pointing us to Adam, Nick, and Katharine, Dan mentions that their service, support, and account management teams also send video messages to customers. It's especially useful for explaining complex topics like how to use specific features of the HubSpot software. Screen recordings show the steps and walk people through it, rather than making them read through it. All in all, video "is a great way to have that small-company feel, even if you have more than 3,000 employees," says Dan.

DOS, DON'TS, AND DISCS

When we're simply delivering information for a transactional purpose, we may not need video for that meeting or that message. But any time there's a relational or emotional aspect, it's time to turn the camera on. Videos "go a long way towards relating to people in a non-business way," says Dan. "We share our thoughts more effectively in a way that's human first—and business a little bit secondary."

From that perspective, here are some simple things that Dan recommends you include and avoid in video messaging, along with a deeper strategy that's driving his remarkable response rates.

Dos

+ Practice to develop your confidence.

+ Before recording, check your framing; try for a simple head-and-shoulders shot.

+ Before recording, define the two or three objectives of your video on paper or in your mind.

+ Personalize the thumbnail and the video title.

+ Keep it short—30 to 45 seconds.

+ Stand up to increase energy.

+ Modulate your voice to enhance understanding of the message.

+ Record in front of a clean, non-distracting background.

+ Show things besides yourself.

Among the things Dan likes to show are the person's LinkedIn profile or website to make it more personal. Or he shows something to support the purpose of the message; for example, a workbook from one of the training sessions he delivers. "The whole idea of a video message is not only being more human, but also doing a better job of conveying either the reason you're reaching out or giving them what they wouldn't get in a text email," says Dan.

Don'ts

+ Don't delay in getting going; start now.

+ Don't be a robot; be more conversational.

+ Don't make the video too long.

+ Don't be redundant within your video.

+ Don't be redundant to the typed-out text that supports your video.

+ Don't use a script but don't completely wing it either.

DISCs

In person and even on video calls, we naturally mirror other people. We tend to match others' tone, posture, facial expressions, and other qualities. This process facilitates empathy, bonding, and emotional contagion.[5] It demonstrates attention and understanding. It creates similarity and liking. How can we create this through video messages when the other person isn't in front of us and we may not have met them yet?

Dan does this by using the Crystal personality platform at CrystalKnows. com, which helps predict people's personality types even if you've never met them before. As Founder and CEO Drew D'Agostino says of the service, "it's like having a coach for every conversation, teaching you to communicate more effectively, be more persuasive, build stronger teams, and improve the overall quality of your professional relationships."[6]

It's based in part on the DISC behavioral framework that defines personality as a plot of higher or lower people-orientation and task-orientation. It helps you determine if people are characterized most by Dominance, Influence, Steadiness, or Conscientiousness.

"Before I call Ethan, I can download my version of Crystal Knows and see his DISC personality type. I realize that if I use big energy, he'll like it. But he wants me to get right to the point," Dan explains. "I know that he's a D-I, so I know what he wants. I'll work that into the video. If instead I see somebody who's an S, my video will be longer than 90 seconds because it's insulting to them if I don't tell them the whole story."

This is similar to mirroring because it helps us think about, understand, and reflect the other person's values.

"If I'm sending to a hard-charging CEO of a financial services company, I'll say, 'Steve, let me get right to the point.' When I do, do you know what happens? In his brain, dopamine drops. He's like, 'Yeah, I like this guy,'" explains Dan. "If I get somebody who is a C? No big energy." For that type of person, Dan plays to their preferences for logic, accuracy, and analysis without any bold emotional expression.

In these hypothetical scenarios, Dan anticipates and serves the preferred level of directness with his tone of voice and degree of seriousness. He tends to play to people's professional titles, as well. Throughout every video, he remains specifically focused on their problem or opportunity.

Dan attributes his 85% response rate to this additional layer of thought and care. He's taking a human-centered approach to his video messages and experiencing a measurable improvement. Success isn't about the tool or the technology, but about the personal touch.

GETTING EVERYONE INVOLVED

When Dan joined HubSpot, he was the first remote employee at the company, operating from his home in Phoenix. He works with people all over the globe. As a result, he's hosted countless video calls with team members, partners, prospects, and customers. Here are some of the things he does to create more conversation and connection through the camera.

When you're live on video, Dan says, "you've got to be centered, you've got to be focused, and you've got to be respectful." You must engage people right away and, unlike a recording, there's no do-over. In addition to reading a personality assessment from Crystal, Dan reads the emotion of the person or the group immediately. He's determining whether to take a few minutes to build rapport or go straight into the facts.

In short: Instead of doing what most of us do (focusing on ourselves, how we look, and what we have to say), he's spending the crucial first moments of the call focusing on other people.

After a warmup of appropriate duration, Dan sets the agenda. He breaks down how the time is going to be spent, then stops and asks for confirmation that it meets everyone's needs and expectations. Like Morgan J Ingram, Dan is creating a conversation, not delivering a presentation. To facilitate that experience, he stops throughout to engage people, directing questions to specific people. He reads faces and offers observations such as, "Amber, it looks like you have a couple of questions." Dan also uses the chat function with the group and with individuals. In one way or another, he makes sure everyone is involved.

To ensure people know he's listening to them and understands them, Dan frequently repeats back in his own words what he heard people say. For example, "Donna, what I heard you say is . . ." This creates the opportunity for confirmation or clarification before proceeding. One caution: It's easy to talk over people on video calls because there's often a slight delay in the video transmission. In person, it's more socially acceptable and more easily ironed out. Virtually, it's often awkward and frustrating. If this happens, simply apologize and clarify your intent.

Many of the skills and habits we have for live, face-to-face meetings are helpful when we go virtual. But it's not a direct parallel. We must adjust some of our behaviors to make sure the people on our screen feel valued and appreciated.

THE RIGHT SIDE

For Dan, being a practitioner of human-centered communication and avoiding digital pollution is "being on the side of right." No matter what's going on in the world, "everybody can use a little bit of humor, a little bit of niceness, and a little bit of connection." That's why he expects video to "explode" over the next few years. And that's why the risk right now isn't that it's not going to work. Instead, "the risk is that the train has left the station and you're not on it."

For everyone's benefit, Dan wants his prediction to come true. So does Steve. So do I. We know that the professional worker receives an average of 120 emails per day.[7] This year should be the year that at least 2.5% of our emails—or three per day—are more personal and more human. It's not too expensive. It's not too hard to learn. And it all starts with a little practice.

The year of video is the year of three per day—in emails, texts, social media, and other messaging platforms. And not just from salespeople using video to prospect more successfully—from anyone and everyone within our business ecosystem. Internally and externally. Checking in. Following up. Giving thanks. Sharing updates. Building culture. Providing nuance. Improving experiences. Being on the side of right.

You've just learned from the experience and expertise of Dan and 10 other leaders in this movement how we can reduce digital pollution and adopt human-centered communication. Ahead in Part Three, view the common themes in their strategies and tactics to develop a roadmap to connect with people more effectively in the years to come.

Part Three

TAKEAWAYS & TOMORROWS

CHAPTER 14

Takeaways:
Strategies and Philosophies

Human-centered communication isn't new. And it isn't radical. It's a restoration.

Efforts to reduce pollution are efforts to return our natural environment to a cleaner and healthier state. Acts to reduce and eliminate digital pollution are acts to make every digital environment a more helpful and more human space. The innovation of human-centered communication is a call to consciously and consistently make what's virtual more personal.

Our communication is created from a set of habits, systems, and processes. Our habits are internal to us; they are our default way of doing things. As a book reader, you're likely the kind of person who sets out to create new healthier habits from time to time. Make this one of them. Set your mind to being more human-centered, put a few ideas into practice, then iterate and build upon them.

Unlike habits, the systems and processes that inform our communication are externally imposed by force or by circumstance. They're designed and installed into our organizations. They're coached and trained into our teams. They're in place to achieve desired outcomes as predictably and efficiently as possible. Our communication processes provide order and support scalability. But, as we've seen, they can have unintended consequences. Now is the time to review and realign our communication practices with long-term success in mind.

There is no sacrifice here. Just as clean air, water, and soil are necessary precursors to healthy people and human thriving, human-centered communication is a necessary precursor to healthy companies and business success. Human-centered communication allows other people to feel seen, heard, understood, and appreciated. All it requires of us is sincerity and intention as we reach out in meaningful and service-oriented ways. It's better for prospects, customers, team members, leaders, managers, partners, suppliers, vendors, and all of the other stakeholders our success depends on.

> Human-centered communication is
> **better** for all of the stakeholders
> our success depends on.

Hacks. Silver bullets. Magic pills and potions. Though we often seek and buy them, there are no shortcuts to true success. They may seem to work in the short run. But, as we've seen, what's "working" may not actually be working. Not if we want open doors, longer views, and better futures. Not as volume-based, automated activity shows signs of diminishing returns. And not in the face of an increasingly noisy, polluted, and untrustworthy digital environment.

Instead, we must recognize that our measurable success is created through our immeasurable qualities—"things like trust, wisdom, character, ethical values, and the hearts and souls of the human beings who play the central role in all economic activity" in the words of John Bogle, founder and former CEO of The Vanguard Group.[1]

The restoration begins here with 10 of the key strategy, philosophy, and mindset recommendations our like-minded experts bring to this important conversation. Like the next chapter, this one is no substitute for those that came before it; each of the previous chapters is loaded with useful information you can put to work today. Use this as a reminder of key ideas and also as a reference to earlier chapters.

1. SEE THE NEED FOR CHANGE

Human-centered communication starts with people. The goal is alignment with the needs and wants of the people affected by it. The process requires a deep understanding of these people. Taking care of humans is tantamount to taking care of desired outcomes. For so many reasons, this perspective is an improvement over a more selfish or mechanical approach to business communication. Today, standing firm in the status quo means losing ground to increasing noise, decreasing trust, and growing commoditization.

By being more human-centered in our work, we can rehumanize people negatively impacted by the overemphasis on specialization, volume, and efficiency. We can still exceed our goals, but we can do it in a way that honors the people our success is built with and for. In this way, we can make the years ahead a decade for sellers to shine, as Lauren Bailey rallied us to do in Chapter 8.

In Chapter 5, Mathew Sweezey reminded us that a process created without people first in mind gives us a mechanized, inhuman experience that isn't good for people. "Hence you end up with a society that is optimized for the wrong thing." He gave us a series of questions to test how human-centered our organizations are right now. His context framework challenges us to create messages and experiences that are organically sought, permission-based, consistently authentic, purpose-driven, and human-to-human in delivery.

In our rush to deploy powerful and inexpensive technologies in our businesses, we too often get things backward. We tend to design the process around the tech. The proper order of events is to design the process in a human-centered way, then find the best technology to augment our people, increase productivity, enhance efficiency, and ensure results. In Chapter 3, Jacco van der Kooij provided this caution with his fishing, farming, and outbounding examples.

Just because something's become normalized within business culture doesn't mean it's good. Innovation and evolution are always needed. We are not calling for change for its own sake; we're addressing the opportunity to improve relationships and results through a pro-human philosophy and practice.

2. RESTORE HUMAN EMOTIONS

Many of the problems in our companies and in the markets we serve are the result of industrial mindsets that haven't adapted to the times. For decades, people like Mike Cooley, E.F. Schumacher, and David J. Schwartz have written about dehumanized work environments. We shared some of their ideas in Chapters 2 and 4. Slowly and surely, mass production, mass markets, mass media, and mass mindsets are giving way to something more personal.

One of the changes needed to improve the experiences of our employees and customers is the restoration of emotional expression. We need to invite whole, integral people into professional contexts, not just businesspeople being business-like by suppressing parts of themselves. The long-standing and artificial divide between your work self and your whole self is coming down. We need to make up for missing all the in-person coffees, lunches, drinks, and dinners that allowed us to be a little more ourselves and to meaningfully connect with others.

As Dan Hill, PhD, observed in the 1990s and as many of us still experience today, emotions are often unwelcomed in professional environments. Should they be expressed, they're to be ignored or dismissed. They slow us down and threaten efficiency. They're messy and unpredictable.

But without emotion, there is no action; emotions drive both memory and motivation.

As a consequence, Dan taught us in Chapter 4 that it's more important to be "on emotion" than it is to be "on message" in our communication. Julie Hansen echoed this in Chapter 6 as she recalled how many people seem to "have left their personalities at the door" in their professional roles and challenged us to find authentic parts of ourselves to invest in every role we play in our lives. In honest, emotional expression, we convey the intent and meaning missing from so much of our business communication.

Related to the suppression of emotion is the imbalance of science over art. Lauren Bailey and Mario Martinez Jr. both cautioned against this in Chapters 8 and 9. A focus on tools and specialization harkens back to our industrial, mech-anized, and dehumanized past. We need efficiency and repeatability, but we can't create recurring impact for customers based on science alone. As Mario shared, "If science says, 'Ask the question,' then art says, 'Ask the question and allow it to be human.'" We need art, not just science.

We must encourage and support a communication style that allows each of our stakeholders to feel seen and heard. We must model behavior that not only validates emotional honesty and personal integrity, but that also invites others to adopt for themselves. Bringing fuller expressions of our whole selves into business contexts may feel unnatural to you initially, but it will feel refreshing to others.

3. HELP, DON'T SELL

More than ever, sales and service share much in common. To sell is to help and to serve. To serve is to create recurring revenue. When we shift into and operate from a service mindset, we begin to take a human-centered approach. We put the emphasis on others—on their needs, interests, struggles, and opportunities. Training and education become a focus when the other person's success is our goal. When our intent to serve is made clear in our communication, our messages and experiences are received as welcome help rather than digital pollution.

In the words of Dan Tyre in Chapter 13, "always be closing" is dead. Instead, we must "always be helping." Though we're not big on pronouncements that specific methods and modalities are dead, Steve and I are definitely with Dan on this one. Closing focuses on your own interests. Helping focuses on everyone's interests and leads to long-term success and strong reputations. This approach honors individuals and market trends.

Adam Contos and Morgan J Ingram both realized years ago that they could help other people, but only if they created visibility and presence, which is why they have cultivated large communication platforms. Mario Martinez Jr., Viveka von Rosen, and the Vengreso team define sales as "the art of helping." Jacco van der Kooij says that recurring revenue only results from recurring impact. And what does it take to create recurring impact for people? We need to help them. In more ways. In deeper ways. In meaningful and measurable ways.

4. MANAGE THE HUMAN TOUCH

Imagine the tech touch and the human touch on opposite ends of a continuum. On one end is a completely self-serve model composed solely of tech touches. On the other is a completely hands-on, white-glove service model built exclusively on the human touch. The vast middle is where most of us operate; we must figure out how to balance the tech touch and the human touch. How to balance the personalized with the truly personal. Volume and value. Efficiency and effectiveness. We must figure out how and when to let machines operate on their own, as well as how and when to have them complement our people to better provide the human touch.

As Shep Hyken reminded us in Chapter 11, "You can't automate a relationship." Loyalty is always driven by emotion and often driven by human-to-human experiences. Not by the mechanics of the offer alone. Lauren Bailey estimated in Chapter 8 that being just 20% more human will differentiate you and your business. And in Chapter 12, Morgan J Ingram observed, "Humanity in the sales process is extremely valuable, even though it should be normal." In our rush to efficiency and scale, we often automate before we properly evaluate where, when, and how to make meaningful touches and emotionally resonant connections.

As technology continues to get less expensive, more powerful, and more pervasive in our lives and in our work, our ability to manage the human touch becomes more important. In reviewing our customer and employee lifecycles across The Bow Tie Funnel, designing our customer and employee experiences, and crafting our stakeholder communication, we must consciously create human-to-human moments—even if they don't scale. As Mathew Sweezey taught us in Chapter

208 HUMAN-CENTERED COMMUNICATION

5, human-to-human messages and experiences are the new pinnacle of personal experience. And the value of what's uniquely human will only increase in value.

5. TAKE THE EXTRA STEP

Treat others as *you'd* like to be treated. The Golden Rule comes from the inside out. We inform our actions with our values and preferences in order to improve the experiences of other people. It applies equally to everyone we encounter. If more people followed this rule with consistency and conscious intent, we'd have a better world to live and work in.

Treat others as *they'd* like to be treated. The Platinum Rule comes from the outside in. We apply what we learn about a person's values and preferences in order to improve the experience of that person. We treat each individual uniquely. If we know and understand someone, we should take the extra step of honoring this rule.

Both rules call us to move from empathy to compassion. Empathizing with others is positive; it's key to being more human-centered. Even better, though, is compassion, which turns thoughts and feelings into actions. The difference is subtle but significant. It's described by the Greater Good Science Center at the University of California, Berkeley in this way: "While empathy refers more generally to our ability to take the perspective of and feel the emotions of another person, compassion is when those feelings and thoughts include the desire to help."[2] Compassion bonds us to others and drives us to help them.

Human-centered communication challenges us to take the extra step. To make things a little easier, clearer, and better for others. For everyone's benefit, including your own. It's reflected in Mathew Sweezey's personal context continuum from mass to segmented to one-to-one to human-to-human, which we discussed in Chapter 5. It's reflected in Mario Martinez Jr.'s call in Chapter 9 to start with a generalized, persona-based script, then to add context, color, and personality as you personalize it for an individual person.

Generalized to specific. Personalized to personal. Persona to person. Conversation to presentation. Identity to verification. Empathy to compassion. For better communication, take the extra step in service of others.

6. CREATE CONVERSATIONS, NOT PRESENTATIONS

This reminder plays as both a strategy and a tactic. Before we write one word, record one second, or create one slide we should have top of mind the E in the GIVER framework . . . engagement. If we're to move people and support transformation, we need conversations, not just presentations.

A presentation presumes that we know what others need and want. A conversation creates an interactive experience driven by humility and curiosity. Recall from Chapter 2 that a deep understanding of those we seek to serve is fundamental to human-centered design. This is what conversation produces.

"Conversations, Not Presentations" came to us from Morgan J Ingram and was immediately resonant. Along with Shep Hyken and Dan Tyre, Morgan provided several ways to improve our video calls, meetings, and presentations by involving all of the participants. In a one-hour session, Viveka von Rosen will ask 10 times for people to "Let me know in the chat" to get direct feedback and create interaction. Getting people to turn their cameras on creates equity in visual and emotional presence; Lauren Bailey shared specific language she uses to encourage people to do so.

A defining characteristic of a healthy conversation is active listening; Julie Hansen gave us insights on being present, providing pauses, and listening with our entire beings. This is why Shep Hyken called for more video calls in customer service and support—undivided attention and better conversation.

When you're hosting a video call, virtual event, or online presentation, your approach is driven by your mindset. When you conceive of it as a conversation before and during the experience, it will be received as such by other people. This is why, as described in Chapter 4, Dan Hill's class taught "in the round" was so highly rated; he made everyone an equal and engaged participant, not an audience member. You can also approach your messages this way. Stay curious, seek input, request replies, and create conversations.

7. FOCUS ON OUTCOMES, NOT ACTIVITIES

Just as Jacco van der Kooij cautioned us against getting things backward by designing our processes around technologies, he cautioned us against volume-based approaches. Calls, emails, videos, and other activities are like technologies; they're means to ends, not ends in themselves. When we focus on activity volume, we can lose sight of the reasons we're performing the activities in the first place. The measured activities may come to supplant the actual goal. Higher volumes also increase the likelihood of negative consequences. Jacco reminded us that volume metrics are deeply ingrained in today's culture and taught us to improve through marginal gains in Chapter 3.

Too often, managers demand that you "go do all these activities," which in Morgan J Ingram's experiences doesn't allow people to be human or to create human-centered experiences for others. Salespeople are being forced to follow prescribed activities in a prescribed manner using words that have been prescribed to them, as Lauren Bailey lamented. The cost is that they become cogs in the machine that aren't connecting with others, building relationships, or adding value.

Instead, we must focus on quality over quantity in our activities. Viveka von Rosen gave the example of generating two deals through five opportunities from 15 to 20 high-quality conversations. This was a far more effective approach than blasting messages to 5,000 people hoping to create those same two deals. Mario Martinez Jr. noted that Vengreso's sales reps have half the activity goal of an average rep, but still reach their ambitious goals.

We all want predictable results with optimal efficiency. But playing the volume game fails to fully empower our people and increases the likelihood of digital pollution and reputational damage. By honoring and serving our recipients and participants, human-centered communication adds a layer of effectiveness. It requires more thought and care, but less volume, to get to mutually beneficial results.

ℐ. BUILD TRUST AND REPUTATION

Through human-centered communication, we can create and reinforce trust. This is inherently good. And it's required for survival in a polluted digital environment. Each message we send and each experience we provide has the potential to enhance people's positive feelings, thoughts, and behaviors. Doing this consistently over time builds our reputation. Humans look for patterns and make predictions. Building trust and reputation through positive loops is the best way to overcome increasing noise and pollution.

Lead with your identity. Provide easy and clear verification. Create engagement. Help, rather than sell. Infuse messages with emotional and visual qualities. Build a sense of "know, like, and trust" through visibility and presence, as Adam Contos and Viveka von Rosen recommended in Chapters 7 and 10.

"Trust is the currency of human relationships," as we learned from Mathew Sweezey in Chapter 5. The more trust our employees, customers, and other stakeholders have with us, the more time and attention they're willing to give us. These are the most valuable things anyone can give. A human-centered approach rewards this commitment and honors these relationships.

9. VALUE THE IMMEASURABLES

What gets measured gets managed. What gets measured gets done. And what gets done gets improved. These truisms can be balanced with respect and appreciation for those things that are immeasurable. Earlier in this chapter, we shared John Bogle's list: trust, wisdom, character, ethical values, and "the hearts and souls of the human beings who play the central role in all economic activity." Few would disagree that these immeasurable qualities drive the measurable results in our businesses.

A failure to be human-centered drives us to see people more as numbers, metrics, and measures. And people feel the difference. Jacco van der Kooij and Mathew Sweezey challenged us to question whether what seems to be "working" is actually working. They advised that we look at the negative metrics, not just the positive ones—the 98.4% failure rate that corresponds with a 1.6% success rate. Not only is this a caution against volume-based activity, it's also a caution against dismissing what can't be measured easily.

The way we make people feel motivates them to reply and engage. It encourages them to say "yes" and helps them decide to buy, buy again, and refer us to others. Recall that 95%–98% of our mental activity is subconscious and that we make most decisions emotionally. Yes, we can engineer solutions to support positive feelings. Yes, we can run surveys to measure trust levels, brand reputation, and emotional sentiment. But our business execution and business results reflect whether or not we treat people like people and value the immeasurable.

10. GET STARTED TODAY

Julie Hansen reminded us that if you have a message that you're passionate about, this approach is for you. Adam Contos simplified the qualification to participate: Anybody can do it. Shep Hyken observed that being more human and more engaging in your communication is cheaper and easier than ever; the opportunity is in front of you right now. Dan Tyre made clear that the risk of a human-centered approach isn't that it's not going to work. Instead, "the risk is that the train has left the station and you're not on it."

If you're worried about being too late by starting today, Morgan J Ingram assuaged your fear by letting you know that we're still very early in this movement; you can still become an early adopter. Mario Martinez Jr. shared that developing these skills not only brings you better results and relationships in the near term, but that it also makes you more valuable in the long term.

No one can force you to change. You have to want it for yourself. No one can practice, try, fail, learn, and grow for you. You have to do these things for yourself. Digital pollution will never go away completely. But you can't just passively sit by and accept it as necessary. The visual, emotional, and human forms of communication described in these pages will become normalized. And today's status quo will come to be seen as archaic.

In short: Today is the day to commit to being more consistent and intentional about communicating in a human-centered way.

With specific things you can do to turn the philosophy into practice, the next chapter gets more tactical and practical.

CHAPTER 15

Takeaways:
Tips and Tactics

You see the need for change and improvement. You share a human-centered mindset and perspective. You've highlighted, underlined, or written down tips and tactics provided in these pages. One critical step between having that vision and making it reality, though, is not to be missed.

To make meaningful improvements in your business, you must cast the vision of human-centered communication with your team.

In times of change, confusion is likely and resistance is natural. Transforming mindsets, habits, and processes requires more than a checklist. We need to create mutual understanding and emotional buy-in. When we get the "why" right through shared beliefs and shared values, the "what" and "how" become things to rally around, rather than things to complain about. We must set the foundation for success.

Here are tips and tactics to cast the vision, empower the hesitant, and keep it real. They're followed by 10 tips and tactics introduced and reinforced throughout the book.

CAST THE VISION

The ideas of digital pollution and human-centered communication feel very familiar, even if the language feels new. To move these ideas out of this book and into the context of your own life and business, follow these four steps. To help facilitate conversations through these steps, we've provided 10 questions for you in a discussion guide.

Download the **discussion guide** at
BombBomb.com/BookBonus

*Step 1: Find, share, and discuss examples of digital pollution created outside
your company.*

In email, social messages, social feeds, and other places, you and your team are
seeing digital pollution. The more you identify it, the more obvious it becomes.

Create a Google Doc, Slack channel, or another place to share examples. Invite
your team to post screenshots, links, or copied-and-pasted text. Ask them to comment on what's being shared. Take time in a meeting to have a conversation about
what you're finding. Classify examples as Innocent, Consequential, or Intentional
and discuss why each fits its type.

Look beyond the negative and egregious examples of digital pollution.
Celebrate the positive and human-centered communication you see, as well.
Create focused discussions in the gray areas.

Doing this as a group creates mutual understanding. Filter the examples
through your team's culture and core values; they'll be clarified and strengthened
in the process. This is the foundation for Golden Rule thinking; you're deciding
how to treat others based on how you're being treated.

*Step 2: Find, share, and discuss examples of digital pollution created inside
your company.*

We're all producing some Innocent or Consequential pollution; remind yourself
of the characteristics of these classifications by revisiting Chapter 1. Create time
to consider and discuss some of the negative external consequences of the way
your team works.

Because the judgment is subjective, it's not just up to you. It's up to the people for whom you're creating messages and experiences. Bring the words of your
prospects and customers into the conversation. Decide how to treat others based
on real feedback.

Add feedback from individuals and accounts to their records in your CRM in order to support Platinum Rule treatment.

Step 3: Audit and improve the human centricity of your most important systems, processes, messages, and experiences.

As you would with journey mapping or a similar exercise, create a list or timeline of moments that matter most to your customers. Inflection points. Situations in which they're making important decisions about their future with you. Experiences that leave them with strong feelings or impressions. To get started, look at The Bow Tie Funnel we shared in Chapter 3 to identify and plot key moments and transitions.

Potential moments might include: during or immediately after an initial sales call with one of your team members, the point of commitment or purchase where there's potential for buyer's remorse, the onboarding experience, or contract or subscription renewals. Line them out and put them in priority order of emotional and business impact. Ask questions like:

+ What's driving those experiences?

+ Have they been set up from a human-centered perspective?

+ Are they being executed that way?

+ Are you just checking the box or are you sincerely operating and communicating in service of others?

+ Are you immersing yourself with and developing a deeper understanding of people in these moments?

+ Are you applying what you're learning through customer conversations and feedback?

Take on the process of improving these moments one at a time. Modify the design and execution in favor of the customer. Whenever possible, create a measure, benchmark the status quo, and drive toward quantifiable improvements.

Step 4: Use the language and have the conversation.

The consequences of digital pollution extend far beyond your business and far beyond what we can cover in a single book. Consider this the early stage of an important conversation that will continue for years to come. Digital pollution threatens trust, authenticity, and connection. Because of the growing width and depth of our digital existence, it challenges the entirety of our human experience and may alter reality itself (more on that in the next and final chapter).

Undertaking the practice of human-centered communication is critical to the long-term health of your business. It's an approach you can take throughout the day every day with every stakeholder you interact with. In this way, we can collectively set the tone and establish new norms within and beyond our professional work. This is how culture changes.

And culture must change. We can't afford to tolerate dehumanization, misinformation, confusion, or frustration in digital spaces. The sooner we create awareness of and resistance to the ills of digital pollution, the better off we all are.

Talk about digital pollution. Call it out. Discuss it. Talk about human-centered communication. Practice it. Be the change. The type of world in which we live and work—and pass on to future generations—is within our control.

EMPOWER THE HESITANT

Digital pollution is all around us. Many of us even create it. In a reasonably healthy organizational culture, having these conversations with team members should be easy and stimulating. Not so easy, though, is getting everyone on camera for video calls and video messages.

Video helps you connect with people in a visual, emotional, and human way; it's fundamental to human-centered communication. To get your team on board, here is some guidance.

Start with people you know

Whether it's you who is hesitant or someone on your team, start your video journey with familiar people like your team, your peers, or even your family. This reduces fear and anxiety and provides psychological safety. On your next video call, practice making more eye contact while still "reading the room" emotionally. Try turning off self-view. Try switching between the speaker view and the view of everyone on the call. Try engaging people through chat who seem disengaged on screen. A lower-threat, lower-consequence environment gives you more security to try, fail, learn, and grow.

Anchor from the familiar

Does your team use live, synchronous video calls? Zoom, Microsoft Teams, Google Meet, Cisco Webex. Most of us use these tools daily.

Answer a few questions for yourself: Why do we use these tools? What are the benefits? What do you like about them? How does it help to be face to face on a video call?

Next, have your team answer these questions. Have a conversation about them. Document and discuss the responses.

Then bring these conversation points into the context of video messages. Teach and train people to start using recorded, asynchronous videos based on the benefits they already recognize about live, synchronous videos. Anchor to what's good about the latter to help people embrace the former.

Acknowledge the difference

There's something different about recording a video message and sending it to people than turning your camera on in a video meeting. Live video comes and goes; it's in the moment. Recorded video has a sense of permanence. You can play it back. You can judge yourself in every frame, scrutinizing how you look and sound.

Many people work their way through these challenges; they're able to silence the inner critic and build confidence through practice. But many people quit before they ever get started. In the face of their initial uncertainty and discomfort, they falsely assume that there are "video people"—and that they're not one of them.

Acknowledge that communicating through video messages is new, different, unnatural, and uncomfortable. The discomfort is caused by vulnerability and the feelings of risk, uncertainty, and emotional exposure. The paradox is that while vulnerability can make video messaging daunting, vulnerability is exactly what makes it so effective. The openness it requires is how and why people relate to you.

Part of being human-centered is relinquishing the digital control to which we've grown so accustomed. Typing and editing emails. Shooting four photos and posting the best one. Typing a comment or publishing a post, then editing or deleting it. We've had an incredible amount of control over our digital personas. We can fuss over and overwrite every little detail.

In video messages, we have to let go with confidence and just be ourselves. Learning to give up some control is extremely liberating and powerful. Not just for your videos, but for your life. Think about what's in it for the other person first and communicate that with confidence and sincerity.

Hear the concerns

> *"What I'm doing right now works just fine."*
>
> *"This seems like a fad or gimmick."*
>
> *"I'm not a video person."*

We've heard these concerns. We have responses for them. But dismissing concerns with pointed arguments won't get people on board. We're talking about people's self-identity and digital likeness. Emotions and confidence. Fears and perceptions. Therefore, we should seek to understand, create engagement, earn trust, and create buy-in.

Ask about concerns and listen to the answers. Ultimately, practice is the answer. Immediately, however, the first step is making sure each person feels heard and validated. Even if someone is more confident and excited than hesitant or resistant, they likely have questions and objections. Help them understand the value and importance of video messages and work toward a shared belief in human-centered communication. As you've read throughout this book, this alignment and self-confidence are key.

Reminder: We addressed the questions "Will this take more time?" and "Can I afford for my team to take this approach?" at the end of Chapter 2.

Start with one use case

As you and your team get started with video messaging, list out all of the ways you'd like to use it across the customer and employee lifecycle. Narrow it down and prioritize it. And choose one. Or at least one per role. Start there. For example, consider having Account Executives start by doing a short "thank you" and recap video after meetings with prospective customers. Share video examples and customer replies within the team. Talk about what you're learning. Develop confidence. Then expand to other uses.

Go in depth

The topic of successfully incorporating video messages into your organization is far too big for one chapter, but we wrote a free 124-page book about it. The Video Adoption Guide walks through getting buy-in and getting through each of the four stages of successful adoption of video messages:

1. Script: Deciding what to say and when to say it.

2. Self: Developing confidence on camera.

3. Structure: Using text and video together in your messages.

4. System: Making video messaging a process and habit.

Get **The Video Adoption Guide** free at
BombBomb.com/BookBonus

When you download this ungated guide, look for more than 50 detailed use cases for video messages with your customers, employees, and network in Stage 1: Script.

KEEP IT REAL

Ironically, many video service providers and video messaging practitioners treat video messaging as a stunt, trick, gimmick, or parlor trick to get attention. In contrast, practitioners of human-centered communication view it as a way to provide clarity and understanding, as well as to build connection and trust. It's not a practice that you'll wear out in 18 months. It's a skill and habit that will serve you and others every day as you blend it into your normal communication mix of text-based emails, text messages, social media posts and comments, social media messaging, phone calls, video meetings, and in-person meetings.

Human-centered communication takes the long view on video.

Because you're reading this far into the chapter and this deep into the book, you likely share our belief that there are no shortcuts, silver bullets, or magic pills. But you might be wondering: How will I know that video messages are working? And when?

Here's a quick list of realistic expectations and recommendations:

+ Your tenth video recording will be better than your first. Your one thousandth video recording will be better than your one hundredth. As with anything, your strength and skill are built through practice and repetition.

+ You may never be completely confident. Tens of thousands of video messages into our journey, both Steve and I still re-record or second-guess ourselves from time to time. It's human.

+ You will not have a 100% delivery rate, 100% open rate, 100% video play rate, or 100% reply rate. You're not achieving that now. You'll likely never achieve these measures. Compare video messages to text-based messages, not to perfection.

> Compare video messages to text-based messages, **not** to perfection.

+ Not every message needs a video; simple, short, and factual messages are likely better as text alone.

+ Start by sending two messages per weekday for two weeks. That's 20 total. Make them simple, human-to-human videos to people you know. In under one minute, say something like, "thank you," "good job," "congratulations," "I was thinking about you," "I just noticed," or "I'm following up on." Look to your social media feeds, your inbox, your team, or your journal for inspiration. Pay attention to the quality and quantity of replies; they'll look and feel different than if you'd sent the same message in plain, typed-out text.

+ Celebrate milestones. Any video count divisible by 10—and later by 100 and eventually by 1,000—is a nice milestone. Each represents your commitment to be more personal and more human in a polluted digital environment. Each provides guidance and learning to you, identity and verification to others, and engagement and relationships for all. Celebrate your team members' milestones as well.

+ Look for the influence of immeasurables on your measurable results. Many teams see the specific lift in A/B tests that compare the original, text-based messages to human-centric videos. You'll almost certainly see measurable improvements, but don't miss immeasurable trust signals like warmth and language choice in replies.

Once your team has a shared understanding and shared vision for human-centered communication in the context of your business, you can start getting practical. Here are 10 top tips and tactics provided by the experts who were kind enough to share them with us.

1. REVIEW YOUR TECH AND PROCESSES

Look at The Bow Tie Funnel featured in Chapter 3. List out key tools, systems, and processes you're using to support each stage of the journey. Identify those with the greatest impact on customers and employees. Plot them on a "how people feel" continuum with "like a human" on one end and "like a number" on the other.

As our businesses grow, there's a tendency to favor the mechanical, repeatable, and scalable. Lauren Bailey observed in Chapter 8 that many of our tools, tech, and processes are dehumanizing. And Mario Martinez Jr. cautioned us about an overreliance on automation and an imbalance between art and science in Chapter 9. This tension has existed since people first sought economies of scale. As E.F. Schumacher wrote in *Small Is Beautiful: Economics As If People Mattered*:

> *Any organization has to strive continuously for the orderliness of order and the disorderliness of creative freedom. And the specific danger inherent in large-scale organization is that its natural bias and tendency favor order, at the expense of creative freedom.*[1]

Here, creative freedom is the space to be human. To operate from a framework rather than a script. To balance art with science. Your challenge is one all of us must undertake. It requires a thorough and honest review of the status quo in our organizations. It requires engaging our teams and even our customers in the effort. The purpose is simply to find ways to be more human centered in our communication with all stakeholders. And to anticipate and mitigate negative consequences of dehumanizing tech and processes.

2. FOCUS ON OTHER PEOPLE FIRST

Focusing on others first is foundational to human-centered communication; it's designed into the Four Pillars and the GIVER framework provided in Chapter 2. Even when faced with repetitive tasks, we should favor connection over efficiency by thinking about each person on the receiving end, as Julie Hansen advised in Chapter 6. When we get past ourselves and focus on understanding the person we're reaching out to, we become emotionally brilliant communicators, as Adam Contos described in Chapter 7.

Dan Hill put us in our recipients' shoes with WIIFM (What's In It For Me?) and Lauren Bailey has us ask ourselves SWIIFT℠ (So, What's In It For Them?). We should be able to answer these questions before we type a single word, record a single second, or start our next meeting. For a human-to-human experience with someone we don't know well, we might consider a service like Crystal, which Dan Tyre and Mario Martinez Jr. use to learn someone's personality type so they can better anticipate and serve their needs.

When you focus on others first, your communication becomes clearer, more valuable, more resonant, and more effective. You're making things easier for people, and they will respond in kind.

3. USE FRAMEWORKS, NOT SCRIPTS

Don't use a script; this advice is available in pretty much every chapter of this book and it's worth repeating here. Scripts create robotic and dehumanizing experiences. Formulas and frameworks help balance the art and science, the order and creativity. Morgan J Ingram recommended the 10-30-10, a formula for an under-one-minute video that combines your reason for sending, the value proposition, and an "interest" call to action. Viveka von Rosen, Mario Martinez Jr., and the Vengreso team taught us PVC (Personalize, Value, Call to Action). Adam Contos suggested the Problem/Agitation/Solution copywriting formula.

Figure out your framework or formula, internalize the message, then share it with your face, voice, and personality. As Dan Hill advised, it's more important to be on emotion than on message: The way we say something gives significant meaning to what we say. A bonus tip from Dan: Help people by using contrast. "Is it in/out, high/low, warm/cold, dark/light? The human mind works off contrasts." Because it's visual, contrast helps orient people quickly and makes your messages memorable.

And another bonus tip: Help people by providing structure. Especially in longer messages, make it easy for others to follow. As Dr. Nick Morgan suggests in *Can You Hear Me?*, "One of the kindest things you can do as a writer for your readers is to let them know where you are in the text. Number your points. Tell your readers what they are in for. Make your progress clear. Tell them you're halfway through, as in 'Let me pause here for a moment at the halfway mark to recap briefly.'"[2] Do this on video calls and in video messages as a gift to people; provide a sense of pace and give a sense of advancement.

To make those longer videos easier for you, put bullet points or an outline on screen or on paper. Refer to it near the beginning to give yourself permission to look at it throughout. You might also use a screen recording video or the screen share function on a call to walk and talk through material on your screen. It will help you and the other person.

4. TURN IT UP A LITTLE

Digital environments dampen our emotional expression. We can't read faces as well. We don't hear voices as clearly. Even expensive equipment and high-speed connections limit our fidelity on screen compared to real life. The solution? Turn it up. Consciously and consistently provide a little extra.

Julie Hansen warned us about "resting business face" and advised us to intentionally increase expressiveness in Chapter 6. Viveka von Rosen described it with "Super Viv" in Chapter 10. We can do this not just when we're speaking, but also when we're listening—with clear head nods and verbal acknowledgment. As Julie and Viveka explained, turning it up is *not* inauthentic. We do it to serve human needs. And we do it to overcome the limitations of digital environments.

5. CREATE ENERGY AND MOMENTUM

You've joined this call before: flat faces, complete silence, and a host that plainly informs everyone that "we're waiting for a few more people to show up." No energy. No momentum. Not much chance of recovery. If the host isn't excited to be there or excited that you showed up, why should you be excited?

The camera doesn't completely capture or convey our energy and emotion. In addition to turning our expressions up a little, we can also overcome this challenge by starting our video meetings and video messages with positive energy and sustaining that momentum. We need and want interest and buy-in from the start. And it's our responsibility to create it.

Dan Hill reminded us that each message or experience seeks to create a series of yeses in Chapter 4. Opening strong gets us the first yes and starts the momentum. And remember, without emotion there's no action. Julie Hansen cautioned us about warming up on our audience's time in Chapter 6. We risk losing their attention as we work to hit our stride. Instead, we should start from the Moment Before, so we have focus and energy right from the start.

6. BUILD CONFIDENCE THROUGH PRACTICE

Like our emotions, our confidence is contagious. Whether in a video message or on a video call, a basic level of confidence is key to our success. But we may not have it on our first, fourth, or seventh try. Practice closes the gap.

+ Practice not watching yourself on screen.

+ Practice actively listening to others.

+ Practice turning up your emotional expression a little.

+ Practice starting with energy and momentum.

+ Practice using a numbered list of tips or ideas.

+ Practice any skill you want to improve.

By practice, we don't mean act like you're recording a video. We mean record it. And we don't mean record a video and delete it. We mean send it. As we suggested earlier in this chapter, practice new ideas and techniques with people you already know and who know you. Pay attention to the quality and quantity of the feedback you get; it should provide the validation you need to gain confidence and keep going.

For reminders on the why and how of building confidence on camera, revisit Chapter 6 with Julie Hansen, Chapter 8 with Lauren Bailey, and Chapter 10 with Viveka von Rosen.

7. WRITE LIKE YOU SPEAK; SPEAK LIKE THEY SPEAK

We're not impressing people when we obfuscate our meaning by being sesquipedalian. See what I mean? Who uses the word sesquipedalian? And what does it mean? Clear beats clever every time; attention is lost the moment we get too clever. Why distract from your message? Why detract from your purpose? Why threaten the positive outcome? Make things easy for people to understand. Human-centered communication seeks to engage people and create trusting relationships, not to impress people and feed our own egos.

Use only as much formality as is necessary and be as simple and conversational as possible. When supporting your video message with text, write like you speak—conversationally. As you engage on video calls and record video messages, use the words and language of your audience. Nothing says "you get me" like appropriately and sincerely using my language as you communicate with me. Think of others in advance. Build a bridge for them. Do the work to make it easier for them to know, like, and trust you.

For a great example of this, let me tell you about Steve's year-long gratitude project. Steve reads stacks of books and listens to hours of podcasts. He's made a habit of reaching out to thank people from whom he's learned something. He records a video message, then sends it in an email or LinkedIn message. He's sent them to CEOs, CMOs, VPs, founders, authors, and others with whom he has no prior relationship. It's cold outreach, but he's not asking for anything. Just expressing gratitude.

Over the course of a year, he sent 125 videos and heard back from 100 people. Some were short, friendly exchanges. Others are ongoing conversations. One thing that quickly became clear to Steve: the shorter and more direct the accompanying text, the better. Another top takeaway: Speak how they speak. With Tiffani Bova, Global Growth and Innovation Evangelist at Salesforce, he referred to "coopetition." For Jeanne Hopkins, CRO at Happy Nest, it was "I don't want 15 minutes or iced tea." And to Jeffrey Perlman, Chief Strategy Officer at Mindvalley: "trigger crystal."

If you don't know what those words mean, that's the point. They're like inside jokes or shared secrets. They're things Steve wouldn't know about each person if he'd not read, listened, and paid attention to them. Using people's first names can be effective, but it's not nearly as effective as using their language. In the supporting text, in the video title, in the video thumbnail, and in the video itself, look for ways to make people feel seen and appreciated. And consider starting a gratitude project of your own! It's a healthy habit.

8. RESPECT TIME AND ATTENTION

In nearly every chapter, you read some variation on this: Keep it short.

Whether you're recording a video message, delivering a video presentation, or hosting a video meeting, take only as much time as necessary to get the job done. From a Platinum Rule perspective, give people who like to warm up with small talk the opportunity to do so. For people to whom small talk's anathema, get right to the point.

Time and attention are the most valuable things people can give us; we must respect both in every interaction. Being clear and concise may require a little more preparation than just showing up, but people will appreciate it. When you do it consistently, they grow to trust your willingness and ability to honor their needs and interests. You develop a reputation as someone who is thoughtful and respectful of their time and attention.

Again, to be human-centered is to put others first. When you prepare in advance and create an appropriate experience, you are prioritizing others' time and attention.

9. CONSIDER PRODUCTION QUALITY

In these pages, you saw a variety of recommendations regarding production quality. Thousands of video messages and video calls into his journey, Dan Tyre still doesn't see the need to invest heavily in tools and equipment. Morgan J Ingram just used his webcam and smartphone in 10,000 videos and counting. Mathew Sweezey and Shep Hyken, however, challenged us to learn to use the newest tools available. Adam Contos shared his DIY journey, starting with his iPhone then slowly acquiring new lights, cameras, and switchers. Viveka von Rosen suggested you upgrade your production quality to the degree it helps your confidence. Mario Martinez Jr. provided compelling reasons to learn how to cleanly execute videos with green screens and virtual backgrounds.

Over the years, Steve and I have recommended simple and authentic production. We've seen too many people use tools, equipment, and quality as reasons (or excuses) not to get started. In the process of writing this book, however, we've realized that making it easier for others to clearly see and hear you by giving some thought and care to your lighting, camera, and microphone is a human-centered act. You're not doing it to make yourself look better; you are helping others understand your emotions, meaning, and intent.

There are no quick or easy answers here. Most of our allies and exemplars acknowledged that any video is better than no video at all. Several acknowledged that emotion and authenticity are more important than video quality. And they all acknowledged that it's an iterative process; you learn as you go. The most important thing to keep in mind is that researching, selecting, buying, and setting up the "right" equipment should not be steps that prevent you from getting started today. People need and want to see you.

10. WORK ON ONE THING AT A TIME

Early in his career, Mathew Sweezey learned from Zig Ziglar the practice of recording his calls, playing them back, and thinking about them through the eyes and ears of the other person. Early in his career, Kobe Bryant made the commitment to focus on a single basketball skill at a time. And later in his career, he learned to watch back a recording of the entire game as soon as it concluded to improve his understanding and performance. Morgan J Ingram shared that with us to help us improve our video presence. Julie Hansen advised the same thing to overcome our fear and build our confidence: Don't focus on the entire video, just focus on the one thing you want to improve right now.

Early in your video journey, you might feel overwhelmed by all the things you want to be better about your video recordings and video calls. Make a list. Work on one thing at a time, whether it's eye contact, smiling, pace of speech, energetic starts, or something else. Think of each skill as a building block. Before long, you'll have a strong foundation and self-confidence. You can do this as both a practitioner and as a coach, helping your team members.

Before you begin reviewing recordings and focusing on areas for improvement, get some practice in and build the habit. Send at least 20 video messages as prescribed at the start of this chapter. Don't analyze your first or second video. Analyze your twentieth or thirtieth. And remember, perfection isn't the goal. Instead, it's to help other people through clarity and sincerity.

Human-centered communication is a journey, not a destination. It's not a check-box item or a task on your to-do list. As our digital environments evolve (or devolve), we will adapt. We will refine the strategies and tactics we've recapped in these last two chapters. What will remain true is the dignity of each of our fellow human beings. What will endure is our willingness to connect and communicate with them in visual, emotional, and authentic ways.

CHAPTER 16

Tomorrows: The Future of Human-Centered Communication

We are proposing a change. A movement away from dehumanization, disconnection, and digital pollution. We propose a movement toward being more personal. Toward deeper connection. More trust. Stronger relationships. Though it's a restoration with ancient roots, this movement is not an inevitable progression within our businesses or our society. In fact, it's part of an ongoing battle.

About halfway through the writing of this book, what we knew was coming finally arrived: fake personalization of video messages.

Picture this: Your otherwise-ordinary, 45-second video message with an artificial "Hello, (first name)" tacked onto the front of it—using your face and your voice. For years, we've been able to personalize text-based emails by automatically slugging in variable data, like the name of a person, company, or industry. Now, you can now personalize videos in a similar way.

You record the video once, then blast it at dozens, hundreds, or even thousands of people. Each person receives a video message in which "you" say their name at the start, even though you never actually said their name. "Hey, James." "Hey, Zoe." "Hey, Josh."

These new services promise to put artificial intelligence and "deepfake" video, as it's being called, to work in your sales process. The term is a portmanteau of "deep learning" and "fake." Using existing audio and video footage of you (the more, the better), machines can be trained to create a fully synthetic deepfake in which you say something you never said and do something you never did. As you might imagine, this is both exciting and terrifying.

What's being offered by these services today are normal video messages, but with a two-second greeting artificially created and tacked on. Only a fraction is actually faked. And it's plugging in just one piece of variable data (your recipient's first name). Those limitations will fade in time, making them more artificial and more personalized.

No need to record unique videos for unique people!

Machines will put the words in your mouth and the expressions on your face!

Awesome, right!?

No, not really.

This approach mistakes video itself as the cause of a video message's success. Though the medium is correlated with that success, it's not the cause. You are the reason a video message is successful or not. Video puts forth your confidence, sincerity, enthusiasm, concern, or whatever you're trying to convey better than other forms of digital communication. It's a gift of your time and attention. It helps you serve others more effectively. The medium isn't the cause of your success—*you* are.

We prefer not to trade authenticity for deception. That trade is wholly inconsistent with human-centered communication. Here's why we'll be avoiding deepfake videos . . .

First, the technology as applied here is a work in progress. The execution in the sales prospecting videos we've seen is laughably bad; the mouth and voice don't match at all. So they're not going to fake many people out. Especially on a budget and at scale. The fun deepfakes featuring celebrities and making the rounds on social media often take months to complete, including significant post-production work.

The process, however, will get much faster and better. Academic research in this area has been going on for years. The faces, voices, movements, and expressions will become much more realistic and convincing. Synthetic video has a wide variety of applications, many of which are positive, creative, and helpful. While this tech has a long way to go, we expect it to move quickly.

Second, these deepfakes introduce a new problem while offering an unnecessary solution. Think about all of the text-based emails you've received with missing, inaccurate, or misused data. The "Dear [$first_name$]" with your name left out. Being greeted by your last name or your company name instead of by your first name. An outdated job title or an incorrect industry name. We've all been on the receiving end of these comical, embarrassing, or offensive errors. Now think about sending something similar, but with your faked face and voice as the delivery mechanism. You'd be pretending to personally greet people to start a conversation, but with missing, inaccurate, or misused data.

The problem they purport to solve is that you don't have enough time to record separate videos for individual people. While that may be true, a simple solution has already been mentioned several times in this book. Just record an evergreen video and send it one-to-one or one-to-many. Send it manually or automatically. The supporting text and broader context can make it feel personal, even though it's for a group of people. Problem solved. No deceit required.

Third, this is where the hordes will migrate, especially as the technology gets more convincing and less expensive. Most people want what's easy and fast. That's why this was inevitable; people will definitely buy and use services like these. To be fair, we may find appropriate use cases for this type of artificial video, especially if we're willing to disclose their synthetic nature rather than trying to pass them off as personal. For now, however, deepfakes turn video prospecting into a gimmick and create both a problem and an opportunity for human-centered videos.

The problem is that there will be a lot more video noise and video pollution, reducing the attention each video gets. At present, the act of sending a video message of any kind stands out. In the future, as the crowd shoots out synthetic, artificial representations of themselves, each video message stands out less and gets scrutinized more. Personal videos may not get the benefit of the doubt or the attention they deserve. We'll have to modify the ways in which we offer identity, provide verification, and create engagement. We'll have to add little touches, details, and turns of phrase relevant to the person that a machine can't produce on its own.

Here's the opportunity: In that environment, a truly personal and authentic message will connect even more. When you let a machine crank out videos on your behalf, you sacrifice the purpose and value of the medium. You give up control of tone, intent, and meaning. The artificial version of you may be on message but won't likely be on emotion. The authentic version of you acting in a human-centered way makes your recipient feel worthy of your time and attention. There should be no mistaking that your video is human-to-human; there should be no confusion that you see, hear, understand, and appreciate the other person.

Finally, it's fake. While some deepfakes are playful and creative, they're also closely associated with non-consensual pornography, fake news, political hoaxes, and financial fraud.[1] They may entertain, but they also deceive and manipulate. Deceit and manipulation are not qualities on which to build your corporate brand or reputation. And they're not qualities you want associated with your personal name or face.

By doubling down on mass mindsets, mass production, and mass blasting, this inauthentic approach is much more likely to pollute than to connect. When put up against Mathew Sweezey's framework defining contextual relevance, these deep-fakes don't fare well. They're a new twist on the same old tactics that may appear to be working even when they're not working.

Human-centered communication wins. Personal beats personalized. And the unscalable beats what's scaled.

Think about an email from a person who really knows you compared to one that's just personalized with variable data plugged into it. You've probably got one of each in your inbox right now. Think about a video from a person who really understands you compared to one that's generically recorded for someone *like* you (as if you're completely defined by your role or industry). Think about a video from a person reading a script compared to one from a person speaking from the heart with sincerity and enthusiasm. What's truly personal is noticeably and meaningfully different.

When we are human-centered and when we create human-to-human messages and experiences, we're playing to our strengths. As artificial intelligence takes over more tasks, our success will be found in being more personal, authentic, and empathetic more often. As Geoff Colvin wrote in *Humans Are Underrated: What High Achievers Know That Brilliant Machines Never Will*:

> *We are designed to empathize. It's part of our essential nature. But in developed economies, we live in an environment that has become hostile to empathy. We hunger for it. We can't get it from computers because that's not what it is. It evolved in us as a human-to-human interaction. The opportunity for us to offer genuine empathy in an empathy-starved world is thus a chance to be truly valuable, to supply something that everyone wants and needs and isn't getting enough of. That's part of why employers are becoming so desperate to find it in employees.*[2]

Personalized scales. It can be done by bots and automation.

Personal doesn't scale. It's delivered human to human.

As you weigh efficiency and effectiveness in any decision-making process, remember something that my friend Sangram Vajre, Cofounder and Chief Evangelist at Terminus, says:

Relationships don't scale. But doing unscalable things builds strong relationships.[3]

The fact that time and attention don't scale is what gives them their meaning and value. They're finite. They're precious. When you focus on other people, connect with them in the moment, and give the gifts of your time and attention, the difference is felt.

WHEN SEEING IS NO LONGER BELIEVING

We don't offer these arguments against fake personal video messages as a teardown of new services, but as cautions. These types of technological advances demand our scrutiny. If we're not thoughtful or careful as new tools and practices enter our market, our culture, and our society, we wind up with unanticipated and undesirable consequences.

"Technology is merely an amplifier of human intention, and so it is being used for good as well as bad,"[4] says Nina Schick, author of *Deepfakes: The Coming Infocalypse*. Use is met with misuse. Information is met with misinformation. To protect authenticity and trust in digital spaces, vigilance must meet whatever attacks and erodes them there.

The "Infocalypse," according to Schick, is "the increasingly dangerous and untrustworthy information ecosystem within which most humans now live."[4] She provides a dystopian view of digital pollution by detailing example after example of misinformation, disinformation, conspiracy, fake news, deepfakes, cheapfakes, and other corrosive tools used against us in personal, business, and geopolitical contexts. It's been going on for decades, but with today's technology, creating confusion, dividing people, and doing harm have become even cheaper, more pervasive, and more effective.

We should find it especially worrying that "the means for AI-powered subversion of audio and video are developing at a time when these media are becoming the *most important* form of human communication—not only for the digitally savvy but for everyone."[4] Manipulation of faces, voices, and likenesses will only get more convincing and less expensive. Soon, both good actors and bad will be able to make anyone say or do anything. Anyone can be targeted. And anyone can become collateral damage.

Seeing is believing, right? Not for long.

In the near future and unlike the past, video will no longer be evidence of anything. Real documentation and synthetic creation will be equally convincing. As more of our experiences occur in digital environments and as more information comes to us through digital media, it will become less clear what and whom we can trust. What and whom will we believe? When and why? In this type of world, what is the basis for truth? Without clear and objective truth, what becomes of our shared reality?

We face both practical and philosophical considerations here. And we need to consider them right now.

A CONSTANT BATTLE

The threats to authenticity, trust, and relationships in a noisy and polluted digital environment are best countered through human-centered communication. Leading with our identity in a sincere, honest, and open way. Providing verification of our identity, intent, and opportunity. Creating engagement and conversation. Investing in trusting relationships. As our digital culture and environment change, the strategies and tactics that support a human-centered approach also require change. This is why the pillar of guidance is so important.

The battle between human-centered communication and digital pollution won't end; but we can vote for the future we want through our thoughts, words, and actions.

We see this type of battle everywhere—wherever technology is involved and human nature is in play. It's a push and pull. A game of cat and mouse. Deepfake generators versus deepfake detectors. Cyberattacks versus cybersecurity. Advertising-based platforms versus ad-blocking software. Spam versus spam filters. Mis- and disinformation campaigns versus truth and cohesion.

When we judge a technology as good or bad, we're primarily making judgments about the ways people are using it. And it's a reflection of human nature. Social media, email marketing, sales engagement, digital media creation, app development—the same tools used to create pollution online are also being used to serve humans and benefit humanity. Within this tension, policy, technology, and business communities can tip the scale in favor of kind and fair use. But selfishness and maliciousness are ever-present, tipping it the other way.

As with environmental pollution, managing digital pollution requires trade-offs. For example, how do we balance security with privacy? In the real world, we've acted upon but not yet resolved that question with regard to domestic and international terrorism. And we're far from having that balance figured out in the digital world. Trade-offs require compromise, a word that's often and unfairly used pejoratively. The compromise is where the purist meets the pragmatist; we must honor the purity of our values and ideals, but we must also pragmatically get to work and get things done.

In this battle, we can hold to our human-first ideals while operating within practical constraints. We can balance the needs of people (desirability), the possibilities of technology (feasibility), and the requirements for business success (viability). To serve others, build trust, and enhance our reputations, we need a pragmatic, both/and approach, not just a purist either/or approach.

Mass communication is still useful. Mass customization is not an oxymoron, but rather an effective way to serve people's needs and wants. Machine-driven messages are not necessarily pollution; machines can help make messages more relevant and valuable. Human-to-human touches are not necessarily inefficient; tech can enable our team members to be themselves more often.

As you create and refine a healthy, human-centered approach, keep your options on the table, but always start with people first in mind.

A NEW BALANCE

Nature depends on diversity, thrives on differences, and perishes in the imbalance of uniformity. Healthy systems are highly varied and specific to time and place. Nature is not mass-produced.[5]

So wrote environmentalist, entrepreneur, and author Paul Hawken in *The Ecology of Commerce* more than 25 years ago. In contrast to healthy, natural systems, mass production thrives on uniformity, standardization, and homogeneity. Interchangeable parts, processes, and people. One size fits all. Waste and pollution are inherent to this industrial process.

Though we're well aware of their ills, we're still wandering our way out of the mass mindset and culture in which we've lived for a couple of centuries now. Remnants abound. Still today, people are met with interruption marketing, managed by command and control, relegated to cogs in the machine, and treated like means to ends, rather than beings with intrinsic value. Through system and circumstance, we've normalized the dehumanization of people. For so many reasons, we should no longer tolerate or accept this.

Just as we work to restore the balance of nature that's been upset by environmental pollution, we must work to restore the primacy of people in response to digital pollution. Hawken's view of healthy systems—highly varied and specific to time and place—matches Mathew Sweezey's view of contextual relevance. Both are aligned with human-centered communication. See, hear, and appreciate individual people. Help them uniquely in the moment. For stronger relationships and healthier businesses.

In the move away from a purely industrial approach, we're rehumanizing markets, businesses, people, and communication. We're finding a new balance. Between art and science. Between creativity and order. It's technology-enabled and human-centered. Healthier and more natural. Varied and imperfect. It values people as people, not as interchangeable parts.

As business analyst, journalist, and author Christopher Locke wrote in *The Cluetrain Manifesto* more than 20 years ago:

> *The future business of businesses that have a future will be about subtle differences, not wholesale conformity; about diversity, not homogeneity; about breaking rules, not enforcing them; about pushing the envelope, not punching the clock; about invitation, not protection; about doing it first, not doing it "right"; about making it better, not making it perfect; about telling the truth, not spinning bigger lies; about turning people on, not "packaging" them; and perhaps above all, about building convivial communities and knowledge ecologies, not leveraging demographic sectors.*[6]

A WAY TO BE RICH

Treating people like people and adopting human-centered communication is the right direction in the present. For you, your team, your customers, and all your stakeholders. Right now, it's the fastest and best way to attract and retain the best people and partners. Today, it's the fastest and best way to build trusting relationships and an enduring reputation. In that way, it's the right direction for the future as well, where competition for attention and the value of trust both grow exponentially.

You can pursue a human-centered approach on moral or ethical grounds; it can and should be undertaken for its own sake. If so, we appreciate the purist in you. But you can also pursue it pragmatically; it can and should be undertaken for the benefit of your business (note: Sincerity is required). Visual and emotional in nature, it speaks to and connects with humans more deeply and effectively than faceless, digital communication. Transparent, valuable, and customer-centric, it meets or exceeds what the market demands, unlike much of what's currently being provided.

Relationships are the goal. Using a real, human voice to create conversations with people based on their interests and goals lays the foundation. It's good for people and good for business. When we lose sight of this, we're likely to pollute. Hence the need to consciously and consistently develop human-centered communication. Until personal habits are formed and organizational culture is changed, we must be intentional about what we're doing, how we're doing it, and why we're doing it. In the transition, we're still meeting our goals, but we're also restoring balance, valuing people, and building a foundation for a healthy future.

"We can just as easily have an economy that is based on healing the future instead of stealing it. We can either create assets for the future or take the assets of the future. One is called restoration and the other exploitation," wrote Paul Hawken in the introduction to the Revised Edition of *The Ecology of Commerce*. "And whenever we exploit the earth, we exploit people and cause untold suffering. Working for the earth is not a way to get rich; it is a way to be rich."[5]

As it is with our physical environment and natural capital, so it is with our digital environments and social capital. We can dehumanize ourselves and others with digital pollution. Or we can work in service of people. Not just to get rich, but also to be rich. We hope your investment of time and attention here has been rewarded. We hope that you'll join us in the conversation, exploration, and restoration that is human-centered communication.

Notes

Chapter 1: Digital Pollution

1. Rinkesh Kukreja, "Top 19 Most Polluted Rivers in the World in 2020," *Conserve Energy Future* (blog), posted July 14, 2020, https://www.conserve-energy-future.com/most-polluted-rivers-world.php.

2. Nsikan Akpan, "Great Pacific Garbage Patch weighs more than 43,000 cars and is much larger than we thought," PBS NewsHour, March 22, 2018, https://www.pbs.org/newshour/science/the-great-pacific-garbage-patch-weighs-more-than-43000-cars-and-is-way-bigger-than-previously-thought.

3. *Templafy* (blog), "How many emails are sent every day? Top email statistics for businesses," posted August 2020, https://info.templafy.com/blog/how-many-emails-are-sent-every-day-top-email-statistics-your-business-needs-to-know.

4. Joseph Johnson, "Global spam volume as percentage of total e-mail traffic from January 2014 to September 2020, by month," Statista, February 16, 2021, https://www.statista.com/statistics/420391/spam-email-traffic-share/.

5. Joanna Szabo, "Why Am I Getting Spam Text Messages?," Top Class Actions, November 3, 2020, https://topclassactions.com/lawsuit-settlements/lawsuit-news/888395-why-am-i-getting-spam-text-messages/.

6. Louis Columbus, "2020 Roundup Of Cybersecurity Forecasts And Market Estimates," *Forbes*, April 5, 2020, https://www.forbes.com/sites/louiscolumbus/2020/04/05/2020-roundup-of-cybersecurity-forecasts-and-market-estimates/?sh=47e8efd3381d.

7. "Uses for Oil," Canada's Oil & Natural Gas Producers, accessed March 15, 2021, https://www.capp.ca/oil/uses-for-oil/.

8. "A World of Minerals in Your Mobile Device," United States Geological Survey, last modified September 22, 2016, 08:26, https://pubs.usgs.gov/gip/0167/gip167.pdf.

9. Estelle Camizuli, Renaud Scheifler, Stéphane Garnier, et al. "Trace metals from historical mining sites and past metallurgical activity remain bioavailable to wildlife today," *Scientific Report* 3436, no. 8 (February 2018): https://doi.org/10.1038/s41598-018-20983-0.

10. Benjamin Ross and Steven Amter, *The Polluters: The Making of Our Chemically Altered Environment Illustrated Edition* (Oxford: Oxford University Press; Illustrated edition, 2012), 9.

11. "Study Session 7 Pollution: Types, Sources and Characteristics," The Open University, accessed March 15, 2021, https://www.open.edu/openlearncreate/mod/oucontent/view.php?id=79946&printable=1.

12. Nick Visser, "Microplastics Have Invaded Some Of The Planet's Most Remote Places," *Huffpost*, May 7, 2019, https://www.huffpost.com/entry/ocean-plastic-remote-places-on-the-planet_n_5ccfb8c5e4b0e4d75734aed8.

13. Dr. Ramakrishnan Nara, "Microplastic Contamination of the Food Supply Chain," *Food Safety Magazine*, December 14, 2018, https://www.food-safety.com/articles/6053-microplastic-contamination-of-the-food-supply-chain.

14. Jill Neimark, "Microplastics Are Turning Up Everywhere, Even In Human Excrement," NPR, October 22, 2018, https://www.npr.org/sections/thesalt/2018/10/22/659568662/microplastics-are-turning-up-everywhere-even-in-human-excrement.

15. Antonio Ragusaa, Alessandro Svelatoa, CriseldaSantacroce, et al., "Plasticenta: First evidence of microplastics in human placenta," *Environment International* 10674, no. 146 (January 1, 2021): https://www.sciencedirect.com/science/article/pii/S0160412020322297.

16. Steve Cohen, "The Human and Financial Cost of Pollution," *State of the Planet* (blog), Columbus University, October 23, 2017, https://blogs.ei.columbia.edu/2017/10/23/the-human-and-financial-cost-of-pollution/.

17. "Environmental Laws Impeded by Lack of Enforcement, First-ever Global Assessment Finds," International Institute for Sustainable Development, January 29, 2019, https://sdg.iisd.org/news/environmental-laws-impeded-by-lack-of-enforcement-first-ever-global-assessment-finds/.

18. "Benefits and Costs of the Clean Air Act, 1970 to 1990 - Study Design and Summary of Results," Clean Air Act Overview, United States Environmental Protection Agency, accessed March 15, 2021, https://www.epa.gov/clean-air-act-overview/benefits-and-costs-clean-air-act-1970-1990-study-design-and-summary-results.

19. Ian Urbina, "Think Those Chemicals Have Been Tested?," *The New York Times*, April 13, 2013, https://www.nytimes.com/2013/04/14/sunday-review/think-those-chemicals-have-been-tested.html.

20. The website of Google Sustainability, the "Our Commitments" page, https://sustainability.google/commitments/#.

21. The website for the University of Cambridge Judge Business School, Cambridge Bitcoin Electricity Consumption Index, the "Comparisons" page, https://cbeci.org/cbeci/comparisons.

22. Raynor de Best, "Bitcoin network average energy consumption per transaction compared to VISA network as of 2020," Statista, March 2, 2021, https://www.statista.com/statistics/881541/bitcoin-energy-consumption-transaction-comparison-visa/.

23. The Week Staff, "An epidemic of loneliness," *The Week*, January 6, 2019, https://theweek.com/articles/815518/epidemic-loneliness.

24. Stephen Marche, "The Epidemic of Facelessness," *The New York Times*, February 14, 2015, https://www.nytimes.com/2015/02/15/opinion/sunday/the-epidemic-of-facelessness.html.

25. "Researchers Find Link Between Excessive Screen Time and Suicide Risk," *Social Work Today*, Great Valley Publishing Company, accessed March 15, 2021, https://www.socialworktoday.com/news/dn_121317.shtml.

26. John Love, "A Brief History of Malware—Its Evolution and Impact," *Lastline* (blog), Lastline Inc., April 5, 2018, https://www.lastline.com/blog/history-of-malware-its-evolution-and-impact/.

27. Rob Smith, "40 years on from the first spam email, what have we learned? Here are 5 things you should know about junk mail," Web Economic Forum, May 4, 2018, https://www.weforum.org/agenda/2018/05/its-40-years-since-the-first-spam-email-was-sent-here-are-6-things-you-didnt/.

28. "History of Phishing," Cofense, accessed March 15, 2021, https://cofense.com/knowledge-center/history-of-phishing/.

29. "A Byte Out of History: $10 Million Hack, 1994-Style," Stories, Federal Bureau of Investigation, January 31, 2014, https://www.fbi.gov/news/stories/a-byte-out-of-history-10-million-hack.

30. "Business E-mail Compromise The 12 Billion Dollar Scam," Public Service Announcement, Federal Bureau of Investigation, July 12, 2018, https://www.ic3.gov/Media/Y2018/PSA180712.

31. Bob Sullivan, "Identity theft hit an all-time high in 2016," Personal Finance, *USA Today*, February 6, 2017, https://www.usatoday.com/story/money/personalfinance/2017/02/06/identity-theft-hit-all-time-high-2016/97398548/.

32. "Top Policy Trends 2020: Data privacy," PwC, accessed March 15, 2021, https://www.pwc.com/us/en/services/consulting/risk-regulatory/library/top-policy-trends/data-privacy.html.

33. Cynthia Brumfield, "12 new state privacy and security laws explained: Is your business ready?," *CSO*, December 28, 2020, https://www.csoonline.com/article/3429608/11-new-state-privacy-and-security-laws-explained-is-your-business-ready.html.

34. Cynthia Brumfield, "Passage of California privacy act could spur similar new regulations in other states," *CSO*, November 12, 2020, https://www.csoonline.com/article/3596295/passage-of-california-privacy-act-could-spur-similar-new-regulations-in-other-states.html.

35. Brian Keeley, *Human Capital: How What You Know Shapes Your Life*, (OECD Insights, 2007, chap. 6, https://www.oecd.org/insights/37966934.pdf.

36. "Americans are worried about the declining level of trust citizens have in each other," U.S. Politics & Policy, Pew Research Center, July 18, 2019, https://www.pewresearch.org/politics/2019/07/22/the-state-of-personal-trust/prc_2019-07-22_trust-distrust-in-america_2-01/.

37. Roderick M. Kramer, "Rethinking Trust," *Harvard Business Review*, June, 2009, https://hbr.org/2009/06/rethinking-trust.

38. Judy Estrin and Sam Gill, "The World Is Choking on Digital Pollution," *Washington Monthly*, February 12, 2019, https://washingtonmonthly.com/magazine/january-february-march-2019/the-world-is-choking-on-digital-pollution/.

39. Dr. Erik J. Huffman, "The Making of a Cyber Victim, Human Hacking: The Psychology Behind Cybersecurity, Cyberpsychology," TED Conferences, September, 2019, https://www.ted.com/talks/dr_erik_j_huffman_the_making_of_a_cyber_victim_human_hacking_the_psychology_behind_cybersecurity_cyberpsychology.

Chapter 2: Human-Centered Communication

1. "Golden Rule," Norman Rockwell Museum, March 27, 2018, https://www.nrm.org/2018/03/golden-rule-common-religions/.

2. Donald J. Robertson, "The Golden Rule in Stoicism," *Stoicism: Philosophy as a Way of Life* (blog), Medium, December 18, 2019, https://medium.com/stoicism-philosophy-as-a-way-of-life/the-golden-rule-in-stoicism-d2dc2d8b8e.

3. "'Golden Rules' in World Religions and Philosophies," Unitarian Universalist Fellowship of Hendersonville, 2017, https://uufhnc.org/wp-content/uploads/2017/08/Golden-Rules-Marc-Mullinax-Presentation-8.20.17.pdf.

4. Markham Heid, "Does Thinking Burn Calories? Here's What the Science Says," *Time*, September 19, 2018, https://time.com/5400025/does-thinking-burn-calories/.

5. Karamjit S. Gill, "Architect or Bee? Mike Cooley: the human spirit," *AI & Soc* 31, (August 2016): 435–437, https://doi.org/10.1007/s00146-016-0675-2.

6. Ernst F. Schumacher, *Small Is Beautiful: Economics As If People Mattered* (New York: Perennial Library - Harper & Row, 1975).

7. The website for IDEO Design Thinking; the "History" page, https://designthinking.ideo.com/history.

8. The website for IDEO Design Thinking; the "FAQ" page, https://designthinking.ideo.com/faq/whats-the-difference-between-human-centered-design-and-design-thinking.

9. Caroline Forsey, "Using Human-Centered Design to Create Better Products (with Examples)," *Marketing* (blog), Hubspot, Inc., June 14, 2018, https://blog.hubspot.com/marketing/human-centered-design.

10. IEDO.org, *The Field Guide to Human-Centered Design* (New York: IEDO.org, 2015), 17-25.

11. LUMA Institute, *Innovating for People: Handbook of Human-Centered Design Methods* (Pennsylvania: LUMA Institute, 2012).

12. "Ergonomics of human-system interaction," International Organization for Standardization, 2019, https://www.iso.org/obp/ui/#iso:std:iso:9241:-210:ed-2:v1:en.

13. Nick Morgan, *Can You Hear Me?: How to Connect with People in a Virtual World* (Massachusetts: Harvard Business Review Press, 2018), 18.

14. "Life's Most Persistent and Urgent Question Is, 'What Are You Doing for Others?,'" Quote Investigator, January 18, 2016, https://quoteinvestigator.com/2016/01/18/altruism/.

15. Rutger Bregman, *Humankind: A Hopeful History* (Massachusetts: Little, Brown and Company, 2020), 385,378.

16. Adam Grant, "Are you a giver or a taker?," YouTube, January 24, 2017, https://www.youtube.com/watch?v=YyXRYgjQXX0.

17. Baris Korkmaz, "Theory of Mind and Neurodevelopmental Disorders of Childhood," *Pediatr Res* 69 (2011), 101–108, https://doi.org/10.1203/PDR.0b013e318212c177.

18. Mark W. Schaefer, *Marketing Rebellion: The Most Human Company Wins* (Illinois: Publisher Services, 2019), 42.

19. Marc Benioff and Monica Langley, *Trailblazer: The Power of Business as the Greatest Platform for Change* (New York: Currency, 2019), 187,212-213.

20. John Marshall and Simon Glynn, "Welcome to the Human Era," Lippincott, January 14, 2020, https://lippincott.com/insight/welcome-to-the-human-era/.

Chapter 3: A More Human Funnel

1. "What a Drag: The Global Impact of Bottom Trawling," United States Geological Survey, March 14, 2016, https://www.usgs.gov/news/what-drag-global-impact-bottom-trawling.

2. Winning by Design, "How to do Outbound Right | Sales as a Science #17," YouTube, January 14, 2019, https://www.youtube.com/watch?v=ASlhA3rDhZg.

3. Jacco van der Kooij, "Being kind and assuming positive intent will help you see the world from a different perspective," LinkedIn, https://www.linkedin.com/in/jaccovanderkooij/.

4. Matt Long, "How Bannister trained for and ran his sub-four-minute mile," *Athletics Weekly*, May 6, 2020, https://athleticsweekly.com/performance/how-bannister-ran-sub-four-mile-1039929761/.

5. Stephen Wilson, "AP Interview: Roger Bannister relives 4-minute mile and stays coy on London Olympic flame," *The Associated Press* via Yahoo! News, March 1, 2012, https://news.yahoo.com/ap-interview-roger-bannister-relives-4-minute-mile-231018636--spt.html.

6. Aylin Woodward, "Crowds, costs, and corpses: 16 misconceptions about what it's like to climb Everest," *Business Insider*, May 30, 2019, https://www.businessinsider.com/mount-everest-misconceptions-about-climbing-2019-5.

7. Nathan Brannen, "Only 1,497 humans have ever broken the 4-minute mile—and I'm one of them," *CBC Sports*, June 27, 2018, https://www.cbc.ca/playersvoice/entry/only-1497-humans-have-ever-broken-the-4-minute-mile-and-im-one-of-them.

8. Joseph Johnson, "Global digital population as of January 2021," Statista, March 5, 2021, https://www.statista.com/statistics/617136/digital-population-worldwide/.

Chapter 4: Emotion, Memory, and Motivation

1. David J. Schwartz, *The Magic of Thinking Big* (New York: Fireside, 1987), 366,371.

2. Elizabeth A. Segal, Ph.D., "Power Blocks Empathy," *Empathy* (blog), *Psychology Today*, September 23, 2019, https://www.psychologytoday.com/us/blog/social-empathy/201909/power-blocks-empathy.

3. Valène Jouany & Mia Mäkipää, "8 Employee Engagement Statistics You Need to Know in 2021 [INFOGRAPHIC]" *Smarp* (blog), January 4, 2021, https://blog.smarp.com/employee-engagement-8-statistics-you-need-to-know.

4. Dan Hill and Sam Simon, *Emotionomics: Leveraging Emotions for Business Success* (London: Kogan Page, 2009), 16.

5. Tech2 New Staff, "Researchers Map Free Will, Choice Seconds Before Making Decisions In Brain Scans," *Tech2* (blog), Firstpost, March 12, 2019, https://www.firstpost.com/tech/science/researchers-map-free-will-choice-seconds-before-making-decisions-in-brain-scans-6244621.html.

6. Seth Godin, "Really Bad Powerpoint," *Seth's Blog* (blog), January 29, 2007, https://seths.blog/2007/01/really_bad_powe/.

7. Nick Morgan, *Can You Hear Me?: How to Connect with People in a Virtual World* (Massachusetts: Harvard Business Review Press, 2018), 19-20.

Chapter 5: Noise, Attention, and Trust

1. Ethan Beute, "The Context Marketing Revolution with Mathew Sweezey," *BombBomb* (blog), BombBomb, February 18, 2020, https://bombbomb.com/blog/context-marketing-mathew-sweezey-salesforce/.

2. Marc Benioff and Monica Langley, *Trailblazer: The Power of Business as the Greatest Platform for Change* (New York: Currency, 2019), 22-23.

3. Mark W. Schaefer, *Marketing Rebellion: The Most Human Company Wins* (Illinois: Publisher Services, 2019).

4. Mathew Sweezey, *The Context Marketing Revolution: How to Motivate Buyers in the Age of Infinite Media* (Massachusetts: Harvard Business Review Press, 2020), 104, 115.

5. Nigel Holloway and Dan Armstrong, "The Experience Equation: How Happy Employees And Customers Accelerate Growth," *Forbes*, accessed March 16, 2021, https://c1.sfdcstatic.com/content/dam/web/en_us/www/documents/reports/forbes-insight%20experience-equation%20final-report.pdf.

6. James L. Heskett, W. Earl Sasser, Jr. and Leonard A. Schlesinger, *The Service Profit Chain* (New York: Free Press, 1997).

7. Robert Noggle, "Why the difference between persuasion and manipulation matters," *Fast Company*, August 3, 2018, https://www.fastcompany.com/90212788/why-the-difference-between-persuasion-and-manipulation-matters.

8. Geoff Colvin, *Humans Are Underrated: What High Achievers Know That Brilliant Machines Never Will* (New York: Portfolio, 2015), 4.

Chapter 6: Preparing to Be Present

1. Ethan Beute, "Emotional Intelligence and The Power of Faces," *BombBomb* (blog), BombBomb, May 19, 2020, https://bombbomb.com/blog/emotional-intelligence-faces-dan-hill-sensory-logic/.

2. Mark A. W. Andrews, "Why do we use facial expressions to convey emotions?," *Scientific American*, November 1, 2010, https://www.scientificamerican.com/article/why-do-we-use-facial-expressions/.

3. Cory Stieg, "Making this facial expression can boost your performance by 20%, according to science," CNBC, November 20, 2019, https://www.cnbc.com/2019/11/20/study-making-a-determined-face-improves-cognitive-performance.html.

4. Ethan Beute, "Creating Fans Through Human Connection," *BombBomb* (blog), BombBomb, March 3, 2020, https://bombbomb.com/blog/creating-fans-human-connection-david-meerman-scott-fanocracy/.

Chapter 7: "How Can I Help You?"

1. Annette Choi, "The Parasocial Phenomenon," *NOVA Next* (blog), PBS, Aril 5, 2017, https://www.pbs.org/wgbh/nova/article/parasocial-relationships/.

2. Samantha Rotbart, "On Top In 2020: RE/MAX Ranked No. 1 Real Estate Brokerage Franchise In Franchise 500," RE/MAX, January 14, 2020, https://news.remax.com/on-top-in-2020-remax-ranked-no-1-real-estate-brokerage-franchise-in-franchise-500.

Chapter 8: The Decade for Sellers to Shine

1. Aja Frost, "Only 3% of People Think Salespeople Possess This Crucial Character Trait," *Sales* (blog), Hubspot, Inc., April 29, 2016, https://blog.hubspot.com/sales/salespeople-perception-problem.

2. Geoff James, "According to Neuroscience, Confidence Is Contagious, but Not for the Reasons You Think," *Productivity* (blog), Inc., https://www.inc.com/geoffrey-james/if-youve-got-this-1-character-trait-youll-probably-be-successful-according-to-neuroscience.html.

3. Jessica Bennett, "It's Not You, It's Science: How Perfectionism Holds Women Back," *Time*, April 22, 2014, https://time.com/70558/its-not-you-its-science-how-perfectionism-holds-women-back/.

4. Ken Fujiwara, "Gender And Conversation: Why Are Women More "In Synch" Than Men?," *Character & Context* (blog), Society for Personality and Social Psychology, September 30, 2019, https://www.spsp.org/news-center/blog/fujiwara-gender-conversation.

5. Emma Seppala, "Are Women More Compassionate than Men?," *Greater Good* Magazine, June 26, 2013, https://greatergood.berkeley.edu/article/item/are_women_more_compassionate_than_men.

6. Jon Warner, "Are Women Better Communicators Than Men?," *Communication* (blog), ReadytoManage Inc., June 14, 2013, http://blog.readytomanage.com/are-women-better-communicators-than-men/.

Chapter 10: The Teacher's Take on Connection

1. Reid Hoffman, "Connections with Integrity," *strategy+business*, May 29, 2012, https://www.strategy-business.com/article/00104?gko=ed6ea.

2. Robert Taibbi L.C.S.W., "6 Steps to Leading a Life of Integrity," *Fixing Families* (blog), *Psychology Today*, July 15, 2017, https://www.psychologytoday.com/us/blog/fixing-families/201707/6-steps-leading-life-integrity.

3. Gwendolyn Seidman Ph.D., "Why Do We Like People Who Are Similar to Us?," *Personality* (blog), *Psychology Today*, December 18, 2018, https://www.psychologytoday.com/us/blog/close-encounters/201812/why-do-we-people-who-are-similar-us.

4. Shana Lebowitz, "15 Psychological Tricks To Make People Like You Immediately," *Independent*, October 19, 2020, https://www.independent.co.uk/life-style/sixteen-psychological-tricks-people-like-you-a7967861.html.

5. Alison Prato, "Does body language help a TED Talk go viral? 5 nonverbal patterns from blockbuster talks," *Ted Blog* (blog), TED, May 12, 2015, https://blog.ted.com/body-language-survey-points-to-5-nonverbal-features-that-make-ted-talks-take-off/.

Chapter 11: Always Be Amazing

1. Amy Morin, "7 Scientifically Proven Benefits Of Gratitude That Will Motivate You To Give Thanks Year-Round," *Forbes*, November 23, 2014, https://www.forbes.com/sites/amymorin/2014/11/23/7-scientifically-proven-benefits-of-gratitude-that-will-motivate-you-to-give-thanks-year-round/.

2. "If I Had More Time, I Would Have Written a Shorter Letter," Quote Investigator, April 28, 2012, https://quoteinvestigator.com/2012/04/28/shorter-letter/.

3. Rutger Bregman, *Humankind: A Hopeful History* (Massachusetts: Little, Brown and Company, 2020), 233.

4. Arlin Cuncic, "How to Overcome Eye Contact Anxiety," Verywell Mind, November 9, 2020, https://www.verywellmind.com/how-do-i-maintain-good-eye-contact-3024392.

Chapter 12: People-First Prospecting

1. "Kobe Bryant: Mamba Mentality, NBA Championships, and Oscars," Lewis Howes, October 1, 2020, https://lewishowes.com/podcast/kobe-bryant-mamba-mentality-nba-championships-and-oscars/.

2. Devin Reed, "This (Surprising) Cold Email CTA Will Help You Book A LOT More Meetings," *Gong* (blog), Gong.io, May 27, 2020, https://www.gong.io/blog/this-surprising-cold-email-cta-will-help-you-book-a-lot-more-meetings/.

Chapter 13: The Year of Video?

1. Ethan Beute, "The Biggest Transformation in Prospecting in 30 Years," *BombBomb* (blog), BombBomb, October 15, 2019, https://bombbomb.com/blog/sales-prospecting-video-email-dan-tyre-hubspot/.

2. Movieclips, "Glengarry Glen Ross (1992) - Movie," YouTube, November 12, 2014, https://www.youtube.com/playlist?list=PLZbXA4lyCtqpboym55ebI3Vzm2UhujECK.

3. Dan Tyre, "It's Time to Move From 'Always Be Closing' to This New Sales Mantra," *Sales* (blog), Hubspot, November 9, 2020, https://blog.hubspot.com/sales/always-be-closing-is-dead-how-to-always-be-helping-in-2015.

4. Nick Salzman, "Book More Sales Opportunities In Less Time With Video," *LinkedIn Pulse* (blog), LinkedIn, https://www.linkedin.com/pulse/book-more-sales-opportunities-less-time-video-nick-saltzman/.

5. Shahram Heshmat Ph.D., "Why We Copy Each Other, and 5 Ways It Can Change Us," *Science of Choice* (blog), *Psychology Today*, January 20, 2016, https://www.psychologytoday.com/us/blog/science-choice/201601/why-we-copy-each-other-and-5-ways-it-can-change-us.

6. "Our Story," Crystal, accessed March 17, 2020, https://www.crystalknows.com/about.

7. Matt Plummer, "How to Spend Way Less Time on Email Every Day," *Harvard Business Review*, January 22, 2019, https://hbr.org/2019/01/how-to-spend-way-less-time-on-email-every-day.

Chapter 14: Takeaways: Strategies and Philosophies

1. John C. Bogle and Bill Clinton, *Enough: True Measures of Money, Business, and Life*, (New Jersey: Wiley, 2010), 99.

2. "What Is Compassion?," *Greater Good Magazine*, accessed March 17, 2021, https://greatergood.berkeley.edu/topic/compassion/definition.

Chapter 15: Takeaways: Tips and Tactics

1. Ernst F. Schumacher, *Small Is Beautiful: Economics As If People Mattered* (New York: Perennial Library - Harper & Row, 1975), 229.

2. Nick Morgan, *Can You Hear Me?: How to Connect with People in a Virtual World* (Massachusetts: Harvard Business Review Press, 2018), 137.

Chapter 16: Tomorrows: The Future of Human-Centered Communication

1. Lvxiao Chen, "Deepfake is Here. What Should We Do?," *The Blog* (blog), JIPEL NYU Journal of Intellectual Property & Entertainment Law, February 14, 2020, https://blog.jipel.law.nyu.edu/2020/02/deepfake-is-here-what-should-we-do/.

2. Geoff Colvin, *Humans Are Underrated: What High Achievers Know That Brilliant Machines Never Will* (New York: Portfolio, 2015), 83.

3. "450: Relationships Don't Scale - But Build Them Anyway," #FlipMyFunnel Podcast, accessed March 17, 2021, https://listen.casted.us/public/6/The-FlipMyFunnel-Podcast-05659/031676.

4. Nina Schick, *Deepfakes: The Coming Infocalypse* (Twelve, 2020), 10,30,195.

5. Paul Hawken, *The Ecology of Commerce Revised Edition: A Declaration of Sustainability* (New York: Harper Business, 2010), xxii-xxiii,15.

6. Rick Levine et al., *The Cluetrain Manifesto: The End of Business as Usual* (New York: Basic Books, 2001), 17.

Acknowledgments

Organizing, sharing, and advancing the ideas behind human-centered communication required the thought, care, time, and attention of so many wonderful and helpful humans.

We'll start with Conor McCluskey, Darin Dawson, and the entire BombBomb team; the work we do and the way we do it is challenging, important, and meaningful. Thanks to John Rougeux for guiding our team to the essential language and concepts in these pages. Thanks to Amber Van Schooneveld for providing so much thoughtful provocation, refinement, and editing; this is a much better book because of you. Anna Hayes and Sarah Wagle, thank you both for capturing the spirit of all the work we do together and creating a remarkable look and feel. We also appreciate you, Donna Kelly, for joining us again after all your help on *Rehumanize Your Business*.

This project was built on the expertise of all of our featured contributors. We are so appreciative of your willingness to join us. Thanks to Jacco van der Kooij, Jerimiah Lee Lancaster, Sari Eisendrath, and the Winning by Design team. Thanks to Dan Hill, Mathew Sweezey, Julie Hansen, Lauren Bailey, and Morgan J Ingram. Thanks to Adam Contos, Melissa Ada, and the entire RE/MAX community. Thanks to Mario Martinez Jr., Viveka von Rosen, and Diego Pineda at Vengreso. Thanks to Shep Hyken and Cindy Pass at Shepard Presentations. And thanks to Dan Tyre, Adam Rataj, Nick Saltzman, Katharine Fischer, and Alice Sol at HubSpot. You are all kind and generous in lending your time and attention, sharing stories, providing insights, and leading by example.

This book would not be in your hands without the help of Justin Branch, Jessica Choi, Tyler LeBleu, Neil Gonzalez, and the entire team at Greenleaf Book Group and Fast Company Press, as well as Peter Knox and the Book Highlight crew. Thanks to you all for sharing our vision and partnering with us to bring this important message to market.

From Ethan: Love and thanks to you, Megan and Owen, for your constant inspiration, patience, belief, and support. What you give is immeasurable. Thank you, Steve, for sparking this project and making the whole thing happen—another true joy and meaningful milestone along our journey of learning and growth. And thanks to everyone who invests time, attention, and money into writing books, buying books, and reading books. Our culture is better for it.

From Steve: To Gretchen, Grant, Owen, Sophia, and Winston, you fill me with so much love and energy. Life is always better when we're together! Ethan, I've learned so much from you and I'm a better person both professionally and personally because of our time together. To my family and friends, thank you for all of the support and encouragement you've provided me through the years. I'm also thankful for all of the people who take a human-centered approach to everything they do.

Index

ABOUT THE AUTHOR

ETHAN BEUTE

CHIEF EVANGELIST AT BOMBBOMB

ETHAN BEUTE

Chief Evangelist at BombBomb, coauthor of *Rehumanize Your Business,* and host of The Customer Experience Podcast, Ethan Beute has spent the past decade helping business professionals be more personal and human through simple video messages. He's sent more than 12,000 videos himself. Prior to joining BombBomb, he spent a dozen years leading marketing teams inside local television stations in Chicago, Grand Rapids, and Colorado Springs. He holds undergraduate and graduate degrees from the University of Michigan and the University of Colorado-Colorado Springs in communication, psychology, and marketing. He lives in Colorado Springs with his wife and son.

STEPHEN PACINELLI

A passionate storyteller by nature who measures his success by helping people reach their potential, Steve Pacinelli is Chief Marketing Officer at BombBomb and coauthor of *Rehumanize Your Business*. Prior to joining BombBomb, he was a customer and advocate of personal video for its benefits to his sales teams as Sales Manager, Vice President of Events, and National Speaker for Realtor.com. Steve's presented to more than 1,000 audiences on topics like online marketing, video communication, consumer psychology, and lead conversion. He resides in Downingtown, PA, with his wife, twin boys, and daughter.